Innovation Ecosystems

Martin Fransman presents a new approach to understanding how innovation happens, who makes it happen, and the factors that help and hinder it. Looking at innovation in real time under uncertainty, he develops the idea of an 'innovation ecosystem', i.e. a system of interrelated players and processes that jointly make innovation happen. Examples include: how companies like Amazon, Google, Facebook, Apple, AT&T, and Huawei interact in the ICT ecosystem; four innovations that changed the world – the transistor, the microprocessor, the optical fibre, and the laser; the causes of the telecoms boom and bust 1996–2003 that influenced the Great Recession from 2007; and the usefulness of the idea of innovation ecosystems for Chinese policymakers. By delving into the complex determinants of innovation, this book provides a deeper, more rigorous understanding of how it happens. It will appeal to economists, social scientists, business people, policymakers, and anyone interested in innovation and entrepreneurship.

MARTIN FRANSMAN is Professor Emeritus of Economics at the University of Edinburgh. He won the 2008–2010 Joseph Schumpeter Prize for his book *The New ICT Ecosystem* (Cambridge University Press, 2010). His other book prizes include the Wadsworth Prize for the best business book published in the United Kingdom for *Telecoms in the Internet Age – From Boom to Bust to ... ?* and the Masayoshi Ohira Prize for *The Market and Beyond* (Cambridge University Press).

T0320904

Innovation Ecosystems
Increasing Competitiveness

MARTIN FRANSMAN

University of Edinburgh

CAMBRIDGE
UNIVERSITY PRESS

CAMBRIDGE
UNIVERSITY PRESS

University Printing House, Cambridge CB2 8BS, United Kingdom

One Liberty Plaza, 20th Floor, New York, NY 10006, USA

477 Williamstown Road, Port Melbourne, VIC 3207, Australia

314–321, 3rd Floor, Plot 3, Splendor Forum, Jasola District Centre, New Delhi – 110025, India

79 Anson Road, #06–04/06, Singapore 079906

Cambridge University Press is part of the University of Cambridge.

It furthers the University's mission by disseminating knowledge in the pursuit of education, learning, and research at the highest international levels of excellence.

www.cambridge.org
Information on this title: www.cambridge.org/9781108472463
DOI: 10.1017/9781108646789

© Martin Fransman 2018

First published 2018

Printed and bound in Great Britain by Clays Ltd, Elcograf S.p.A.

A catalogue record for this publication is available from the British Library.

Library of Congress Cataloging-in-Publication Data
Names: Fransman, Martin, author.
Title: Innovation ecosystems : increasing competitiveness / Martin Fransman.
Description: First edition. | New York, NY : University of Edinburgh, 2019. | Includes bibliographical references and index.
Identifiers: LCCN 2018024265 | ISBN 9781108472463 (hardback : alk. paper) | ISBN 9781108459709 (pbk. : alk. paper)
Subjects: LCSH: Technological innovations. | Research, Industrial. | Industrial productivity centers.
Classification: LCC T173.8 .F785 2019 | DDC 338/.064–dc23
LC record available at https://lccn.loc.gov/2018024265

ISBN 978-1-108-47246-3 Hardback
ISBN 978-1-108-45970-9 Paperback

This book is dedicated, with admiration and gratitude, to Richard Nelson

Contents

Preface

This book is addressed to all those who want to understand innovation better, who want to know how innovation happens, who makes innovation happen, and how innovation is best conceptualised.

Innovation is about creating novelty and injecting it into the socio-economic system. Over time, innovation is the most important driver of socio-economic change.

But the process of innovation is complicated and uncertain. How it happens, who makes it happen, and how it is best conceptualised is by no means obvious. These are the issues into which this book delves. The first introductory chapter gives the reader a fairly lengthy overview of the topics addressed. The overall conclusions drawn are presented in the final chapter.

From the outset it must be emphasised that this book is not intended to be a survey of the literature relating to innovation and systems. To provide such a survey would require another book with another set of objectives. The aim of this book is on the one hand more limited but on the other more focused. More specifically, the aim of this book is to explore the idea of what is referred to in the book's title as innovation ecosystems.

Innovation ecosystems are socio-economic systems that make innovation happen. The exploration of this concept is undertaken in this book through the close examination of what may appropriately be thought of as two relatively unrelated schools of thought. The first school is the 'systems of innovation' school and the second the 'business ecosystems' school.

The method that has been adopted is to examine the ideas and main publications of several selected pioneers of each of these schools. These pioneers have set out the terrain, as it were, which has provided the fertile soil within which other writers have developed their own contributions. In so doing, these pioneers have shaped their field whilst leaving it to later-comers to make their own additions. This book does not attempt to follow the many threads that weave their way through these two schools of thought. Rather, it explores a number of important issues that are raised by the conceptualisations of innovation and systems contained in the work of the pioneers of the two schools. The most important of these are the questions of how does innovation happen and who makes innovation happen?

Since intellectual output always stands on the shoulders of many others, acknowledgements and debts are due. My first debt is to my mother and father, Dee and Elie, who were always encouraging and supportive. Intellectual acknowledgements must also be made since without the people named, this book would not have been possible.

Chronologically, my first intellectual debt is to my first teacher of economics, Ludwig Lachmann at the University of the Witwatersrand in Johannesburg. It was Lachmann who taught me that ultimately economics is about people, not super-competent calculators, but fallible people like you and me, trying to do what seems best for ourselves but largely muddling through in a world where certainty is the exception rather than the rule.

An important influence on this book, as will readily be evident to the reader, is a contemporary of Lachmann's, Joseph Schumpeter. Although they focused on different issues, there is a significant degree of compatibility in their thinking.[1] Both Lachmann and Schumpeter were convinced that mainstream economics does not provide sufficient room for a rigorous analysis of the issues that they felt were fundamental for a proper understanding of the capitalist economy. For Schumpeter, the main issue was how novelty is created and diffused within the forever restless capitalist system. It was this concern that led him to an analysis of the role of innovation.

---

[1] This is brought out in my contribution paper, titled 'Lachmann and Schumpeter: Some Reflections and Reminiscences', to the memorial conference, 'The Legacy of Ludwig Lachmann: Interdisciplinary Perspectives on Institutions, Agency, and Uncertainty', held at the University of the Witwatersrand, Johannesburg, 11–13 April 2017.

Two contemporary Schumpeterians have also been important influences. The first is Richard Nelson, founder with Sidney Winter of modern Schumpeterian-evolutionary economics. It is to Dick that this book is, with gratitude, dedicated. Dick's many rich contributions provided a beacon for the young and gradually older scholar who has written the present book.[2] The second is Stanley Metcalfe, whose insightful common sense about the workings of the capitalist economy has always provided inspiration.

I also want to acknowledge with gratitude the understanding and support of Simon Clark, head of the School of Economics at the University of Edinburgh.

Crucially, however, the intellectual contributions of scholars, important though they have been, have not been sufficient. Equally important have been the many contributions made by key decision-makers in the great number of companies – both large and smaller in many countries around the world – with whom I had the great fortune to discuss. In a crucial sense, it is they who were my teachers.

Although it is extremely difficult to select names, it would be remiss of me if I did not mention the following. The first is Arno Penzias, former Vice President of AT&T, President of Bell Laboratories, and Nobel Laureate. I met and briefly worked with Arno at a key point in the history of Bell Labs, arguably the most important corporate research laboratory of all time. Arno was in the midst of rethinking and reorganising Bell Labs when for the first time in its history AT&T was forced by regulatory changes to confront competition from designated new entrants. The issues that Arno had to deal with and the solutions that he created deeply influenced my subsequent thinking about innovation.

Japan and leading Japanese companies have also been a crucial formative influence. As the main post-war catch-up country, the

---

[2] The conclusions that Nelson arrived at regarding the importance and approach of Schumpeterian-evolutionary economics and why it has not been more widely accepted by mainstream economics are very similar to my own as is evident in the present book. See his seminal article, Nelson, R.R., 2012. 'Why Schumpeter has had so little influence on today's main line economics, and why this may be changing'. *Journal of Evolutionary Economics*, 22, 5: 901–16.

experiences of innovation in this country are of particular interest. Here I must mention, with deep gratitude for the enormous amount of time coupled with intense, stimulating discussion over many years, the contributions of Botaro Hirosaki, Executive Vice President and head technology officer at NEC, and his successor, Katsumi Emura, Executive Vice President and current CTO, as well as Norio Wada, CEO and then Chairman of Japan's largest telecoms company, NTT, and Sadahiko Kano, Vice President of NTT. Another important influence was Didier Lombard, CEO of France Telecom.

Closer to home I must also thank Ian McCoull and his innovation colleagues at Scottish Enterprise. Their commitment and practical activities aimed at helping companies based in Scotland to improve their performance through innovation has also been a source of both stimulation and inspiration.

The role of these and other key company decision-makers was crucial in injecting aspects of the real world into my thinking, which, in the academic environment which was mine, could all too easily have lost touch with reality.

Mention must also be made of the generations of students whom I had the good fortune to teach over my many years as a university teacher. Their youth and enthusiasm were always a joy. Being students in a conventional economics department, their questioning and fresh insights were often stimulating.

I must also acknowledge, with profound thanks, the generous Leverhulme Fellowship which allowed me to take off one year to write this book. Without this help the present book simply would not have been written.

Finally, gratitude is due to my family and particularly my wife, Tammy, who has graciously put up with the prospect of 'yet another book' and the grumpiness that inevitably accompanies a bad day's writing.

To all these, and the others not mentioned here, I express my deepest gratitude.

I Introduction

What is innovation? To innovate, coming from the Latin word *innovare*, means to introduce something new.

The ability to introduce something new is an evolved capability. A crucial transformational moment in the history of humankind occurred with the emergence of the ability of *Homo sapiens* to introduce something new (although we are not yet sure how this ability evolved). From this moment on humans were not entirely constrained by what already existed. They were now able to some extent and in some areas to create the novelty that would change what existed. The evolutionary emergence of this ability would fundamentally alter not only what it meant to be human, but also the world in which humans existed.

What does the ability to introduce something new consist of? Most importantly it involves *the ability to imagine* something which does not yet exist but which might come to exist; that is, the ability to imagine what might be. The next step in human endeavour was to try to bring into existence what had been imagined.

But the ability to bring into existence is limited, not only by physical factors, but also by socioeconomic factors. Thus the ability to innovate differs in hunter-gatherer, feudal, and capitalist societies, to take three examples.

In capitalist societies, for instance, the ability to introduce something new is considerably enhanced by the ability to obtain and harness complementary resources such as money and people. Institutions, for example, the laws of property and contract, are further facilitators. The context within which innovation occurs, therefore, is crucial, shaping the innovation which is created under these conditions.

THE IDEAS OF JOSEPH SCHUMPETER

We begin this book by contextualising innovation through a discussion of the role that innovation plays in capitalist economies. This discussion is based on the approach adopted in Schumpeterian-evolutionary economics.

Joseph Schumpeter is commonly regarded as one of the greatest of twentieth-century economists. Through his study of economics Schumpeter was struck by the incessant change and restless characteristic of the capitalist economy. This change involved the continual creation of the new accompanied by the destruction of the old.

What is the main driver of this change? The main driver, according to Schumpeter, is innovation. Innovators, a subset of the population, begin by imagining something new. This they embody in an innovation hypothesis. The hypothesis is that the new something, if successfully introduced, will produce beneficial effects.

Schumpeter identified four kinds of innovation which he felt were individually, and in combination, very important drivers of creative-destructive change in the capitalist system. Innovators' imaginings and innovation hypotheses are embodied in these four kinds of innovation. The four are the following:

- new products and services
- new processes and technologies
- new ways of organising people and things
- new markets, ways of marketing, and business models.

How do these four kinds of innovation drive change? The answer is through substitutability and complementarity effects. The improved new substitutes for the inferior old. The improved new produces demands for complementary additions. Aggregated across the whole economy, these innovations drive restless change.

In Chapter 2 we examine the essentials of the framework that Schumpeter developed to understand the restless capitalist system, how it works, and some of the consequences. As we shall see, innovation lies at the heart of this framework. This examination is undertaken by developing a number of logically related propositions that, taken together, explain Schumpeter's framework.

INNOVATION AS A SYSTEMIC PHENOMENON

How does innovation happen? The imagined innovation hypothesis is only the beginning of the innovation process. Further activities are necessary (taken in tandem or in parallel and with feedbacks being generated). The hypothesis needs to be implemented (or in Schumpeter's words, 'carried out'). As part of the implementation process the hypothesis must be tested to establish its validity. Finally, the innovation (for example, a new product or service) must be taken to 'market', i.e. delivered to the customer-user. The latter might be either outside or inside the innovating organisation.

Carrying out these activities will in most cases require the inclusion in the act of innovation of many other factors. Collectively we will refer to them as 'players and processes'. Often, for instance, the innovator or the innovation team will need to raise money for the innovation project and/or will need additional expertise. These may be provided by other players such as venture capitalists or university researchers. Processes of various kinds will also be required to harness these additional resources.

As this simple example illustrates, the implementation of an intended innovation involves far more than an imagining innovator even though this is the usual starting point of the innovation process.

In the last thirty years or so a conceptual breakthrough was achieved when several analysts with an interest in innovation came up with the idea that the many determinants of innovation were best understood from a systems perspective. That is, these determinants were best viewed as being part of a system with interdependent, interacting components. Two clusters of literature emerged pursuing this line of reasoning. These two clusters are the main focus of Chapter 3.

The National Innovation Systems Approach

The first cluster will be referred to in this book as the 'national innovation systems' approach. The pioneers and main contributors to this approach consist largely of Schumpeterian-evolutionary economists with an interest in long-term economic growth and development.

Dissatisfied with the approaches adopted by mainstream economics, which they regarded as oversimplified, they set out to develop a more robust approach, more in touch with the empirical realities of growing economies. They were also interested in related questions such as why growth rates differ between countries and why companies from different countries dominate different global industries. Their shared belief was that an understanding of economic growth requires primarily a deep understanding of the innovation processes that are the main drivers of growth.

We begin Chapter 3 with an in-depth discussion of the pioneering work of Christopher Freeman, whose book on Japan gave birth to the national innovation systems approach. Freeman was impressed with the performance of Japan which succeeded after the Second World War in rapidly catching up with the United States and Europe, the global leaders. Freeman asked questions such as the following: How did Japan manage to achieve this remarkable performance? What role was played by Japan's ability to master and harness the radical information and communications technologies that heralded the new information age? What role was played by the various organs of the Japanese state? How important were the contributions made by the main Japanese companies?

Since the approaches of mainstream economics had little to contribute in answering questions such as these, Freeman began to create his own approach, publishing his seminal book in 1987. This approach he called the 'national system of innovation' approach.

In subsequent years Richard Nelson and his collaborators elaborated on and further developed Freeman's work. In Chapter 3 two contributions in particular are closely examined. The first is an edited volume on the different national innovation systems of different countries published in 1993. The second is a collective study of industrial leadership in seven industries published in 1999 which uses the notion of innovation systems to explain this leadership.

Amongst the many contributions made by the national innovation systems approach, two are of particular importance. The first, as already discussed, is the demonstration that the determinants of innovation are best understood as being part of a broader system. In short, innovation is systemic.

The second contribution is the significant role played by institutions conceived of as including not only the 'rules of the game' adopted by a nation's (or sector's) innovation system but also the noncompany facilitators (and, at times, frustrators) of the innovation process. These institutions provide companies with the knowledge and money they need to implement their innovation hypotheses. In this way institutions such as universities and government research institutes; banks, venture capitalists, and angel investors; laws relating to matters such as intellectual property; and government policymakers and regulators become key components of innovation systems shaping outcomes.

The Business Ecosystems Approach

The second cluster of literature that also took a systemic approach to innovation emerged and evolved entirely independently of the first. It is referred to in Chapter 3 as the 'business ecosystems' approach.

The first to pioneer this approach was James Moore in an article published in 1993 and a book in 1996. Moore was interested in business strategy and competition and worked closely on and with large American companies. As his work progressed he came to feel increasingly strongly that the approaches to strategy and competition then used in the leading business schools had lost touch with the practices of the companies that he studied.

Rather than individual companies going head-to-head in particular industries, he observed that groups of cooperating companies often tended to coalesce around emerging new innovations using and then further advancing these innovations in the products and services that they sold. Frequently, competition between companies was more a matter of competition between groups of companies unified around particular innovations. To conceptualise this process, he turned to the analogy of biological ecosystems where species and organisms cooperated and competed and by so doing co-evolved.

Innovation was central to Moore's narrative. Innovation provided the main rationale for a company to get together in the first place with a group of other companies, coalescing around a group of new innovations. Furthermore, subsequent rounds of innovation resulted as the companies, often motivated by competitive pressures, sought additional value-adding improvements.

Whilst Moore, who was the first to rigorously introduce the ecosystems idea into the business literature, felt that the biological ecosystems analogy was helpful in providing insights, he recognised that it could not be pushed too far. The reason was that whereas biological species and organisms are constrained by their genes, and the length of their lifespan limits how quickly advantageous characteristics can be reproduced within populations, this does not hold for companies. In strong contrast, companies can make relatively rapid changes to their behaviour, including strategies.

Marco Iansiti and Roy Levien, writing in the aftermath of the collapse of the Internet economy, wanted to understand better the ways in which complex networks of companies were managed. Like Moore, their concerns were also with company management, strategy, and competition. Their key article and book in this field were published in 2004.

Drawing significantly on Moore's work, however, and whilst also employing the biological ecosystems analogy, Iansiti and Levien focused their attention on the strategic decisions of a company's business units. Their reason is that it is mainly at the business unit level that a company's strategic decisions relating to their products and services are made. Different business units in the same company, they pointed out, may belong to different business ecosystems.

One of their contributions that led to a rich seam of subsequent literature was the development of the idea of 'platforms' that was already nascent in Moore. Platforms they defined as services, tools, or technologies provided mainly by the so-called keystone players in the ecosystem to other members of the ecosystem which enabled the latter to develop solutions to some of the main problems that they confronted working within the ecosystem. These other members include niche players in the system.

Innovation enters Iansiti and Levien's narrative in two main ways. First, through the creation, largely by keystones, of 'integration innovations' that allow members of the ecosystem to leverage resources, including technologies, available in the ecosystem. In this way keystones seek to enhance the collective value-creation of the ecosystem as a whole whilst securing their own ability to appropriate part of this value. The second way is through the innovative activities of niche players attempting to safeguard and strengthen their positions in the ecosystem (whilst possibly also creating openings in other rival ecosystems) by allowing them to differentiate themselves.

Comparisons and Reflections

In Chapter 3 the similarities and differences between the national innovation systems and business ecosystems literatures are examined. It is emphasised that their seminal contribution lies in their demonstration that innovation can be fruitfully conceptualised and analysed as a systemic phenomenon.

However, it is also shown that neither of these approaches considers in detail how innovation happens; that is, what innovators do and the questions and challenges that they must deal with to bring about the innovations they are attempting to create and implement. On the whole, these kinds of issues remain external to their analyses. This prevents a fuller picture of the innovation process being portrayed.

In Chapter 6 the question of *how* innovation happens is pursued further. This is done through a detailed examination from an ex ante perspective focusing on the real-time decisions that were made by those who created four key innovations. Together these four innovations crucially facilitated the emergence of the Internet and its supporting technologies and in this way changed the world. The four innovations are the transistor, the microprocessor, the laser, and optical fibre.

Also missing in the national innovation systems and business ecosystems literatures is a detailed consideration of *who* makes innovation happen. This question is taken up in Chapter 7 which includes a detailed discussion of the role of entrepreneurs and the entrepreneurial function and asks whether the entrepreneur has become obsolete.

INNOVATION ECOSYSTEMS

To focus more directly on the evolving innovation process, including the how and who questions, it is proposed also in Chapter 3 that the idea of an 'innovation ecosystem' might be fruitful. The innovation ecosystem is defined as the collection of players and processes that through their cooperative and competitive interactions make innovation happen and, by so doing, co-evolve. The conceptualisation of the innovation ecosystem with its emphasis on the how and who questions draws significantly on the closely related conceptualisations of national innovation systems and business ecosystems. However, a different appellation is used to emphasise that how innovation happens and who makes it happen are at the heart of the conceptualisation of the ecosystem and its functioning.

In Chapter 4 the idea of innovation ecosystems is explored further through a detailed analysis of what is referred to as the information and communications technologies (ICT) innovation ecosystem. A layer model of this sector innovation ecosystem is developed bringing together four groups of interdependent players who through their interactions produce the products and services of the ICT sector whilst at the same time generating the innovations that drive both this sector and the wider economy.

The four groups of players are the following: in Layer 1, the ICT equipment suppliers (who supply semiconductors, computer hardware and software, telecommunications equipment, etc.); in Layer 2, the network operators (i.e. telecoms, cable, satellite, and broadcasting operators who use the ICT equipment provided by the first layer players to construct their networks); in Layer 3, the platform, content, and applications providers (including the Internet players such as Google, Amazon, eBay, and Facebook); and in Layer 4, the final customers who consume ICT products and services. The cooperative vertical relationships and competitive horizontal relationships between these players are analysed, providing a more detailed picture of the context within which ICT innovations happen and the players who make it happen.

Chapter 5 contains an interview with the present author in which the conceptualisation and policy implications of innovation ecosystems are discussed.

HOW DOES INNOVATION HAPPEN?

As already mentioned, in Chapter 6 this question is explored through a detailed ex ante examination of the innovation processes involved in the innovation of the transistor, microprocessor, laser, and optical fibre. This examination results in the distillation of nine propositions which together provide a richer answer to the key question addressed in this chapter: How does innovation happen? These propositions are incorporated in the analysis of the ICT innovation ecosystem undertaken in Chapter 4.

WHO MAKES INNOVATION HAPPEN?

Schumpeter's answer is that it is the entrepreneur who makes innovation happen. According to his definition, anyone who makes innovation happen is an entrepreneur.

However, as we will show in Chapter 7, he distinguishes the entrepreneur from other players who also contribute to innovation happening. These players are inventors (who create the initial idea(s) for innovation), managers, and the providers of capital.

But Schumpeter goes even further, arguing that an additional function of entrepreneurship, which provides a further rationale for the existence of entrepreneurs, lies in overcoming the resistances to innovation that frequently exist. These resistances are examined in detail in Chapter 7.

Perhaps surprisingly, Schumpeter also argued that in modern capitalist societies the role of the entrepreneur is becoming obsolete. His reasoning is that in modern large companies, innovation is becoming routinised and is being undertaken by cooperating teams. Schumpeter's arguments are examined in detail and their limitations revealed.

But Schumpeter's observations raise far broader and crucially important questions: How is the process of specialisation and the division of innovation labour changing in capitalist economies, what are the consequences for entrepreneurship, and who makes innovation happen?

To explore this question in more detail we draw on some of the ideas of three famous economists: Adam Smith and Alfred Marshall (who wrote well before Schumpeter), and Friedrich Hayek (who was a contemporary of Schumpeter's). The relevance of their ideas is explored through a discussion of the division of innovation labour in modern large companies.

Taking the discussion even further, Chapter 7 ends with a critical examination of a widely referenced contemporary book which purports to teach companies and not-for-profit organisations how to make innovation happen. This examination makes use of the ideas previously discussed in this chapter. This book is Eric Ries's *The Lean Startup*.

Chapter 7 concludes with an answer to the question: Is the entrepreneur obsolete?

INNOVATION AND FINANCIAL INSTABILITY

As already discussed, the innovation process typically begins with the creation by the innovator of an innovation hypothesis. This is the first of the nine propositions that emerge from the analysis of four key innovations in Chapter 6. The innovation hypothesis embodies the innovator's subjective expectations regarding the intended innovation.

But subjective expectations about innovations also play a crucial role in other domains. One particularly important domain is in financial markets. The reason is that innovations create opportunities such as opportunities for investors and consumers. The more important the innovation, the greater the opportunities. In turn, investment and consumption are two key drivers of economic output and employment.

What is the transmission mechanism linking innovation with financial markets? The answer is that the expected opportunities created by an innovation may affect the value of financial assets, both existing assets and new assets. For example, the shares of companies that are expected to benefit from the opportunities that innovation provides may rise as buyers purchase these assets in anticipation of realising gains.

An important recent case is the so-called telecoms and dot-com boom and bust 1996–2003. The innovation (or, more accurately, cluster of innovations in this case) was the advent of the Internet, which began to make a widespread commercial impact from about 1995. Several parts of the present book are devoted to a deeper understanding of the innovations and innovation processes that gave birth to the Internet. Chapter 6 deals with how innovation happened in the cases of the transistor, microprocessor, laser, and optical fibre, innovations without which the Internet would have been impossible. Chapter 4 provides a detailed examination of the structure and functioning of the ICT innovation ecosystem which created, and in turn was fundamentally influenced by, the Internet. The primary concern of Chapter 8, however, is the connections between innovation and financial markets.

Chapter 8 is devoted to a detailed, blow-by-blow account of the telecoms boom and bust, analysing the precise causes of the boom and its eventual collapse into panic and bust. Lessons are derived from this important experience which also had longer term consequences, arguably influencing the great financial global crisis from 2007.

For the purposes of the present book, however, the main importance of the telecoms boom and bust is its illustration of the links that may occur between innovation ecosystems and the markets of financial ecosystems. It is subjective expectations regarding the consequences of innovation that lie beneath these links.

INNOVATION ECOSYSTEMS POLICY: THE CASE OF CHINA

What are the implications of innovation ecosystems thinking for government policy? This question is pursued in the case of China in Chapter 9. The occasion for a more detailed examination of this important question was presented when the present author was invited by the incoming Chinese government of Xi Jinping to participate in a programme established as part of several efforts to prepare the new government for office. In this programme the Chinese government invited selected Fortune 500 companies to prepare reports in four areas proposing actions that should be undertaken by the new government. Innovation was the topic for the first of these areas and the present author was invited to join this group.

Chapter 9 begins with an account of the specific questions that were asked of the companies preparing the innovation report. The rest of the chapter consists of the report that the present author was invited to prepare. The main topic of this report is the role that innovation ecosystems thinking might play within the Chinese context.

INNOVATION AND ECONOMIC THEORY: KEYNES'S *GENERAL THEORY*

As noted in this book, over time innovation is the main driver of socioeconomic change. In the case of the economy it is innovation that determines productivity, competitiveness, and economic growth and employment. And as the present book shows, innovation happens through the systemic activities of players and processes. But this raises an interesting puzzle. Why is it that arguably the most important book ever written about the economy and its functioning,

The General Theory, produced by John Maynard Keynes, says virtually nothing about innovation?

In the penultimate chapter in this book, Chapter 10, attention is turned to the question of innovation and economic theory. The specific issue examined is the role that innovation plays in Keynes's magnum opus, *The General Theory*, or, more specifically, why Keynes excluded an analysis of innovation in this book and how he might have added innovation had he chosen to do so.

There is widespread agreement that Keynes was the greatest economist of the twentieth century. A notable feature of *The General Theory*, however, is the absence of discussion of innovation. The words 'innovation' and 'technical change' are absent from the index to this book. This is in strong contrast to the writings of Joseph Schumpeter, another of the twentieth century's great economists, with which Keynes's work is often compared. Innovation was central in Schumpeter's analysis of the dynamics of the capitalist system, as is shown in many parts of the present book. How is this contrast to be explained?

In Chapter 10 it is suggested that the most relevant part of *The General Theory* in which a discussion of innovation could have been located is chapter 12, titled 'The State of Long-Term Expectation'. It is this chapter that would have provided a natural home for an analysis of the relevance of innovation had Keynes chosen to include it. But why did Keynes not decide to do so? This is the main question pursued in Chapter 10.

CONCLUSIONS

The final chapter, Chapter 11, draws several conclusions from the discussions and analyses contained in the present book.

2 Contextualising Innovation

The Schumpeterian-Evolutionary Approach to Economic Change[*]

In this chapter the context within which innovation occurs in capitalist systems is examined. This is done through a discussion of the Schumpeterian-evolutionary approach to economic change. This approach is based on the writings of Joseph Schumpeter.[1] Schumpeter is usually thought of as one of the greatest economists of the twentieth century along with John Maynard Keynes. Keynes, however, had very little to say about innovation.[2] In strong contrast, innovation was central for Schumpeter. For it is innovation, he argued, that is the main engine driving the capitalist system and causing its restlessness. Schumpeter's framework provides a useful context for the discussions in this book around the themes of innovation ecosystems and how innovation happens.

In the 1980s Dick Nelson and Sidney Winter injected a new stimulus into Schumpeterian thought by marrying the thought of Schumpeter and Darwin to enrich the analysis of the process of change in capitalist systems.[3] Innovation remains central in this

---

[*] The author would like to acknowledge, with thanks, comments on an earlier version of this chapter from Cristiano Antonelli, Dick Langlois, Stan Metcalfe, and Dick Nelson.

[1] See, for example, Schumpeter, J. A., 1961. *The Theory of Economic Development.* New York, NY: Oxford University Press, and Schumpeter, J. A., 1943. *Capitalism, Socialism, and Democracy.* London: Unwin.

[2] The index to Keynes's most famous book, for example (Keynes, J. M., 1961. *The General Theory of Employment, Interest and Money,* London: Macmillan), does not contain the words 'innovation' or 'technical change'. For a discussion on how Keynes could have incorporated an analysis of innovation into the *General Theory,* had he chosen to do so, see Chapter 10 of the present book.

[3] Nelson, R. R. and Winter, S. G., 1982. *An Evolutionary Theory of Economic Change.* Cambridge, MA: Harvard University Press. Dick Nelson is also the author of significant work on 'national innovation systems' discussed in Chapter 3.

marriage. Their work stimulated a large corpus of theoretical and empirical research.

To explain briefly but rigorously the Schumpeterian-evolutionary approach to economic change, the analysis in this chapter is presented in the form of several propositions that, taken together, illuminate the system of thought at the heart of this approach.

PROPOSITIONS

1. Capitalism as a Restless System

1.1 For Schumpeter, *the* key characteristic of capitalism is its restlessness. It is a system in a *constant* process of change. This feature constitutes an indubitable starting assumption about the nature of the system.

1.2 But this poses the question: what causes this restlessness?

1.3 Schumpeter's answer to this question is that the cause of the restlessness is the constant injection of *novelty* into the system.

1.4 The introduction of novelty creates new possibilities and opportunities to which some players in the system respond.

1.5 But at the same time the novelty also destroys some old practices, rendering them obsolete.

1.6 The change that accordingly is brought about appears as restlessness.

2. Novelty and Innovation

2.1 What is the 'novelty' that is constantly injected into the capitalist system?

2.2 Schumpeter identified what he called four 'prime movers' or innovations that together drive the process of change:

    2.2.1 New products and services

    2.2.2 New processes and technologies

    2.2.3 New forms of organisation

    2.2.4 New markets, ways of marketing, and business models.

2.3 In short, it is these four forms of innovation that are the engine of economic change as they generate substitution and complementarity effects.

3. Innovation and the Entrepreneur

3.1 But who introduces innovation into the system?

3.2 Schumpeter's answer is that this function is provided by the entrepreneur. In Schumpeter's words, it is the entrepreneur who 'carries out' – i.e. implements – innovation, in this way injecting the new into the system.

3.3 However, the entrepreneur is not necessarily the inventor who introduces the new idea in the first place. It is the entrepreneur who commercialises the idea, facilitating its diffusion and economic impact.

3.4 The entrepreneur is also not necessarily the provider of capital who is the risk-taker.

3.5 Furthermore, the entrepreneur is not a manager. Whilst the entrepreneur introduces the new, the manager seeks to optimise the efficiency of the enterprise using known processes.

4. The Odd Character That Is the Entrepreneur

4.1 The entrepreneur, however, is a distinctive player in the system. This is so for two reasons:

4.1.1 Entrepreneurs 'see' opportunities that others do not. Only a small minority of the players in the system are entrepreneurs.

4.1.2 Entrepreneurs are often wrong! In Schumpeter's words:

> 'a majority of would-be entrepreneurs never get their projects under sail and, of those that do, nine out of ten fail to make a success of them'.[4]

4.2 Are entrepreneurs therefore 'rational' in their decision to become entrepreneurs?

5. Why Entrepreneurs and Mainstream Economics Make Poor Travelling Companions

5.1 The entrepreneur is noticeably absent from the vast majority of theories and models in mainstream economics. Why is this the case?

5.2 The reason is that entrepreneurship is incompatible with the assumptions, explicit and implicit, and analytical procedures adopted in mainstream economics.

5.3 Concepts such as optimisation, maximisation, and equilibrium all imply that there is a 'right' outcome.

5.4 But as we have seen, the ex-ante world of the entrepreneur is characterised by *uncertainty* (in the sense of Frank Knight where uncertainty, as opposed to risk, is unmeasurable[5]). This is why entrepreneurs are often wrong.

---

[4] Schumpeter, J. A., 1939. *Business Cycles*. New York, NY: McGraw Hill, p. 117.
[5] Knight, F. H., 1921. *Risk, Uncertainty and Profit*. Boston, MA: Houghton Mifflin.

5.5 In such a world there is no optimal or maximising decision for the simple reason that it cannot be defined. The absence of the entrepreneur is, therefore, not surprising.

6. Is There an 'Engine of Change' in Mainstream Economics?

6.1 If what has been said so far is correct, mainstream economics faces a significant problem: it lacks a realistic 'engine of change'.

6.2 This is so because it lacks a realistic theory of how novelty happens. Without such a theory, mainstream economics is confined to the 'given'. For it is the injection of novelty that *changes* the 'given', making it other than what it was and forcing players to adapt to the new. This is what change in the capitalist system is all about.

6.3 In the world of the 'given', essentially a static world, there *are* 'right' outcomes and decisions. It is in such a world that concepts such as optimisation, maximisation, and equilibrium make sense.

6.4 The problem, however, is that this static world is *not* the restless, uncertain world that is the capitalist system in which we live.

7. Uncertainty, Expectations, and Decision-Making

7.1 As time passes, novelty is injected into the system by entrepreneurs, causing the system itself to change.

7.2 Ex ante, however, we cannot know the nature of these changes. For if we did, the changes, by definition, would not be novel. The result is Knightian uncertainty where probability distributions cannot be defined and cannot, therefore, assist decision-making.[6]

7.3 How do players play in such a world? The answer is that they construct subjective expectations that they know may be wrong. (Entrepreneurs do not make innovation decisions by rolling the dice.)

7.4 But this creates further problems. The reason is that different players in the same circumstances may construct inconsistent expectations. If they do, over time some will turn out to be right, others wrong.

7.5 This presents problems for the notion of equilibrium over time. For if some players turn out to be wrong, they cannot have been in equilibrium earlier when they made their decisions based on incorrect expectations. Under these circumstances equilibrium over time does not make sense.

[6] Ibid.

8. Economy-Wide Equilibrium?

8.1 For these reasons Schumpeter found the notion of economy-wide equilibrium unacceptable.

8.2 Not only is the notion itself inherently unacceptable, it is also misleading. The reason is that unpredictable novelty is *constantly* disrupting the capitalist economic system, disturbing existing expectations and decisions, and replacing them with new ones. Such a process is incompatible with the assumption of a state of rest as players achieve their preferred positions, which is inherent in the notion of equilibrium.

8.3 Accordingly, the concept of equilibrium distorts the reality of decision-making in the uncertain world that is capitalism. By so doing it may make decision-making even less effective than it might be.

9. Entrepreneurial Innovation Decision-Making

9.1 How do entrepreneurs make decisions about innovation? That is, how does innovation happen?

9.2 Innovation happens in a number of ways. The most common (and important for the entrepreneur) is through the generation ex ante of a hypothesis about how value will be created.

9.3 This is a hypothesis about what will add value for consumer-users relative to what is being offered by competitors. It involves 'the imagined deemed possible'.[7]

9.4 But this hypothesis is uncertain. It may, or may not, turn out to be correct. It therefore must be tested, passing through several selection processes, ultimately being subjected to the test of market selection.

9.5 The testing process also provides feedback that may transform the original hypothesis. For this reason, the hypothesis is best thought of as a process evolving over time.

9.6 Emergent innovation refers to the innovation that emerges from these selection processes.

10. An Example of Emergent Innovation: Concorde versus the iPhone

10.1 Both Concorde and the iPhone were highly creative, new products.

10.2 Both represented significant advances in their areas.

---

[7] Loasby, B., 1996. 'The imagined deemed possible', in E. Helmstadter and M. Perlman (eds.), *Behavioral Norms, Technological Progress and Economic Dynamics*. Ann Arbor, MI: University of Michigan Press, pp. 17–31.

10.3 But the hypothesis in the case of Concorde was wrong; in the case of the iPhone it was right.

10.4 Economically, Concorde itself had little impact, whilst the iPhone had a substantial impact. Only the iPhone was an emergent innovation.

10.5 As the example illustrates, *ignorance*, *mistakes*, and *errors* are an inherent part of the evolutionary innovation process. In this process there are not, ex ante, 'right' answers.

11. Schumpeter and Darwin

11.1 Although Schumpeter referred to innovation as an evolutionary process, he neither discussed nor employed Darwin's ideas on evolution.

11.2 This task was left to 'modern' Schumpeterians, Richard Nelson and Sidney Winter, in their seminal book, *An Evolutionary Theory of Economic Change* (1982).

11.3 For Darwin, evolution = variety + selection + reproduction.

11.4 The conceptual link to Schumpeter is made, first, by treating variety as being generated through entrepreneurial innovation. Second, selection is seen as the winnowing process that is brought about as innovation hypotheses pass through the various selection hurdles that end with market selection.

11.5 For both Darwin and Schumpeter, the evolving outcomes of the interaction between variety and selection are ex ante unpredictable.

12. Innovation and Financial Instability

12.1 The link between innovation and the possibility of financial instability is readily made.

12.2 The reason is that innovations create new possibilities and opportunities. Some players seize these and act accordingly.

12.3 Where these players are successful, particularly highly successful, information regarding the possibility of gain is generated affecting the demand for related financial assets.

12.4 It is here that the subjective expectations of other players, held with ex ante uncertainty, enter the story. If the innovations are radical with widespread ramifications and generate significant short-term gain, it is possible that the expectations become 'exuberant' and engender 'greed'. These are fundamentally human and social behaviours that are not well captured in formal mathematical models.

12.5 However, greed may turn into 'panic' as changing realities contradict increasingly unrealistic expectations. Changing realities include the entry of new players, reducing profit margins; coordination failures leading to overinvestment; and unsustainable price–earnings ratios. Under these conditions many sell their financial assets.

12.6 Falling financial asset prices have further knock-on effects, leading eventually to economic downturn.

13. Explaining Economic Growth

13.1 Significantly, all schools of thought in economics agree that innovation is the main driver of increasing productivity and growth.

13.2 Where the disagreement enters is in explaining how this growth happens and the analytical tools that are appropriate in analysing it.

13.3 The Schumpeterian-evolutionary approach to analysing the innovation that leads to increasing productivity and growth was examined above.

13.4 From a Schumpeterian perspective, the explanations of growth provided in the mainstream exogenous and endogenous growth theories[8] in economics are unconvincing. The reason is that, lacking a robust understanding of innovation, they do not come adequately to grips with how growth happens in particular contexts at particular times, even though they may include some of the mechanisms that exist.

13.5 Common analytical tools, such as aggregate production functions,[9] are also thought to be inadequate since they treat the process of innovation as a 'black box' with the result that output becomes an ex post given, lacking any credible causal antecedents.

13.6 In response to these shortcomings, Schumpeterian economists have developed the concept of 'national innovation systems' that incorporate institutions as well as firms in explaining innovation and growth and formulating appropriate policies.[10] Significantly, this concept is widely used in international organisations such as the OECD and government ministries such as the UK Ministry of Business, Innovation and Skills.

14. Why Has Schumpeterian-Evolutionary Economics Received so Little Attention from Mainstream Economics?

14.1 In the present author's view there are several reasons.

---

[8] In an exogenous growth model, the causes of growth are outside the model. In an endogenous growth model, the causes are internal to the model.

[9] An aggregate production function relates aggregate output to the aggregate of all the inputs.

[10] The literature relating to national innovation systems is examined in Chapter 3.

14.2 First, the Schumpeterian approach, as indicated here, logically leaves little room for concepts such as maximisation, optimisation, and equilibrium that are key analytical tools for much mainstream theorising. To really take Schumpeter on board would require questioning the usefulness of these concepts.

14.3 Second, the logic of the Schumpeterian approach – with its emphasis on concepts such as Knightian uncertainty, the likelihood of inconsistent subjective expectations, and the ubiquity of ignorance, mistakes, and errors – implies a degree of unpredictability that the mainstream is unwilling to accept. In effect, physics rather than biology is seen as the role model in mainstream economics.

14.4 Third, the Schumpeterian emphasis on history, the nonquantitative empirical 'appreciation' of complex socioeconomic determinants, and the willingness to see mathematical models as possible aids to human reasoning, rather than as acceptable depictions of the real world, is the cause of further tension.

14.5 Will this change in the near future? The one glimmer of hope comes from the centrality of innovation itself. This centrality makes it essential that academics, other analysts, and policymakers 'get a handle' on innovation in order to understand how it happens. And to do so, as this chapter has made clear, it will be necessary to depart in significant respects from what currently is the dominant approach in mainstream economics.

3 'National Innovation Systems', 'Business Ecosystems', and 'Innovation Ecosystems'

One of the most important ideas in the field of innovation studies is that innovation is systemic. That is, the many determinants of innovation are best viewed as being part of a system. The idea of an 'innovation ecosystem', the key concern of the present book, is derived from this way of understanding innovation.

In this chapter, attention is focused on some of the seminal contributions that have given rise to two clusters of literature that have a close bearing on the notion of innovation being a systemic phenomenon. These are the 'national innovation systems' and 'business ecosystems' literatures. In each case the main contributions of some of the founders of each approach are examined in detail. Reflections are offered on these contributions.

Two conclusions emerge from this examination. The first is that in these literatures, great strides have been made, increasing the richness and robustness of our understanding of innovation. Second, despite these advances, many further questions, of key importance to the understanding of innovation, remain to be explored in greater detail.

In particular, two questions are identified. The first is: How does innovation happen? That is, what are the processes that facilitate the creation of innovations that increase competitiveness, a common concern in both approaches? The second question, closely related to the first, is: Who makes this innovation happen? That is, which players actually do what must be done to make competitiveness-enhancing innovation happen and what is the division of labour amongst them?

To analyse these questions in more detail, endogenising them in the conceptualisation of the system, a third approach is suggested, namely the innovation ecosystems approach. Whilst making the most of the strengths and insights of both the national innovation systems and the business ecosystems approaches – so that there is a significant overlap between these two approaches and the innovation ecosystems approach – the latter delves more deeply into the 'how' and 'who' questions.

In Chapter 4, an example is given of a sector innovation ecosystem analysis. This involves a study of the information and communications technologies (ICT) innovation ecosystem.

Chapter 6 discusses in far more detail how innovation happens, taking the innovation of the transistor, microprocessor, optical fibre, and laser as examples. Chapter 7 is devoted to an analysis of who makes innovation happen. This includes discussion of the role of the entrepreneur and entrepreneurship, the argument that the entrepreneur has become obsolete, and the continuously evolving division of labour in making innovation happen.

INTRODUCTION

There is widespread agreement across most schools of thought that innovation is the main driver over time of the productivity, competitiveness, and growth of both countries and companies.

But *how* does innovation happen? In other words, what must be done to make innovation happen? Without an answer to this question we cannot have a complete explanation and understanding of improvements in the productivity, competitiveness, and growth of countries and companies.

There is agreement regarding *what* innovation is. In answering this question, the major international organisations such as the OECD have followed Joseph Schumpeter, who, as we saw in Chapter 2, included not only new products and services, and new processes and technologies, but also new forms of organisations, new markets and ways of marketing, and new business models.

There is also some agreement regarding *who* makes innovation happen. This is a question that is examined in detail in Chapter 7. For Schumpeter, as we will see, it is the entrepreneur who innovates, and innovation, accordingly, is the function of entrepreneurship. Subsequent literature in the Schumpeterian tradition has also emphasised the important role in innovation played by institutions of various kinds.

Since the 1980s two important concepts have been developed and widely adopted, by academics, companies, and policymakers, to get a better 'handle' on the determinants of innovation. The first is the concept of 'national innovation systems'. The second is the concept of 'business ecosystems'.

This chapter has four aims:

1. To explore the origin of these two concepts
2. To identify the core components of each concept
3. To examine whether either or both of the concepts gives a satisfactory answer to the question of how innovation happens, and
4. To explore a new concept of 'innovation ecosystems', which provides additional understanding of how innovation happens and, relatedly, who makes innovation happen.

NATIONAL INNOVATION SYSTEMS

Christopher Freeman

Christopher Freeman was a leading thinker in the economics of innovation. After spending some time at the OECD, Freeman went to Sussex University in the United Kingdom where he established the Science Policy Research Unit, which became one of the world's leading academic institutes specialising in science, technology, and innovation theory and policy.

Freeman was one of the initiators of the concept of national innovation systems. This he did in a book titled *Technology Policy and Economic Performance: Lessons from Japan*,[1] published in 1987.

---

[1] Freeman, C., 1987. *Technology Policy and Economic Performance: Lessons from Japan*. London: Pinter.

Freeman's 'World View'

Writing in the tradition of Joseph Schumpeter, Freeman saw innovation as the 'prime mover' of the global (and national) economy. Innovation creates new opportunities for both investment and consumption, and these drive economic change. At the same time as creating the new, innovation destroys some or all of the old. It is this that makes capitalism the restless, continually changing, 'creative-destructive' (to use Schumpeter's terminology) system that it is.

From a longer-term perspective, Freeman, like Schumpeter, saw radical innovation emerging periodically in clustered bursts. These clusters of innovation drive long-term waves of economic activity (often referred to as Kondratieff waves after the Russian statistician who studied these waves). In all, since the Industrial Revolution, which began in Britain in the 1770s, there have been five such long waves – in textiles, steam and railways, steel and heavy engineering, oil and the car, and information and communications technologies. But there is also a downside to radical innovation that causes instability. As Freeman and Carlotta Perez[2] showed, financial markets frequently respond with excessive exuberance to the radically new opportunities, resulting in mania that, as the innovations diffuse and rates of profit in the new industries fall, turns to panic and pessimism and hence falling asset values.

But innovation, as defined earlier, does not exist in a vacuum. It needs, if it is to be economically effective, to be supported by institutions, e.g. financial, research, and training institutions, rules of the game, and infrastructure. This creates openings for following countries to catch up since the leading countries, whose economic performance has been based on previous waves of innovation, often find it difficult to adapt their institutions and create new ones sufficiently quickly to support the new wave of innovations. Follower countries, in contrast, lacking the institutions of earlier waves, may be able to

---

[2] Perez, C., 2002. *Technological Revolutions and Financial Capital: The Dynamics of Bubbles and Golden Ages*. Cheltenham: Edward Elgar.

move more quickly to effectively develop the new institutions supporting the new wave. This may result in catch-up. It is this problem-
atic that made Freeman particularly interested in Japan.

Technology Policy and Economic Performance: Lessons from Japan,
by Chris Freeman

From Freeman's point of view and at the time that he was writing,
Japan was particularly important. At the very beginning of his book he
states, 'This book is about innovation and the diffusion of innovations. Following Schumpeter, it argues that technical and related
social innovations are the main source of dynamism and instability
in the world economy and that technological capacity is the main
source of the competitive strength of firms and nations.'[3]

From this perspective, Japan was highly significant. Referring to
the 'astonishing Japanese progress', Freeman points out that Japan is
'that country which has been the most successful in accelerating the
rate of technical change over the past 30 years'.[4]

From today's vantage point, however, this statement might
seem dated. After all, not only has Japan's economy slipped into third
place after China's, most of the Japanese companies that Freeman
praises, having caught up with the global leaders by the time Freeman
wrote, since the bursting of the Japanese bubble economy in 1990,
have fallen significantly behind in terms of indicators such as market
share, profitability, and growth. But to understand Freeman's ideas it
is necessary to understand Japan as it was at the time he perceived it.

An iconic contemporary book published in 1989, two years after
Freeman's, makes this perception of Japan clearer. This book is *Made
in America: Regaining the Productive Edge*,[5] edited by Michael Dertouzos, Richard Lester, and Robert Solow for the MIT Commission on
Industrial Productivity. Based on detailed studies of eight sectors of

---

[3] Freeman (1987), p. 1.   [4] Ibid., p. 2.
[5] Dertouzos, M. L., Lester, R. K., and Solow, R. M. 1989. *Made in America: Regaining
the Productive Edge*. Boston, MA: MIT Press.

the US economy – automobiles; chemicals; commercial aircraft; computers, semiconductors, and copiers; consumer electronics; machine tools; steel; and textiles – the Commission concluded, 'The verdict is that American industry indeed shows worrisome signs of weakness. In many important sectors of the economy, U.S. firms are losing ground to their competitors abroad.'[6]

Although in some sectors such as computers, chemicals, and commercial aircraft the main threat to US companies did not come from Japan, in most of the remaining sectors it did. For example, in microelectronics the Commission pointed out that 'Japanese companies hold 75 percent of the market. Today the three leading merchant semiconductor companies are all Japanese: NEC, Toshiba, and Hitachi.'[7] In machine tools, the Commission noted, 'the Japanese are pushing up from the low end … The Japanese success is based on a policy coordinated by the Ministry of International Trade and Industry (MITI).'[8] In consumer electronics the Japanese industry '[i]n just four decades … has progressed from making a few cheap, low-quality parts and radios to leading the world in market share and technology. Japan's ascendancy has come primarily at the expense of the U.S. industry.'[9]

So much for the phenomenon and empirical evidence for Japanese catch-up. But how is this Japanese performance to be explained and understood? Crucially, it was in answer to this question that Freeman, an economist, felt that he needed a new concept, one substantially different from what was available from mainstream economics, which he felt did not provide a sufficiently robust explanation. The concept that he proposed was that of a 'national innovation system'.

In the first chapter of his book, Freeman noted, 'In particular [the book] attempts to develop the idea of "national systems of innovation" associated with pervasive changes in technology.' Several paragraphs later, he provided his definition of this concept:

[6] Ibid., p. 8.   [7] Ibid., p. 9.   [8] Ibid., p. 20.   [9] Ibid., p. 28.

> The network of institutions in the public and private sectors whose activities and interactions initiate, import, modify and diffuse new technologies may be described as 'the national system of innovation'. This study is about some features of the Japanese system of innovation and their implications for other countries.[10]

Later in the first chapter, Freeman summarises the 'four main features' of the Japanese innovation system:

1. the role of the Ministry of International Trade and Industry (MITI);
2. the role of company research and development strategy in relation to imported technology and 'reverse engineering';
3. the role of education and training and related social innovations; and
4. the conglomerate structure of industry.[11]

Coming at the issue from the perspective of long waves of innovation, as noted earlier, it is no surprise that Freeman focused particularly on what he saw as the superior Japanese ability to adopt, adapt, diffuse and eventually to create the latest generation of technology: 'One of the most notable features of the Japanese system has been the speed with which Japanese firms and Japanese policymakers in MITI and elsewhere identified the importance of information and communication technology (ICT) and embarked on measures to diffuse the new technology very rapidly to more traditional industries, such as machinery and vehicles.'[12]

Richard Nelson and Colleagues

Richard Nelson together with Sidney Winter is regarded as the founder of modern Schumpeterian-evolutionary economics. He has held professorial appointments at Yale and Columbia universities.

---

[10] Freeman (1987), p. 1.   [11] Ibid., p. 4.   [12] Ibid., pp. 4–5.

Nelson is best known for his seminal book with Sidney Winter, *An Evolutionary Theory of Economic Change*,[13] published in 1982, which launched modern Schumpeterian-evolutionary economics. In the preface to this book it is noted that 'For Nelson, the starting point was a concern with the processes of long-run economic development. Early on, that concern became focused on technological change as the key driving force and on the role of policy as an influence on the strength and direction of that force.'[14]

National Innovation Systems: A Comparative Analysis, edited by Richard Nelson

Whilst *An Evolutionary Theory of Economic Change* was primarily concerned with economic theory and with a critique of the dominant paradigm in economics, neoclassical economics, Nelson edited another seminal book, titled *National Innovation Systems: A Comparative Analysis*, published in 1993.[15] The latter book contains a comparative study of technological change and economic development in several countries.

The introductory chapter to this book, written by Nelson and Nathan Rosenberg, explains the 'climate' within which the book was written: 'The slowdown of growth since the early 1970s in all of the advanced industrial nations, the rise of Japan as a major economic and technological power, the relative decline of the United States, and widespread concerns in Europe about being behind both ... has given rise to the current strong interest in national innovation systems, and their similarities and differences, and in the extent and manner that

---

[13] Nelson, R. R. and Winter, S. G., 1982. *An Evolutionary Theory of Economic Change*. Cambridge, MA: Harvard University Press.

[14] Ibid., p. vi. For a summary of the Nelson and Winter approach and a comparison with other neighbouring theories, see Fransman, M., 1994. 'Information, knowledge, vision and theories of the firm'. *Industrial and Corporate Change*, 3, 2: 1–45, reprinted in G. Dosi, D. J. Teece, and J. Chytry (eds.), *Technology, Organisation, and Competitiveness: Perspectives on Industrial and Corporate Change*. New York, NY: Oxford University Press, 1998.

[15] Nelson, R. R., (ed.), 1993. *National Innovation Systems: A Comparative Analysis*. New York, NY: Oxford University Press.

these differences explain variation in national economic performance.'[16] As this quotation makes clear, the context of this book was
broadly the same as that which informed Freeman's 1987 book.

Although a good deal of research had been done on national innovation systems since the publication of Freeman's book, Nelson and
Rosenberg felt that this work was 'seriously' constrained by 'the absence
of a well-articulated and verified analytic framework linking institutional arrangements to technological and economic performance'.[17]

In explaining the 'basic terms and concepts' used in their book
Nelson and Rosenberg elaborate on what they mean by 'system': 'the
concept is of a set of institutions whose interactions determine the
innovative performance ... of national firms ... the "systems" concept is that of a set of institutional actors that, together, plays the
major role in influencing innovative performance'.[18]

'Innovation' they interpreted 'to encompass the processes by
which firms master and get into practice product designs and manufacturing processes that are new to them, if not to the universe or even
to the nation'.[19] In the book's concluding chapter Nelson elaborates
further on what is meant by 'innovation': 'We have defined innovation
broadly so that the term basically stands for what is required of firms
if they are to stay competitive in industries where technological
advance is important ... staying competitive requires continuing
innovation.'[20]

The Institutional Actors Comprising the National Innovation System

Firms Who are the 'institutional actors' that Nelson and Rosenberg
include in their national innovation system and how do they relate to
one another?

The authors point out that '[t]echnological advance proceeds
through the interaction of many actors ... we have considered some
of the key interactions involved, between component and systems

---

[16] Ibid., p. 3.   [17] Ibid., p. 4.   [18] Ibid., pp. 4–5.   [19] Ibid., p. 4.   [20] Ibid., p. 509.

producers, upstream and downstream firms, universities and industry, and government agencies and universities and industries ... in virtually all fields one must understand technical advance as proceeding through the work of a community of actors'.[21] However, it is necessary to bear in mind that the 'important interactions, the networks, are not the same in all industries or technologies'.[22]

The first set of actors identified by Nelson and Rosenberg are 'firms and industrial research laboratories'. There are two points worth noting about this conceptualisation. The first is that reference is to a *plurality* of firms rather than single firms. The second is the reference to research laboratories as a key component of firms.

Regarding the first point, already in *An Evolutionary Theory of Economic Change*, Nelson and Winter make the key distinction between *firms* and *industries* and stress that it is the latter in which they are really interested, although they accept that industries are comprised of firms and that decision-making at firm level, both strategic and routine, is important in its own right.

In this book they point out that 'as in [mainstream economics], the characterization of individual firms in evolutionary theory is primarily a step toward analysing the behaviour of industries or other large-scale units of economic organization. The models in this book are of "industries" – that is, situations in which a number of broadly similar firms interact with one another in a market context characterized by product demand and input supply curves.'[23] This distinction between firms and industries is important, as we shall later see, when it comes to comparing the concepts 'national innovation systems' and 'business ecosystems'.

The specific identification of industrial laboratories as a key component of firms, the second point, is also important. The reason is that although 'the industrial laboratory, rather than university laboratories or government facilities, became the dominant locus of

---

[21] Ibid., p. 15.   [22] Ibid.   [23] Nelson and Winter (1982), p. 18.

the R&D part of innovation',[24] researchers are not the only players within firms who are involved in innovation. 'The lines between R&D, and other activities, such as designing products for particular customers, problem solving on production processes, or monitoring a competitor's new products, are inherently blurry ... In developing countries ... reverse engineering is very much like R&D.' They conclude, therefore, that 'even if it is defined quite broadly, R&D usually is only a small part of the resources and problem solving that go into innovation'.[25]

Other Institutional Actors In the first chapter of *National Innovation Systems* Nelson and Rosenberg identify the following institutional actors included in the national innovation system:

1. Universities
2. Government laboratories
3. 'a nation's system of schooling, training and retraining';
4. Patterns of labour-management relations
5. Financial institutions
6. Firm governance and control, and
7. 'users of the system'.[26]

Reflecting on the findings of this collective study, Nelson concludes that there are three 'matters we are sure about'.[27] The first is that 'in manufacturing at least, the efforts of governments and universities may support, but cannot be a substitute for, the technological efforts of firms'. Second is 'the importance of a nation's education and training system'. And third, 'a nation's fiscal, monetary and trade policies must spur, even compel, national firms to compete on world markets'.[28]

---

[24] Nelson (1993), p. 10.
[25] Ibid., p. 11. In *National Innovation Systems* reference is to 'real world' firms in the countries studied. How 'firms' are modelled in Schumpeterian-evolutionary economics is a separate matter. For an analysis of how firms are modelled in Nelson and Winter's *An Evolutionary Theory of Economic Change*, see Fransman (1994c).
[26] Nelson (1993), pp. 11–14.   [27] Ibid., p. 20.   [28] Ibid.

Significantly, however, Nelson confesses that '[w]e are far less sure about another central issue.' This is 'the extent to which the particular features of a nation's technical innovation system matter centrally in affecting a nation's overall economic performance in such dimensions as productivity and income and their growth, export, and import performance'.[29]

Unfortunately, this very important qualification has not received the attention it deserves, neither from the authors of this volume nor from those who have drawn upon it. As we have noted in detail earlier, it is precisely the attempt to understand better the relationship between innovation and long-term economic perform- ance, growth, and development that motivated the introduction and use of the concept of a 'national innovation system' by Freeman, Nelson, and others. Nelson's qualification poses but does not answer the question of the extent to which the concept of national innovation systems throws light on these key outcomes.

Finally, it is also of interest that the Nelson book takes issue with Freeman's characterisation of the Japanese innovation system, particularly with the significance of the role of the Japanese MITI referred to earlier. In his concluding retrospective chapter, Nelson discusses the importance of 'active coherent industrial pol- icies',[30] examining both sides of the debate. He notes that 'the pos- ition taken by our Japanese authors on MITI' is that the importance of 'government leverage has been exaggerated and that where strong policies have been executed, they as often lead to failure as to suc- cess'. His final conclusion regarding MITI is agnostic: 'Without a better understanding of technological innovation than we now have, there is no way of resolving this debate in a way that will persuade all people.'[31]

The conclusions discussed in the last three paragraphs point implicitly to an important methodological issue that arises in this significant area of analysis. This is the difficulty of assigning causality

---

[29] Ibid.   [30] Ibid., p. 515.   [31] Ibid.

and effects in systems as complex as national innovation systems. Whilst this difficulty by no means negates the importance, indeed the necessity, of this kind of research – since the discipline of economics as a whole has nothing better to offer in explaining the causal relationship between innovation and the performance of countries and companies, and arguably has had much less to contribute – it is necessary to be aware of the challenges that remain in applying the concept of national innovation systems in order to obtain more robust explanations of outcomes.

Sources of Industrial Leadership: Studies of Seven Industries, edited by David Mowery and Richard Nelson

If *National Innovation Systems* is primarily about *countries*, *Sources of Industrial Leadership* is mainly about *industries*.[32] This difference in focus raises the important question of the appropriate unit(s) of analysis in explaining the causal connection between innovation and economic performance.

As we saw in the last section, in *National Innovation Systems* Nelson and Rosenberg identify 'firms' as the first set of 'actors' in national innovation systems. But what is the relationship between 'firms' and 'industries' and what role do these different units of analysis play in the explanation of innovation and economic performance?

Essentially, *Sources of Industrial Leadership* consists of in-depth studies of seven industries in which technological change is a key driver. The industries selected are: semiconductors, computers, software, machine tools, chemicals, pharmaceuticals and molecular biology, and diagnostic devices. The objective of each study is to identify global leadership of the industry and then to explain the determinants of this leadership. As Mowery and Nelson explain, 'The term *industrial leadership* prevents any presumption as to whether industrial leadership is determined by strengths that firms

---

[32] Mowery, D.C. and Nelson, R.R. (eds.), 1999. *Sources of Industrial Leadership: Studies of Seven Industries*. Cambridge: Cambridge University Press.

build for themselves, by their national environment, or by something in between (e.g. regional factors or institutions or other factors that are specific to an industry).'[33]

In discussing the determinants of industrial leadership Mowery and Nelson distinguish three different viewpoints according to whether the causal forces are located (1) at national level, (2) the level of firms, or (3) somewhere in between, i.e. at the sector level.[34]

Having examined the seven industries from these three vantage points, they conclude, 'The picture of the locus of industrial leadership that emerges from our industry studies ... is complex' in that the locus or loci are to be found in different places in different industries. However, this complexity has not prevented the authors from drawing three conclusions from the industry studies:

> First, the issue is not whether it is firms themselves, or the broader national environment in which they reside, that produces industrial leadership. Both the environment, and what firms make of that environment, matter.
>
> Second, although many comparative analyses assume that the institutional environment of firms is determined largely by forces beyond the reach of firms, in fact, firms often exert significant influence on industry-level supporting institutions and policies.[35]

Sectoral Innovation Systems

The authors' third conclusion has significant implications for another closely related conceptualisation of innovation systems, namely sectoral innovation systems:

> Third, to a considerable extent, the sources of industrial leadership reside in structures intermediate between nations and firms. We refer to these as 'sectoral support systems'.[36]

---

[33] Mowery and Nelson (1999), p. 2.   [34] Ibid., pp. 8–10.   [35] Ibid., p. 368.
[36] Ibid.

Referring specifically to 'sectoral innovation systems', the authors concluded, 'One lesson that can be drawn from many of the specific industry studies is the importance of national institutions that are highly specific to particular sectors and of sectoral systems more generally. Although they are embedded in and supported by broader national institutions, in many cases the key sectoral ones have a structure and a life of their own.'[37] The implication is that '[t]he study of sectoral innovation systems and how they differ across industries, countries, and eras ought to be high on the research agenda of economists and other scholars interested in the sources of industrial leadership'.[38]

Diffusion of the 'National Innovation System' Concept

The OECD

The concept of 'national innovation systems' diffused rapidly and widely. One example documenting this is an OECD publication titled National Innovation Systems published in 1997.[39] Exhibit 3.1, taken from this publication,[40] reproduces the definitions of 'national innovation systems' given in some of this literature (with the present author highlighting in italics some of the key terms in these definitions).

EXHIBIT 3.1 **Definitions of National Innovation Systems**

A national system of innovation has been defined as follows:

- 'the network of *institutions* in the public and private sectors whose activities and interactions initiate, import, modify and diffuse new *technologies* ' (Freeman, 1987)

---

[37] Ibid., p. 369. [38] Ibid., p. 370.

[39] OECD, 1997. *National Innovation Systems*, OECD: Paris. www.oecd.org/science/inno/2101733.pdf.

[40] On p. 10.

EXHIBIT 3.1 **(cont.)**

- 'the *elements and relationships* which interact in the production, diffusion and use of new, and economically useful, *knowledge* ... and are either located within or rooted inside the borders of a nation state' (Lundvall, 1992)
- 'a set of *institutions* whose interactions determine the innovative performance ... of *national firms* ' (Nelson, 1993)
- 'the national *institutions*, their incentive structures and their competencies, that determine the rate and direction of *technological learning* (or the volume and composition of change generating activities) in a country' (Patel and Pavitt, 1994)
- 'that set of distinct *institutions* which jointly and individually contribute to the development and diffusion of *new technologies* and which provides the framework within which governments form and implement policies to influence the innovation process. As such it is a system of interconnected institutions to create, store and transfer the *knowledge, skills and artefacts* which define new technologies' (Metcalfe, 1995)

The UK Department of Business, Innovation and Skills

A more recent example is *Innovation and Research Strategy for Growth*,[41] a foundational strategy paper published by the UK Department for Business, Innovation and Skills in 2011 that is indicative of the substantial impact that this body of academic work has had on some policymakers. In this paper the following definition is provided:

> One of the most persistent themes in modern innovation studies is the idea that *innovation of all kinds is systemic*. That is, enterprise-level innovation is more than a matter of independent decision-making at the level of the business firm. There are multiple external institutional, organisational and infrastructure factors shaping the behaviour of enterprises. Taken together these factors

---

[41] UK Department of Business, Innovation and Skills, 2011. *Innovation and Research Strategy for Growth*. London: Department of Business, Innovation and Skills.

make up a system, and system conditions can have a serious impact on the extent to which enterprises can make innovation decisions, and on the modes of innovation which are undertaken. Innovation occurs within the corporate sector and in public sector organisations. Both are affected by a wider system where institutional structures, administrative and regulatory frameworks, educational and scientific capabilities, and physical and knowledge infrastructures all interact to shape the innovation environment. These elements of the innovation system are specific to local and national contexts.[42]

BUSINESS ECOSYSTEMS

The second cluster of literature discussed in this chapter is based on the idea of 'business ecosystems'. This literature draws inspiration from the analysis of biological ecosystems. However, it is stressed that there are limitations to this analogy arising from the ability of human beings to change, to a significant extent, their own knowledge, beliefs, and behaviour in sharp contrast to biological organisms, which are severely constrained by their own DNA and, over time, its mutation. The work of two pioneers in this field who have put the idea of business ecosystems on the research map – James Moore, on the one hand, and Iansiti and Levien, on the other – will be examined.

James F. Moore

Moore began professional life as a business consultant with a prime interest in business strategy. He formed his own consulting company. Later he became more involved with social causes with various attachments at Harvard University. Iansiti and Levien, whose work is discussed later in this chapter, refer in their book to 'authors who have shaped this field [of business ecosystems], most importantly,

---

[42] Ibid., p. 28, emphasis in original.

James F. Moore, who pioneered the application of biological ecosystems to the business context'.[43]

'Predators and Prey' and *The Death of Competition*, by James F. Moore

Moore's main contributions are an article in *Harvard Business Review*, 'Predators and Prey: A New Ecology of Competition',[44] and a book, *The Death of Competition: Leadership and Strategy in the Age of Business Ecosystems*.[45] As the titles of both pieces indicate, for Moore business strategy and competition are closely interlinked. Being interested in, and working closely with, large American companies, Moore became aware that the way in which many large companies competed had changed significantly.

Specifically, these companies were increasingly cooperating with other companies to compete more effectively. This change, however, did not fit into the traditional analytical 'frame' used to analyse competition. 'Most managers', Moore pointed out, 'still frame the problem [of competition] in the old way: companies go head-to-head in an industry, battling for market share. But events of the last decade, particularly in high-technology businesses, amply illustrate the limits of that understanding'.[46]

This raised an important question: How can the process of competition be more appropriately conceptualised? In thinking about this question Moore was influenced by the ideas of an anthropologist, Gregory Bateson, who had written about the process of 'coevolution'. As Moore put it: 'Bateson describes coevolution as a process in which interdependent species evolve in an endless reciprocal cycle – in which [quoting Bateson] "changes in species A set the stage for the

---

[43] Iansiti and Levien (2004a), p. 225.
[44] Moore, J. F., 1993. 'Predators and prey: a new ecology of competition'. *Harvard Business Review*, May–June 1993.
[45] Moore, J. F., 1996. *The Death of Competition: Leadership and Strategy in the Age of Business Ecosystems*. New York: Harper Business.
[46] Moore (1993), p. 75.

natural selection of changes in species B″ – and vice versa.′[47] The example that Moore used was that of predators and their prey.

Definition of Business Ecosystem

Using this way of thinking in order 'to extend a systematic approach to strategy' and, it should be added, competition, Moore went on: 'I suggest that a company be viewed not as a member of a single industry but as part of a *business ecosystem* that crosses a variety of industries.′[48]

What does Moore mean by a 'business ecosystem'? 'In a business ecosystem, companies coevolve capabilities around a new innovation: they work cooperatively and competitively to support new products, satisfy customer needs, and eventually incorporate the next round of innovations.′[49]

It is important, particularly in view of the concern of the present book with innovation, to notice the role that innovation plays in Moore's conceptualisation of a business ecosystem. Note that in Moore's view it is a 'new innovation' that gives birth to a business ecosystem as companies respond to the new opportunities provided by the innovation and 'coevolve' their capabilities around it.[50]

Innovation also enters the business ecosystem in a second way as, at a later point in time, having made efforts to benefit from the new innovation, companies 'eventually incorporate the next round of innovations'.

But how does this second round of innovation happen? In his book published three years later, Moore explains: 'Profits from the

---

[47] Ibid., p. 75.   [48] Ibid., p. 76.

[49] Ibid. This definition of business ecosystems is repeated more or less word for word in Moore (1996), p. 15.

[50] This idea of an innovation providing a foundation for emergent cooperation between multiple players was subsequently developed in a stream of literature analysing the importance of 'platforms' that play precisely this role. See, for example, Gawer, A., and Cusumano, M. A., 2002. *Platform Leadership: How Intel, Microsoft, and Cisco Drive Industry Innovation.* Boston, MA: Harvard Business School Press.

core products and services (those having strong economies of scale) are reinvested in further additions to capabilities and in developing future generations of offers. A continuing "innovation trajectory" of decreasing prices and expanding performance is established. End customers and allies become convinced that this core business will bring them the future – in addition to being there for them in the present.'[51]

Accordingly, Moore concludes: 'The lesson of the business ecosystem is that you must have value, economies of scale, and continuing innovation, and you must invest in an expanding community of allies.'[52]

As this discussion makes clear, therefore, innovation plays a key role in the dynamics of change in business ecosystems according to Moore's conceptualisation. Not only does innovation provide the rationale for the group of cooperating and competing companies in the ecosystem to come together in the first place, it also creates the engine for the further evolution of the ecosystem.

Later in his book, Moore elaborates on his definition of a business ecosystem:

> An economic community supported by a foundation of interacting organizations and individuals – the organisms of the business world. This economic community produces goods and services of value to customers, who are themselves members of the ecosystem. The member organisms also include suppliers, lead producers, competitors, and other stakeholders. Over time they coevolve their capabilities and roles, and tend to align themselves with the directions set by one or more central companies. Those companies holding leadership roles may change over time, but the function of ecosystem leader is valued by the community because it enables members to move towards shared visions to align their investments, and to find mutually supportive roles.[53]

---

[51] Moore (1996), p. 31.   [52] Ibid., p. 32.   [53] Ibid., p. 26.

The Players in the Business Ecosystem

Having given this definition, Moore poses two questions: What are a business ecosystem's components? And what are the boundaries of a business ecosystem?

In answering these questions, he begins by identifying four 'primary species[54] of the ecosystem':

1. Customers
2. Market intermediaries (including agents and channels and those who sell complementary products and services)
3. Suppliers, and
4. Oneself [i.e. the reader of his book, presumed to be an employee of a company participating in a business ecosystem].[55]

But this list does not exhaust the players in the business ecosystem. In addition, there are, first of all, 'the owners and other stakeholders of these primary species'. Second, there are 'powerful species who may be relevant in a given situation', including:

5. Government agencies and regulators
6. Associations and standards bodies representing customers or suppliers, and
7. Your direct competitors, along with companies that might be able to compete with you or with any other important members of the community.[56]

---

[54] Interestingly, while he refers here to 'species', in his definition of business ecosystems given one paragraph earlier Moore makes reference to 'organisms'. An organism refers to an individual (e.g. an individual lion or antelope), whilst a species refers to a population of organisms (e.g. the population of lions and antelope coexisting in the savannah ecosystem). Moore does not explain the significance of this change in terminology. However, in biological ecology and evolution, reference is usually to species (i.e. populations of organisms). The reason is that it is in populations that the variety is generated by mutation, which, together with selection and reproduction, drive the evolutionary process. Moore's discussion, however, does not explicitly deal with the variety of generation and selection processes that over time drive the evolution of business ecosystems. This is an important omission. Instead, he simply states, 'Every business system develops in four distinct stages: birth, expansion, leadership, and self-renewal – or, if not self-renewal, death' (Moore [1993], p. 76) and focuses on the strategies that company players, particularly the ecosystem's leaders, should adopt. The incorporation of variety and selection could have given him a more robust explanation for the changes within each stage as well as the transition from one stage to another.

[55] Moore (1996), p. 27.   [56] Ibid.

According to Moore it is the coevolutionary interactions of these players, driven by innovation-related capability accumulation, and increasing scale, that constitute the dynamics of the ecosystem.

Reflections
Two comments may be made about this conceptualisation of business ecosystems. The first is that the analysis provided by Moore is not sufficient to answer the second question that he poses just after defining business ecosystems, namely, 'What are the boundaries of a business ecosystem?'

The reason is that there is considerable ambiguity regarding precisely which entities should be included from the list of seven groups of players (particularly from group 7, which is very broad). Given this ambiguity, it is inevitable that different analysts may well come up with different entities in specifying the relevant players to be included in a particular business ecosystem (for example, the personal computer ecosystem, which is one of Moore's examples). Significantly, this implies that different analysts will construct different boundaries for the business ecosystem in question.

This highlights an important characteristic of business or innovation ecosystems that is stressed in several places in the present book: a business or innovation ecosystem is not an empirical entity that can be seen, measured, and analysed; rather, it is an observer-dependent analytically constructed entity. Different analysts will come up with different constructions even when referring to the same field. This observation has very significant implications, which are discussed at different junctures in this book (for example, in Chapter 5).

The second comment is that Moore's list of players adds considerable complexity to the functioning of the business ecosystem, a complexity that Moore himself appears not to recognise. It is some comfort, however, that this problem, far from pertaining to Moore alone, is inherent in any attempt to define the relevant 'players' in a socioeconomic ecosystem, business and innovation ecosystems included.

This important point becomes clearer if we take Moore's example of the companies (leading companies as well as followers), which are key members of his 'primary species of the ecosystem'. As we saw, going beyond these primary players Moore also includes in his business ecosystem 'the owners and other stakeholders of these primary species'. As shown in his key diagram depicting a business ecosystem (figure 2.1, p. 27), owners and stakeholders include 'investors and owners, trade associations, labour unions'.

This categorisation presents considerable challenges for an analyst wanting to analyse the coevolutionary interactions that drive the dynamics of the ecosystem. For example, how is the analyst to understand and explain the interactive decisions made by a particular leading company in a business ecosystem? And what is the appropriate unit of analysis in order to do so? Is it the board of the company, the CEO, the shareholders (and which shareholders?), the employees (or trade unions), some of them, or all of them? Indeed, given the complexity, is it possible to provide an explanation of the decisions made or is the analyst restricted to mere description based on an observation of the final outcome?

This problem is inherent in the notion of a 'player' (or 'organism' or 'species'). This notion is a simplification based on an abstraction. And the problem is not unique to the field of business or innovation ecosystems.

For example, reference in many other fields is often made to 'firms' as players. But what is a 'firm' and what do we mean when we say that a firm decided to do something? In both cases the problem arises because the 'player' or the 'firm' is an aggregation of individual people. The same is true for 'stakeholders' and other similar bodies that influence this entity's decisions and behaviour. Each individual member of the player, firm, or stakeholder, has their own knowledge, information, beliefs, and expectations. But not all the individuals involved have equal power to influence the final decisions and behaviours. Furthermore, individuals, coexisting in the same situation, usually differ regarding what should be done.

In view of this complexity, it is by no means surprising that we resort to abstract simplifications by conceptualising aggregated entities such as 'players' or 'firms' and focusing primarily on the final decision of that entity. But we should always be aware, first, that these notions are abstractions and, second, that different analysts may have different aggregations and abstractions in mind when they use the same term, such as player or firm. If we are not careful, this could become a source of confusion.

Marco Iansiti and Roy Levien

Iansiti was professor of business administration at the Harvard Business School. His interests included technology strategy, the managing of product development, and starting new ventures. He had worked with many leading US companies including IBM, AT&T, and Microsoft. He founded a consulting company focused on the implementation of technology strategy in large companies. Levien trained initially as a biologist and worked for seven years at Microsoft in the area of technology development. He too was involved with a consulting company that consulted in the area of networks.

The Keystone Advantage: What the New Dynamics of Business Ecosystems Mean for Strategy, Innovation, and Sustainability and 'Strategy as Ecology' by Iansiti and Levien

Iansiti and Levien's main contributions in this area are a book, *The Keystone Advantage*,[57] and an article published in *Harvard Business Review*, 'Strategy as Ecology',[58] both published in 2004. In the first chapter of their book they explain their motivation: 'The collapse of the Internet economy – the few successes, the many failures, and the many lessons drawn from the evolution of traditional firms – provides

---

[57] Iansiti, M. and Levien, R., 2004a. *The Keystone Advantage: What the New Dynamics of Business Ecosystems Mean for Strategy, Innovation, and Sustainability*. Boston, MA: Harvard Business School Press.

[58] Iansiti, M. and Levien, R., 2004b. 'Strategy as ecology'. *Harvard Business Review*, March, 1–10.

the perfect opportunity to reflect on, research, and finally learn how to manage complex networks of firms.'[59] Their focus, accordingly, was on company management, networks, and strategy.

Drawing significantly on the work of James Moore, they too were convinced of the usefulness of the ecosystems metaphor although they were also at pains to point to the limitations of this comparison in the case of human systems less constrained by genetic determinants.

Definition of Business Ecosystem

How do Iansiti and Levien conceptualise their business ecosystem?

> Like biological ecosystems, business ecosystems are formed by large, loosely connected networks of entities. Like species in biological ecosystems, firms interact with each other in complex ways and the health and performance of each firm is dependent on the health and performance of the whole. Firms and species are therefore simultaneously influenced by their internal capabilities and by their complex interactions with the rest of the ecosystem.[60]

Players in the Business Ecosystem

Who are the players in Iansiti and Levien's business ecosystem? They include 'suppliers, distributors, outsourcing firms, makers of related products or services, technology providers, and a host of other organisations [that] affect, and are affected by, the creation and delivery of a company's own offerings'. Elaborating further, they continue:

> Your own business ecosystem includes, for example, companies to which you outsource business functions, institutions that provide you with financing, firms that provide the technology needed to carry on your business, and makers of complementary products that are used in conjunction with your own. It even includes

---

[59] Iansiti and Levien (2004a), p. 8.   [60] Ibid., p. 35.

competitors and customers, when their actions and feedback affect the development of your own products and processes. [As in Moore,] The ecosystem also comprises entities like regulatory agencies and media outlets that can have a less immediate, but just as powerful, effect on your business.[61]

Business Units

However, even though Iansiti and Levien share with Moore a concern with the strategic challenges facing managers, they depart significantly from him in the way in which they deal with company players. Rather than dealing with 'companies' or 'firms' as a whole, their interest in managers' decisions leads them to disaggregate these entities and instead focus on the strategy of their relevant business units:

> Ultimately, our interest lies in the operational decisions made by managers. Our focus will therefore not be on the business units themselves, but on the patterns of behaviors that characterize those business units: the operational strategies of business units. The key analogy we draw is between the characteristic behavior of a species in an ecosystem and the operating strategy of a strategic business unit. It is important to keep this in mind when we refer to a firm as 'being' a dominator, for example: This should be understood as shorthand for the fact that a firm has business units that are pursuing dominator strategies.[62]

This is an important point of departure. In effect, we are being invited to conceptualise a business ecosystem where the key players are not the species as defined (which include firms – see earlier discussion) but strategic decision-makers within them. Indeed, Iansiti and Levien go so far as to suggest that different business units in a company may be members of different business ecosystems.

---

[61] Iansiti and Levien (2004b), pp. 1–2.   [62] Iansiti and Levien (2004a), p. 36.

On occasion, however, there appears to be some inconsistency in their use of the term 'species'. At one point, for example, they state that 'the companies, products, and technologies of a business network are, like the species in a biological ecosystem, increasingly inter-twined in mutually dependent relationships outside of which they have little meaning'.[63] Whilst companies and their internal units contain managerial decision-makers, the same is obviously not true of products and technologies. It would make more sense, therefore, to exclude products and technologies from the category 'species'.

Business Domains

A further important departure from Moore is Iansiti and Levien's notion of 'business domains'. This is a potentially helpful distinction, although it does come at the price of increasing conceptual complex-ity. They explain their rationale for making this distinction:

> How do we simplify the vast complexity of an ecosystem? It is often useful to subdivide an ecosystem into a number of related business *domains* as a matter of convenience for performing analysis. These domains can be thought of as groups of organisations engaged in similar activities and may sometimes be similar to conventional industries. Each ecosystem thus encompasses several domains, which it may share with other ecosystems.[64]

An example will make the notion of business domains easier to understand. In Iansiti and Levien (2004a)[65] a depiction is provided of what is referred to as the 'Microsoft software ecosystem'. This is divided into a number of business domains, the largest of which are the domains of systems integrators, development service companies, campus resellers, and independent software vendors.

However, although the authors state that the notion of business domains is introduced in order to 'simplify the vast complexity of an

---

[63] Iansiti and Levien (2004b), p. 5.   [64] Iansiti and Levien (2004a), p. 43.
[65] Figure 3-1, p. 45.

ecosystem', it is by no means obvious that the distinction serves this purpose. As noted above, the aim of the book is to help business managers understand and negotiate the interdependent cooperative and competitive interactions between the many players in the ecosystem. But to achieve this aim, it is necessary that the manager knows where to focus.

Iansiti and Levien suggest the focus should be on the business domain. However, they also point out that business domains are part of larger business ecosystems. To the extent that business domains are influenced by the ecosystems of which they are a part, it will also be necessary for managers, at least for some purposes, to be cognisant also of the broader ecosystem. But to decide how much of their scarce attention they should devote to the broader ecosystem, they will need to know the nature of the interdependence between the ecosystem and the business domain.

Furthermore, there is the problem of deciding which of the business domains to enter and what strategy to pursue in each of them. In Iansiti and Levien's words:

> It is also important to understand that a given firm may act as a keystone in one domain while acting as a dominator or a niche player in others; in fact, as we shall see, firms may adopt contradictory stances, with one business unit pursuing a keystone strategy while another pursues a niche or dominator strategy. The firm may even serve as a keystone in several domains.[66]

It is not clear, therefore, whether the notion of business domains achieves its simplifying goal. But perhaps, to the extent that the idea of business domains helps managers to match their capabilities, which draw on the collective resources of the ecosystem, and the

---

[66] Iansiti and Levien (2004a), p. 104. The book identifies three kinds of players according to their positioning in the business ecosystem. Keystones dominate the business ecosystem but create the conditions for mutual benefit for all the ecosystem's players. Dominators are preoccupied with their own objectives and benefits, paying little or no attention to the well-being of other players in the ecosystem. Niche players are differentiated specialists who create viable places for themselves in the ecology of the ecosystem.

markets where these capabilities will yield the highest expected returns, the notion will help them to negotiate the complexity of the business ecosystem if not reduce it.

Platforms in Business Ecosystems

A further contribution of Iansiti and Levien is to develop the notion of platforms already nascent in Moore. They provide their definition of platforms that contributed to a stream of subsequent literature in this area:

> A *platform* is a set of solutions to problems that is made available to the members of the ecosystem through a set of access points or interfaces. In software these interfaces are called APIs (application programming interfaces). Although the API terminology is not usually used in other domains, the same basic approach is followed: Platforms serve as an embodiment of the functionality that forms the foundation of the ecosystem, packaged and presented to members of the ecosystem through a common set of interfaces. Ecosystem members then leverage these interfaces as a kind of toolkit for building their own products and think of them as the starting point for their own value creation ... The platform is the 'package' through which keystones share value with their ecosystems.[67]

More broadly, platforms refer to 'services, tools, or technologies ... that other members of the ecosystem can use to enhance their own performance'.[68]

Ecosystem Boundaries

In contrast to Moore, Iansiti and Levient are adamant that defining the boundary of a business ecosystem is problematical. Indeed, at one point they go so far as to suggest that '[d]rawing the precise boundaries

---

[67] Iansiti and Levien (2004a), pp. 148–9.   [68] Iansiti and Levien (2004b), p. 1.

of an ecosystem is an impossible and, in any case, academic exercise'.[69] Elsewhere, however, they take a more pragmatic approach:

> as with biological ecosystems the boundary of a given ecosystem is often difficult to establish. Organisms may interact with each other through many indirect connections even if they are separated in space or time ... Similarly, firms may interact with each other even if they appear distant at first glance. Therefore, rather than establishing a static and clear boundary between ecosystems, as we often do for the boundary between industries, it is better to gauge the *degree* of interaction between different firms and to depict ecosystems as communities of firms characterized by a given level and type of interaction (e.g. market relationships, technology-sharing and licensing agreements).[70]

Keystones, Dominators, and Niche Players

As the title of their book indicates, Iansiti and Levien are largely concerned with the role that so-called keystone players play. These are companies that have made the strategic decision to create a business ecosystem and cultivate its well-being. The latter is done by providing platforms – services, tools, and technologies – that can be leveraged by all the players in the business ecosystem.

Keystones are to be contrasted with dominators who, on the contrary, through strategies such as vertical integration, try to capture as much of the collective value created by the ecosystem as possible. In Iansiti and Levien's view, their role is ultimately destructive since they do not create a win-win outcome for all the ecosystem's players and therefore they find it increasingly difficult to leverage the resources and creativity of the other players.

Enron is cited as a good example of a dominator. Interestingly in retrospect, however, so is Apple. According to the authors, 'Apple is an example of a classic dominator.'[71] The reason, they suggest, is that

---

[69] Ibid., p. 2.   [70] Iansiti and Levien (2004a), p. 40.   [71] Ibid., p. 74.

'in creating an integrated "appliance computer", Apple courted a dominator role: It controlled everything from operating system to hardware, from applications to peripherals.'[72] But, of course, this was before the iPhone and iPad and Apple's recruitment of independent applications providers who helped turn Apple into one of the world's most valuable companies even though these appliances themselves are produced as a relatively closed system.

Niche players are the third kind of player in the business ecosystem. Whilst depending on the keystone, niche players are able to survive largely by differentiating themselves through specialising and innovating. In this way these players, constituting the greatest number of players in the ecosystem and contributing collectively a significant part of its total created value, make an important contribution to its competitiveness and growth.

Value Creation in Business Ecosystems

One of the most important questions about a business ecosystem relates to the way in which it creates value. Value creation is necessary to have value capture by the individual players in the ecosystem, the source of their revenue, growth, and incentive. How do Iansiti and Levien see value being created in a business ecosystem?

In their view it is the keystone that makes the foundational contribution, creating the conditions that allow the other players to make their contribution:

> A keystone strategy systematizes value creation in a large [ecosystem] by creating what we call *operating leverage*. By this we mean a series of assets that can be easily scaled and shared by a broad network of business partners. These assets may be physical, as in the case of a large and highly efficient manufacturing network; intellectual, as in the case of a broadly available software platform; or financial, as in the case of a venture capitalist's portfolio of investments.[73]

---

[72] Ibid., p. 117.   [73] Ibid., p. 92.

It is crucial, however, that the benefits flowing from the creation of these assets exceed the cost:

> The key to creating leverage is to make sure that the value of these assets divided by the cost of creating, maintaining, and sharing them increases rapidly with the number of ecosystem members that share them. This enables the keystone player to effectively generate more value than it 'needs', and thus to effectively create the potential for sharing this surplus with its community.[74]

But this largely exclusive focus, in specifying the creation of value by a business ecosystem, on the keystone's creation of 'assets' that may be leveraged is overly inward looking, paying too much attention to the creating of the conditions needed to obtain the effective cooperation of the other players in the ecosystem. Surely, à la Moore, it is also necessary to focus at the same time on the importance of the creation of additional value by *all* the ecosystem's players, keystones included, for their own customer-users? The failure to analyse the latter is an important limitation. This raises the question of innovation.

Innovation and Competitiveness

How do Iansiti and Levien deal with the issue of innovation? How do they deliver on the implicit promise contained in the subtitle of their book: 'What the new dynamics of business ecosystems mean for strategy, *innovation*, and sustainability' (emphasis added)?

To explore the answer to these questions, a good place to start is where Moore began. Moore's starting point was competition: How do companies compete? This is a good starting point for the simple reason that it is imperative that firms, operating in markets where there is competition, are competitive. Failure to be competitive certainly means that firms will not thrive and they may not survive.

What must companies do to increase their competitiveness? The answer is they must increase the value that they offer their

[74] Ibid.

customers *relative to their competitors*. The most important way that they can do this is by innovating. In this book, innovation, following Joseph Schumpeter, is defined as new products and services, new processes and technologies, new ways of organising people and things, and new markets, ways of marketing, and business models. It is not *any* novelty in products and services etc. that matters. It is only novelty that results in added value for the company's customers relative to what is being offered to them by competitors.

It seems that Iansiti and Levien's treatment of the question of innovation was influenced by their critique of the then-prevailing business literature on innovation. They suggest that much of the work in this innovation management literature 'has focused on the fragile nature of competitive advantage in situations of significant technological and market upheaval ... but the nature of the change has generally been treated as an exogenous variable. Authors have analysed changes that are competence destroying, attacking the firm's "core"; architectural, fundamentally changing its organization; or disruptive to the firm's business model.'[75] Here they make reference to Henderson and Clark (1990) and Christensen (1997).[76]

According to Iansiti and Levien, the problem with this literature, however, is that 'in virtually all cases, the changes were analysed as an exogenous shock or trend that influenced a single firm (or even a single organisation within the firm). The critical interaction between that firm and its network of business partners was left largely untouched ... the network [of firms] is seen largely as a source of inertia, not as a dynamic factor that can enhance productivity and innovation.'[77]

Nevertheless, Iansiti and Levien acknowledge that a newer stream of literature has underlined 'the importance of industry

---

[75] Ibid., p. 64.
[76] Henderson, R. M. and Clark, K. B., 1990. 'Architectural innovation: the reconfiguration of existing product technologies and the failure of established firms'. *Administrative Sciences Quarterly*, 35: 9–30 and Christensen, C. M., 1997. *The Innovator's Dilemma: When New Technologies Cause Great Firms to Fail.* Boston, MA: Harvard Business School Press.
[77] Iansiti and Levien (2004a), p. 64.

fragmentation and industry networks'. In this connection they mention Baldwin and Clark (2000) and Gawer and Cusumano (2002).[78] Writings such as these, they suggest, 'clearly highlight that distributed industries behave differently'.

However, they argue, 'the implications of this difference for the formulation of strategy and for the management of innovation and operations are still underdeveloped. This leaves unexplored the challenges of managing innovation or operations in ... very large, loosely connected networks.' Accordingly, 'In this book we attempt to fill some of the gap by formulating a framework for understanding and analysing operating strategy in a networked environment.'[79]

The attempt of firms, operating in business ecosystems, to improve their competitiveness is most clearly dealt with by Iansiti and Levien in their treatment of niche players, one of the three kinds of player in business ecosystems that they identify, the others being keystones and dominators.

Iansiti and Levien argue that niche players are crucial 'drivers of innovation' in business ecosystems: 'Because many niche players locate at the "fringes" of the ecosystem, where new innovations are actively being pursued and where new products and services are being developed and new markets explored, they are critical drivers of innovation. These "edge firms" are vital to the health of the ecosystem because they are the locus of precisely the kind of meaningful diversity that we believe is essential to its robustness.'[80]

Furthermore, the contribution of niche players to the business ecosystem comes from their continual innovation. Continual innovation was also identified by Moore, as we saw, as a key requirement for the evolution and growth of business ecosystems, although he assumed that all players would be playing this role.

---

[78] Baldwin, C. Y. and Clark, K. B., 2000. *Design Rules: The Power of Modularity.* Boston, MA: MIT Press; and Gawer and Cusumano (2002).
[79] Iansiti and Levien (2004a), p. 65.   [80] Ibid., pp. 124–5.

But how do niche players make this innovation happen? According to Iansiti and Levien, 'Whether dealing with one or multiple keystones, the heart of technology strategy for a niche player is to continually innovate by integrating technology available from the ecosystem to sharpen the niche offering that it is crafting.'[81]

Indeed, they go even further, suggesting that niche players have an innovation advantage relative to the other players in the business ecosystem: 'Firms that pursue a focused niche strategy have an ultimate advantage in the creation of novelty. This is partly because a focused new idea can more closely correspond to a new firm than is possible in vertical or modular industry structures: Everything beyond the scope of the firm can be integrated from external sources, or, conversely, a new product or technology offered by the firm can be easily integrated into the existing ecosystem as an extension or addition to its capabilities.'[82]

As is clear from these quotations, Iansiti and Levien believe that the most important way of making innovation happen in business ecosystem player-firms is through integrating resources (including technologies) available from the ecosystem. Highlighting this point, they refer to the 'importance of integration':

> Because a company operating in today's networked setting can use resources that exist outside of its own organization, integration now represents a critical form of innovation. This fundamentally changes the capabilities needed and the structure of corporate functions in areas including business operations, R&D, strategy, and product architecture ...
>
> The broad scattering of innovation across a healthy ecosystem and the diversity of organizations in it also change the nature of technological evolution. Rather than involving individual companies that are engaged in technology races, battles in the future will be waged between ecosystems or between ecosystem

---

[81] Ibid., p. 135.   [82] Ibid., pp. 139–40.

domains. Increasingly, the issue won't be simply 'Microsoft versus IBM', but rather the overall health of the ecosystems that each fosters and depends on.[83]

Indeed, Iansiti and Levien go even further, insisting that 'integration capability has become essential to innovation'; that is, it is necessary such that innovation cannot happen without this integration.[84] 'Integration capability' they define as 'an organization's capacity to combine the impact of different competencies, both internal and external to the firm. This capacity affects a variety of key business processes, influencing both innovation and day-to-day operations, effectively tying together old and new capabilities. If platforms provide a base on which to construct new products and services, integration provides the glue with which to add new concepts and technologies.'[85]

Crucially, it is not only niche players who benefit from such integration. The same is true for the other two types of player in business ecosystems, keystones and dominators: 'the process of technology integration provides a critical engine of business evolution, as the capabilities and technological components provided by ecosystem participants are recombined to create constantly improving product and service offerings. The process is crucial to dominators ... to keystones ... and to niche players.'[86]

As we saw earlier, this is precisely the same conclusion that Moore arrives at, although Iansiti and Levien make considerable progress in spelling out what integration within the context of business ecosystems involves.

Reflections

Iansiti and Levien clearly make a good case regarding the important opportunities, of relevance to innovation, provided by integration capabilities nurtured within the context of business ecosystems. But

---

[83] Iansiti and Levien (2004b), p. 10.   [84] Iansiti and Levien (2004a), p. 169.
[85] Ibid., p. 170.   [86] Ibid., p. 173.

is this sufficient in explaining the connection between business eco-systems, innovation, and competitiveness, which, it will be recalled, is the starting point that we adopted in this section on innovation, following Moore? There are several reasons for suggesting that it is, indeed, not sufficient.

The first point is that it is important not to confuse means and ends. Integration as envisaged by Iansiti and Levien is a means rather than an end. What is the end? The end, à la Moore, is to increase competitiveness or at least maintain it. Over time the attainment of this end is crucial, not only for all the players in the business ecosys-tem, but also for the whole ecosystem itself if it is to survive compe-tition from other competing business ecosystems. The problem is that integration *may* be an effective means in achieving this end, but on the other hand it may not. Integration may even be necessary (although under some conceivable circumstances even this may not be true); but it is not sufficient.

Second, one of the main problems with Iansiti and Levien's analy-sis of integration and innovation is that it focuses exclusively on the supply side, that is, the ability of the business ecosystem to provide inputs for innovation. However, it ignores the demand side, that is, whether the output and outcome succeed ultimately in achieving the end, namely the increase in value provided to the player's customers.

To take this one step further, innovation too is a means rather than an end. Innovation (as defined in the present book) may lead to an increase in competitiveness, but it may not.

In the Iansiti and Levien argument, integration leads to innov-ation, which leads to increased competitiveness and performance. But achieving the first two steps in this chain of causation does not guarantee the achievement of the final step, the aim of the process. Indeed, ignoring the demand side and the whole series of issues that arise in the complex and time-consuming process of eventually coming up with products and processes that actually do add value for customers relative to that offered by competitors makes it less likely that the aim will ultimately be achieved.

Third, as a result of the omission of the customer demand side, it is reasonable to conclude that in effect the innovation process and its outcomes remain *exogenous* in Iansiti and Levien's conceptual system. That is, whether successful innovation occurs that succeeds in adding value for customers or not is determined outside this conceptual system.

To put this in other words, Iansiti and Levien's conceptualisation of business ecosystems does not explain *how* competitiveness-increasing innovation happens. This follows from their failure to analyse the interactions between the ecosystems suppliers of products and services and their customer-users who have the option of switching to the products and services of competitors. However strong their 'integration capabilities', these suppliers will not increase their competitiveness if they are unable to add value for their customer-users relative to what is offered to them by competitors.

Fourth, and relatedly, they also do not tell us *who* should make successful innovation happen. They do inform us that their target audience is primarily 'business unit managers'. But if successful innovation is to happen, we need to know far more about who needs to do what and how. This requires a detailed discussion of all the people in the business unit involved in the unit's innovation, not only managers. To answer these questions, however, it is necessary to go beyond the Iansiti and Levien conceptualisation.

NATIONAL INNOVATION SYSTEMS AND BUSINESS ECOSYSTEMS: DISCUSSION

How do the two approaches discussed so far in this chapter – namely the national innovation systems (NIS) approach and the business ecosystems (BE) approach – compare?

Similarities

First of all, both approaches attempt to explain the competitiveness over time of companies. In the case of NIS, as we saw, the companies were either part of country economies or part of particular industries. For BE, the companies were part of broader networks.

Second, both approaches acknowledge that innovation is the main driver of this competitiveness. In NIS, innovation is the result of the activities of companies, intercompany learning and transfer of knowledge, and institutions (which may facilitate and/or frustrate innovation). For BE, innovation is facilitated by the generation and use by BE players of competence-integrating assets. (This is asserted by Iansiti and Levien; Moore has less to say about how innovation comes about).

Third, both approaches agree that innovation is a systemic phenomenon. That is, the innovation that takes place in the system is the result of the interactions, both cooperative and competitive, of a number of players whose interdependence justifies the use of the system concept.

Finally, both approaches concur that noncompany players are a necessary component of the system. Having said this, however, it is reasonable to add that although both approaches are in agreement about this, in practice NIS pays more attention and gives greater weight to players such as universities, government research laboratories, finance providers, and regulation and other government measures aimed at influencing outcomes.

Differences

There are also, however, important differences between the two approaches.

The first difference relates to objectives. The objective for NIS is explaining the performance of countries and industries. For BE, however, the objective is to propose competitiveness-enhancing strategies to the key decision-makers in companies.

The second difference is background and perspective. NIS writers tend to come from a background of university research informed by a Schumpeterian-evolutionary perspective. On the other hand, BE authors tend to be based in university business schools and work actively also as business consultants.

Third, each approach tends to have different consumer-users. The main users of the work of NIS writers are usually government policymakers and analysts with an interest in government policy. BE users are generally managers in companies.

These three factors in combination, inevitably, shape the concerns and arguments of these two approaches.

The Exogenous Innovation Process
One of the conclusions of the examination of these two approaches in this chapter is that in both approaches the innovation process itself is largely exogenous. That is, the processes that lead to competitiveness-enhancing innovation as well as their determinants remain largely external to the system being theorised.

In the case of NIS, great attention is paid to the companies and institutions (including universities, government research institutes, financial providers, laws, and regulators) that jointly shape the innovation process. But the details of how the innovation process happens, what the process consists of, and who is involved in this process are omitted.

BE also does not get into these kinds of issues. This is particularly true of Moore. Although his account of business ecosystems assigns a key role to innovation, the details of *how* innovation happens (i.e. what needs to be done to make competitiveness-increasing innovation happen) and *who* makes it happen are omitted. Iansiti and Levien go into some more detail. But as shown, they stop at the creation and use of integration assets and do not delve into the details of the processes leading to competitiveness-increasing innovation and their determinants including the many interactions that occur between ecosystem players and their customer-users.

It seems reasonable, therefore, to suggest that in both approaches how competitiveness-increasing innovation happens (i.e. the processes that are needed) and who makes it happen tend to remain exogenous to the system being conceptualised.

This raises the question of whether it is possible to formulate an 'innovation ecosystem' approach that embodies many of the strengths of the NIS and BE frameworks whilst endogenising, to a greater extent, the innovation process through the inclusion of an examination of how innovation happens and who makes it happen.

Some thoughts on this question are set out in the following section.

INNOVATION ECOSYSTEMS

Caveat

In undertaking this exercise, it is necessary to bear in mind a point made several times in the present book, that socioeconomic ecosystems are not real observable objects; rather, they are conceptual constructs that serve the purpose of their creators. Accordingly, there are many possible ways that 'innovation ecosystems' could be conceptualised. This section elaborates on some ways that this could be done.

Definition of an Innovation Ecosystem

An innovation ecosystem consists of a group of interdependent *players* and *processes* who together, through their interactions, make innovation happen. This innovation changes the products and services that are produced by the ecosystem. Over time the innovation ecosystem as a whole evolves, as do its players and processes, as the variety of new products and services produced are subjected to various selection forces, market selection being the ultimate selection mechanism. Those players who produce successful products and services are rewarded with increasing revenue, profit, and growth.

At the same time, market selection provides players with important feedback that serves as an input into their subsequent rounds of innovation. In this way, over time, the innovation ecosystem further evolves and changes.[87]

---

[87] This brief account of the evolutionary process in innovation ecosystems draws heavily on the seminal book by Nelson and Winter (1982).

The 'How' and 'Who' Questions

A key concern for the analyst of an innovation ecosystem is to understand the answers to two important questions: *How* does innovation happen? (That is, what is done to make competitiveness-increasing innovation happen?) And *who* makes this innovation happen? It is not sufficient simply to state that innovation happens or to identify some of the factors that influence the innovation process. A more holistic account is required.

It must, however, immediately be recognised that the 'how' and 'who' questions are very complicated. This is one reason why they are usually omitted in most discussions of innovation in ecosystems. But if we are to provide a more robust understanding of the innovation processes that make the capitalist system the restless, forever-changing system that it is, and in this way endogenise innovation, it is essential that these two questions are examined.

Chapter 6 of the present book is devoted to an examination of *how* innovation happens, taking the examples of the innovation of the transistor, microprocessor, optical fibre, and laser, innovations that individually, jointly, and through combinations in broader systems literally changed the world. In Chapter 7 the question of *who* makes innovation happen is examined.

The Players in an Innovation Ecosystem

Who are the players in an innovation ecosystem? A broad distinction separates for-profit companies from other noncompany players. Regarding companies, an important question is: Who are the company players in innovation ecosystems?

This question has been tackled in the NIS and BE literatures, as was shown earlier in this chapter, and we are therefore able to draw on these discussions. Company innovation ecosystem players may be distinguished by level of aggregation. The purpose of the analyst and the questions being asked will determine which level(s) is appropriate.

At the highest level of aggregation, the 'player' consists not only of the whole company itself, but also of its stakeholders that influence that company's decisions and behaviour. This level was identified by Moore in his discussion of business ecosystems.

The second level, going down in aggregation terms, is the company as a whole. Here use may be made, for example, of the decisions and resource allocations make by companies (e.g. as appears in company announcements).

Iansiti and Levien, however, go one step further down to the third level through their focus on managers in a company's business units. As they note, the business unit becomes the 'player', and different business units in a company may be members of different ecosystems.

However, if we are to endogenise innovation by delving in greater detail into the 'how' and 'who' questions, it will often be necessary to go to even lower levels of aggregation, to the people who actually take the decisions involved in making innovation happen and who implement these decisions. These are not only the managers of business units identified by Iansiti and Levien, but also others who are involved in activities such as the generation of innovation hypotheses, the selection of these hypotheses for further development, design, production, marketing, and sales. Chapter 7 of the present book contains a detailed discussion of who makes innovation happen, including a consideration of the role of entrepreneurs and the changing division of labour in making innovation happen.

The selection of noncompany players for inclusion in the innovation ecosystem will depend on the purpose of the analysis, the questions being asked, and the kind of innovation ecosystem that is being envisaged. Included below is a categorisation of some different kinds of innovation ecosystem. Typically, however, noncompany players in innovation ecosystems will include the providers of knowledge (e.g. universities, government research institutes), finance (e.g. investment banks, private equity, venture capital), and institutional 'rules of the game' that influence and constrain the way players play and interact.

The Boundaries of the Innovation Ecosystem

We agree with Iansiti and Levien that the boundary of socioeconomic ecosystems is difficult to define. But it is not impossible, as they suggest (see earlier discussion). The reason is that, as we have pointed out, such ecosystems are not real observable objects but conceptual constructs. As conceptual constructs the appropriate boundary of the innovation ecosystem will be determined by the analyst who constructs the ecosystem and the purposes and questions that have been chosen for examination.

This does mean, however, that different analysts, even when examining the same empirical phenomenon, may well come up with different innovation ecosystems, players, and boundaries. This does imply that care must be taken in comparing and discussing different accounts of innovation ecosystems.

The Processes in an Innovation Ecosystem

Innovation does not happen automatically. It must be made to happen. To make it happen, people and processes are necessary. To make innovation happen, it is necessary for a player's decision-makers to decide who should do what, and how. However, there are many different possible answers to these questions. This is one key reason that players and their innovation processes differ. And it is these differences that provide grist for the evolutionary mill.

'Processes' as conceived here also include 'artefacts' that are an important part of processes and coevolve with them. Artefacts include 'machines' of various kinds, hardware, and software. They are the 'tools' of the innovation process. They therefore must be included in the conceptualisation of 'processes'.

Types of Innovation Ecosystem

Amongst the many types of innovation ecosystem that may be conceived are the following:

- National innovation ecosystems
- Sector innovation ecosystems
- Regional innovation ecosystems

- Focal company innovation ecosystems
- Product, service, or technology innovation ecosystems
- Societal challenge innovation ecosystems.

The first three types of innovation ecosystem – national, sector, and regional – are already well known from the national innovation system literature discussed earlier in this chapter. Most of what has already been said about them in this literature will remain relevant in the case of innovation ecosystems. The main difference is that greater attention will be paid in the innovation ecosystems approach to the 'how' and 'who' questions in order to endogenise to a greater extent the innovation process and its determinants. In Chapter 4, an example of a sector innovation ecosystem is given and analysed, namely the ICT innovation ecosystem.

Focal company innovation ecosystems, as we have seen, feature prominently in the business ecosystems literature. Once again, most of what has been said in this literature remains relevant in the innovation ecosystems approach. The distinguishing feature of the latter approach, however, is the greater attention paid to the 'how' and 'who' questions. This involves endogenising, to a greater extent, the innovation process and its determinants.

The many detailed descriptive studies that have been done of the evolution over time of products, services, and technologies could, in principle, be relatively easily recast within an innovation ecosystems framework. The value that might be added by so doing could arise from a more rigorous examination of questions such as who are the relevant players, what are the relevant processes, how do they interact, how does innovation happen, and who makes it happen?

The innovation ecosystems approach can also be usefully deployed within the context of societal challenges. This is discussed further in the case of China in Chapter 9.

CONCLUSIONS

The purpose of this chapter has been to explore the idea that innovation is systemic, that is, that the many interacting determinants of innovation can best be understood as the components of a system. This exploration has involved the examination of two sets of literature. The first is the national innovation systems approach. The second is the business ecosystems approach. These two approaches were first examined on their own merits and then compared.

This examination has revealed the hugely significant contribution that these two approaches have made to the understanding and explanation of innovation and its various determinants. It has also been shown, however, that neither approach goes in sufficient detail into the questions of how innovation happens (that is, the processes that are usually followed in making innovation happen) and who makes innovation happen (that is, the players who actually do what is needed to make innovation happen and the division of labour amongst them). As a result, it was concluded that in both approaches innovation to a significant extent remains exogenous to the systems being conceptualised.

This led to the proposal of a third approach to innovation, namely the innovation ecosystems approach. This approach draws significantly on the strengths of both the national innovation systems and the business ecosystems approaches. There is, therefore, a significant overlap between both these approaches and the innovation ecosystems approach. However, the latter delves in more detail into the 'how' and 'who' questions.

In Chapter 4, an example is given of a sectoral innovation ecosystem, namely the ICT innovation ecosystem. Chapter 6 discusses in far more detail how innovation happens, taking the innovation of the transistor, microprocessor, optical fibre, and laser as examples. Chapter 7 is devoted to an analysis of who makes innovation happen. This includes discussion of the role of the entrepreneur and entrepreneurship, the argument that the entrepreneur has become obsolete, and the continuously evolving division of labour in making innovation happen.

4   The ICT Innovation Ecosystem[*]

In this chapter the idea of an information and communications technologies (ICT) innovation ecosystem is explored. An ICT innovation ecosystem is defined as a set of players and processes that, through their interactions, make innovation happen and by so doing coevolve.

The chapter begins with brief introductory comments about the usefulness of an analysis of innovation at the sector level. It is noted that the sector is unfortunately a neglected unit of analysis. Its neglect has resulted in a failure to understand much of the dynamics of change in capitalist economies since many of the determinants of these dynamics, including innovation, are generated at sector level.

The analysis of the ICT innovation ecosystem begins by identifying the main vertical cooperative innovation relationships that characterise this ecosystem. The organising principle deployed is to identify which players create knowledge in the ecosystem (embodied in their products and services) and which players use that knowledge.

This leads to the identification at an aggregated level of four groups of players: (1) ICT equipment providers; (2) network operators who use the equipment to construct their networks; (3) platform, content, and applications providers whose products and

---

[*] This chapter draws on two of my previous publications: Fransman, M., 2010. *The New ICT Ecosystem: Implications for Policy and Regulation*. Cambridge: Cambridge University Press; and Fransman, M., 2014. *Models of Innovation in Global ICT Firms: The Emerging Global Innovation Ecosystems*. JRC Scientific and Policy Reports -EUR 26774 EN. Seville: JRC-IPTS. https://ec.europa.eu/jrc/sites/default/files/jrc90726.pdf.

services 'sit on' the networks; and (4) final consumer-users of the ecosystem's output of ICT goods and services.

These players are organised into a hierarchically structured organisational architecture. This is conceived of as a model consisting of four layers, one for each of the four groups of players. Each group of players interacts with all the other groups. This gives a total of six symbiotic ('living together') relationships in the ICT innovation ecosystem. In the final part of the chapter it is shown that these symbiotic relationships constitute part of the context within which innovation hypotheses, which start the process of innovation, are created.

Another important part of the innovation context in the ICT innovation ecosystem is the set of horizontal competitive innovation relationships. These occur primarily within layers as players compete within the markets (where substitutable products and services are sold) into which the layer is divided. The longer-run competitiveness of these intra-layer competing players is determined by their ability to create innovations that increase the value the player is able to offer its customer-users relative to that provided by its competitors.

Each layer also contains layer-specific organisational structures that influence innovation processes within the layer. An example discussed is the Internet innovation platform, which facilitates low cost entry, potential access to global customer-users, and innovation by entrepreneurial digital Internet-based companies. This has created a hotbed of activity in Layer 3 – the platform, content and applications layer – and has given rise to Internet-based companies that have come to dominate this layer globally.

Where do the R&D and capital investment engines of the ICT innovation ecosystem reside? These questions are explored next. It is shown that whilst the R&D engine is located primarily in layer 1 (the ICT equipment layer), the capital investment engine is located mainly in layer 2 (the network operator layer). The section contains a detailed examination of the role of R&D in the ICT innovation ecosystem. This includes the surprising finding that 'Apple is not a high-tech company'.

It is shown, however, that there are serious drawbacks in any attempt to understand innovation in the ICT innovation ecosystem solely through the prism of R&D. This leads to the penultimate section, which asks: How does innovation happen in this ecosystem? The answer is based on a discussion of how innovation hypotheses, which start innovation processes, are created and tested within the context provided by the ICT innovation ecosystem. An example examined is the fruitful innovation relationship forged by Huawei, the Chinese leader in the telecoms equipment market of layer 1, and BT, the incumbent UK telecoms operator in layer 2.

The chapter ends with an important caveat regarding the use of the innovation ecosystem concept. It is shown that innovation ecosystems are not empirical entities. It is not possible to see an innovation ecosystem. Rather, they are conceptual constructs existing only in the minds of the analysts who construct them. The implications of this important word of caution are examined. This makes a crucial link to Chapters 6 and 7 of this book, which discuss *how* innovation happens in the case of the former chapter and *who* makes innovation happen in the case of the latter.

INTRODUCTION

The Sector as Unit of Analysis

The sector, as this chapter will demonstrate, is a crucial unit for understanding the dynamics of change in the capitalist economic system. However, the sector is, unfortunately, much neglected.

An example illustrates the importance of analysis at the sector level. Take the following two sectors: financial services, on the one hand, and information and communications technologies (ICT) on the other. As we all know, in 2007 the financial services sector almost collapsed in a severe crisis, the end result of numerous antecedents, threatening the entire global economy. At the same time the ICT sector has performed remarkably and consistently well.

Think of the extraordinary improvements in mobile networks, smartphones, and the massive increase in the global quantity of data communicated, processed, and stored without barely a hiccough. Think of how ICT-based innovations such as social media have grown and transformed economic, social, and political relationships. The fortunes of these two sectors over the same time period could hardly be more different. The same is true of their dynamics. Yet little if any of these contrasting dramas is evident in the aggregated macroeconomic data and analyses that dominate discussion and debate about the economy.

In part this is due to the fact that one of the blind spots in mainstream economics is the sector. The sector falls foul of the conventional binary organisation of knowledge in economics – the primary distinction in the discipline between macroeconomics, the study of the economy as a whole, and microeconomics, the study of individual key decision-making units such as the firm and the consumer. The sector sits uneasily within, and is excluded by, this binary distinction.

This blind spot is unfortunate. The reason is that it precludes an understanding of some of the crucial dynamics that are an integral part of the process of economic change in capitalist economies. The problem with macroeconomics is that it aggregates the effects of economic behaviour and decision-making in an attempt to present a picture of the whole economy. But in so doing it excludes from view much of the dynamics that drives economic change, dynamics that are best understood at the sector level. In reality, the whole economy consists of its various sectors, individually and in combination. But at any point in time very different things are happening in the economy's different sectors, differences that are aggregated away, and therefore disappear, in the aggregated measures such as output and employment.

Analysis of the sector has also been hampered by the conventional theoretical treatment of 'the firm' in standard microeconomics.

To begin with, standard microeconomics usually begins with reference to 'the representative firm'. Yet one of the key characteristics of the firms in any sector is that they differ from one another. The reason is that to survive and thrive in markets that have more or less competition, they must differ to some extent. Otherwise, they will face the fate of very small profit margins. It is variation amongst firms that, together with multiple selection processes, drive the evolution of the whole system.

Furthermore, the analysis of firms is imprisoned by the straitjacket of assumptions usually made in much microeconomics. Thus, firms are assumed to always make profit-maximising, optimal decisions and are analysed as if they were in equilibrium, that is, in a state of optimising rest. Strikingly absent is the uncertainty (where probability distributions cannot be calculated to assist decision-making), ignorance, and error that bedevils the making of business decisions in the real world.

These assumptions are particularly onerous if the aim and focus of attention is on understanding innovation, the main theme of the present book. As demonstrated throughout this book, innovating firms, making decisions ex ante in their 'moment-in-being' (i.e. the present) constantly face irreducible uncertainty. Under these conditions it is impossible, by definition, to define the optimal decision. The future and the further into the future that the decision-maker is looking is always, to a greater or lesser extent, hazy and unclear. The sharp future imagery implied by concepts such as maximisation and optimisation are entirely inappropriate in such a world.

As shown in detail in the present book, innovation, which injects *novelty* into the economic system, begins as a creative event, as 'the imagined deemed viable'. At its moment of creation, it exists only in the mind of its creator. Furthermore, it exists only as an innovation hypothesis, the outcome of which is uncertain. The innovation hypothesis must still be tested to establish its veracity. The results of these tests may be subject to interpretive ambiguity, perpetuating the uncertainty.

This too-brief and inadequate account of the innovation process will be considerably elaborated upon later in this book, particularly in Chapters 6 and 7, which deal, respectively, with how innovation happens and who makes innovation happen. However, the innovation process is mentioned here in introducing an analysis of the ICT innovation ecosystem because it is, as will be seen, innovation that is the main driver of change, in both sectors and the whole economy. It is innovation that makes these the restless systems that they are, constantly in a process of change, never standing still.

THE ICT INNOVATION ECOSYSTEM (IIE)

The aim in this chapter is to understand the sector determinants of innovation in what will be referred to as the ICT innovation ecosystem (IIE).

What is the ICT innovation ecosystem? It is defined as the collection of *players* (decision-makers) and *processes* that through their cooperative and competitive interactions produce the output of the sector and make innovation happen within it. Through these interactions players and processes coevolve as variety is generated and multiple selection processes select from this variety.

Who are the main players in IIE? They include the providers of semiconductors and other devices; computer hardware and software; telecoms equipment (such as switches, routers, and transmissions equipment); telecoms, cable, satellite, and broadcasting networks, platforms, and services; new media; and Internet platforms, content, and applications.

The Organisation of Players in IIE: Cooperative Vertical Relationships

How are the players in IIE organised? To answer this question, we will use an *organising principle* based on the distinction between those who create knowledge and those who use this knowledge. The knowledge of the former is embodied in the products and services that they

EXHIBIT 4.1 Who Are the Creators and Users of Knowledge in IIE?

produce and sell. These products and services are purchased and used by the latter.

Note that the distinction between creators and users of knowledge is flexible. In some cases, users, by acquiring new knowledge through their use, become the creators of additional new knowledge. Furthermore, creators and users may co-create new knowledge.

The problem to be solved, then, is: How do we distinguish between the creators and users of knowledge? This problem is illustrated in Exhibit 4.1. Taking the brand logos of some of IIE's main players, the question is: How do they fit together as the creators and users of knowledge?

There are a vast number of knowledge creator-user relationships in IIE. Examples include Intel supplying microprocessors for PC makers such as HP and Lenovo; Qualcomm and ARM providing chips for smartphones to players such as Samsung and Apple; ICT equipment makers such as Ericsson and Huawei selling telecoms equipment to telecoms operators such as AT&T, NTT, and Vodafone; telecoms operators supplying telecoms services to Internet platform, content, and applications providers such as Google, Facebook, Amazon, and Alibaba; etc.

In order to make the analysis tractable, we will aggregate these relationships and on the basis of this aggregation will identify four groups of knowledge creators and knowledge users. Note, however, that to answer other questions it may be necessary to disaggregate these relationships.

The four groups are the following:

1. ICT equipment providers (such as Ericsson, Huawei)
2. Network operators (including telecoms, cable, satellite operators, and broadcasters)
3. Platform, content, and applications providers (like Google and Facebook)
4. Final customers (including households, government, and companies from other sectors).

How are the relationships between these players organised? The answer given here (although other conceptualisations are also possible) is that they are organised into a set of hierarchically structured layers. The analogy is that of preparing a building.

First, a foundation is necessary. This provides the basis for the first floor, which, in turn, makes the second, third, and subsequent floors possible. Similarly, it is ICT equipment providers who create the *network elements* (e.g. routers, computers, smartphones, data networks). They populate layer 1. Their knowledge embodied in their products and services is used by the network operators in layer 2 to construct their networks (telecoms, cable, satellite, broadcasting). The platform, content, and applications providers in layer 3 and their products and services 'sit on top' of the networks provided by layer 2.

The companies in these three layers are intermediate consumers of ICT products and services that they buy from other companies in IIE. Layer 4 is populated by final consumers of these goods and services. They include households and companies and users from other sectors.

This layer model of IIE is depicted in Exhibit 4.2.

The Six Vertical Symbiotic Relationships in IIE

The four groups of players relate symbiotically with one another; that is, they 'live together', feeding off each other in a mutually beneficial way. Since each group interacts with all of the others, there is a total of six vertical symbiotic relationships in IIE. This is shown in Exhibit 4.3.

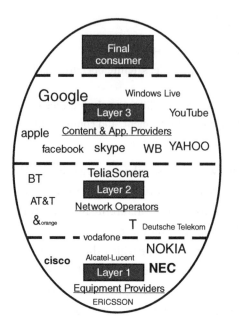

EXHIBIT 4.2 A Layer Model of the ICT Innovation Ecosystem

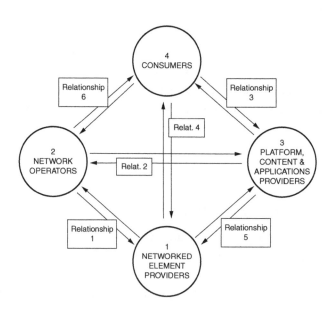

EXHIBIT 4.3 Symbiotic Relationships in the ICT Innovation Ecosystem

The Symbiotic Relationships and Apple's iPhone

The example of Apple's iPhone provides an example of IIE's six symbiotic relationships at work. Apple is primarily located in layer 1 since it is mainly a product maker (e.g. smartphones, iPads, watches) even though it is also active in layer 3 through iTunes and the provision of the iPhone applications (app) platform.

Within layer 1, Apple has approximately 2,000 iPhone component suppliers, most of whom are from Japan, Korea, Taiwan, and China. Foxconn, one of the world's largest electronics products assemblers, owned by the Taiwanese company Hon Hai, does most of the assembly of iPhones in China.

Crucial for Apple, of course, is symbiotic relationship (SR) 4 with its customers worldwide. Also important is SR3, its relationship with content and applications providers such as those who create content available on iTunes and app developers who produce apps for the iPhone, enhancing its value to iPhone users. SR1, Apple's relationships with telecoms operators, is also central. It is these operators who provide the networks necessary for iPhone users. Furthermore, and crucially facilitating Apple's entry into the mobile phone market, it was agreements with major telecoms operators around the world that helped in the beginning to put the iPhone 'on the map'.

Some Characteristics of the Layer Model

Specialisation by Layer

Generally speaking, companies have tended to specialise by layer.[1] For example, companies such as Ericsson, Huawei, HP, Dell, and Cisco have been and remain layer 1 players; AT&T, Verizon, BT, Deutsche Telecom, and Sky are layer 2 players; and eBay, Amazon, Alibaba, Google, and Facebook are in layer 3.

Interestingly, it was new entrants such as Amazon, Google, Facebook, and eBay that first entered layer 3 in the mid-1990s as

---

[1] Specialisation and the division of labour *within* the innovation process is analysed in detail in Chapter 7.

small entrepreneurial start-ups that eventually came to dominate this layer.[2] They are all, essentially, software companies. But it was not the then-dominant software companies such as the telecoms operators or computer companies (like IBM, Fujitsu, and Hitachi) who diversified into layer 3 using their considerable software capabilities.

Why this sustained layer-specific specialisation? To some extent the answer has to do with the 'stickiness' of capabilities, including the difficulty of buying them. This limited diversification into other layers. Furthermore, the software development process in areas such as telecoms was constrained by the immediate need for zero defects for fear that faulty software in network-critical areas such as switching and transmissions would trigger substantial network failure with widespread and significantly negative consequences for companies and households. In contrast, the new software developers had much greater flexibility and therefore it was no surprise that it was they who developed more flexible software development methods such as online beta-testing and the agile methodology for developing new software. These new software methods facilitated their entry into layer 3 and their subsequent rapid scale-up.

However, despite this strong tendency to specialise by layer, many companies have straddled layers whilst remaining primarily dependent on one layer for most of their revenue and profit. An example is Apple, which was primarily a computer maker and is now principally a phone maker, both activities being located in layer 1. However, with iTunes and as a major app platform provider, Apple's activities in layer 3 are also substantial.

---

[2] For a detailed discussion of the entry of these companies into Layer 3 in the mid-1990s, see appendix 7: 'Why do US Internet companies dominate in layer 3?,' in Fransman, M., 2010. *The New ICT Ecosystem*. Cambridge: Cambridge University Press. There information is provided on the entrepreneur's date of birth and country of birth, parents' occupations, company's start date, entrepreneur's prior experience with computers/Internet, universities attended by the entrepreneurs, and source of start-up capital.

Shifting Boundaries between Layers

Over time, layer boundaries have shifted. A good example is the changing division of labour between telecoms operators and their ICT equipment providers.

As is discussed in more detail later, originally telecoms operators such as AT&T, NTT, France Telecom, and BT created and designed their main items of equipment in their own central research laboratories. Over time, however, more and more of the creation, design, and development of equipment was passed over by the telecoms operators to specialised equipment providers like Ericsson, Lucent, Alcatel, and NEC. These specialists benefitted from intense competition globally from their rivals and their specialisation, both of which stimulated their ability to innovate. This meant that with the passage of time the boundary separating layers 1 and 2 shifted upwards, leaving more of the activity to the layer 1 players. The possibility of boundary shift is indicated in Exhibit 4.2 by the broken lines separating the layers.[3]

The Continuously Evolving ICT Innovation Ecosystem

A major problem with the depiction of the ICT innovation ecosystem in Exhibit 4.2 is that, by the nature of a diagram, it is static. It does not show the real-world continuously evolving ecosystem driven by the evolutionary engine of variety generation through innovation coupled with multiple selection processes that select from this variety, causing continual change. This constantly changing ecosystem must be kept in mind in attempting to understand it. It is a system never at rest, never in equilibrium, a system continually being re-created and destroyed and continually being disrupted by innovation.

---

[3] Further details are to be found on the different relationships between telecoms operators and their equipment suppliers – including the differences between AT&T, NTT, and BT – in Fransman, M., 1995. *Japan's Computer and Communications Industry*. Oxford: Oxford University Press, and Fransman, M., 1999. *Visions of Innovation*. Oxford: Oxford University Press.

The Organisation of Players in IIE: Competitive Horizontal Relationships

The layer model diagram shown in Exhibit 4.2 focuses primarily on *vertical* cooperative relationships. But also important, and a key driver of innovation, are *horizontal* competitive relationships.

Each layer can be divided into a number of product or service markets. The competing players in these markets are those who provide substitutable products or services. The forces of competition bring these players into close relationships with one another. Their products and services confront one another as consumer-users select between them. Also to be included are potential entrants who may enter the market, and they, therefore, influence the expectations and behaviour of the incumbents in the market.

An example will illustrate how these horizontal relationships work.

The Example of Telecoms Equipment Providers in Layer 1

The example deals with the changing competitive relationships over time of the major telecoms equipment providers.

Era of Natural Monopoly to Mid-1980s Until the mid-1980s the provision of telecoms services was regarded as being a 'natural monopoly'. The argument was that as a result of the very high fixed costs of establishing telecoms networks, and the ensuing economies of scale that existed in this industry, together with low marginal costs (the cost of adding an extra subscriber to the network), the front-running incumbent would be the first to travel down the long-run average cost curve,[4] thus gaining a significant advantage compared with would-be competitors. Following this line of reasoning, in almost all countries there was one monopoly, usually state-owned, supplying telecoms services.

---

[4] Given the high fixed costs, as the number of subscribers increase, so the fixed cost per subscriber (i.e. the average fixed cost) falls. This can be shown as a falling cost curve relating average fixed costs to the number of subscribers.

Until the 1980s it was the monopoly telecoms operator in the large developed countries (including Japan) that tended to drive the main innovations in telecoms equipment and services. This they did by concentrating the early stages of research, design, and development in their own central research laboratories. Thus AT&T in the United States had its Bell Laboratories, NTT in Japan had the Electrical Communications Laboratories, BT had the Martlesham Laboratories, and France Telecom its CNET Laboratories.

However, the telecoms operators forged different kinds of relationships with their equipment providers. AT&T chose vertical integration with Western Electric, which from the outset was part of AT&T. NTT, however, chose to have a long-term obligational relationship with a family of four selected equipment providers – NEC, Fujitsu, Hitachi, and Oki – known in Japan as the Den Den Family. BT, after an initial period when their main providers included GEC, Plessey, and STC, opted for a more arm's-length relationship with a number of more market-based providers. In short, there was no consensus regarding the most effective way of organising the relationship between telecoms operator and equipment supplier.[5]

Era of Liberalisation of Telecoms Service Provision: From mid-1980s
In the mid-1980s, however, a sea-change occurred in thinking about how telecoms services should be provided. Driven by different political and ideological conditions that emerged for different reasons in the leading telecoms countries, the idea that telecoms services should be provided by monopoly operators was challenged and dropped.

At more or less the same time in the mid-1980s, the United States, Japan, and the United Kingdom introduced limited competition to their incumbent telecoms operators. In the United States, MCI and Sprint were given regulatory permission to compete with AT&T; in Japan, DDI, Japan Telecom, and Teleway Japan competed with

---

[5] See Fransman 1995 and 1999 for further details.

NTT; and in the United Kingdom, Mercury competed with BT. At the same time in the United States, AT&T, formerly a privately owned but state-regulated monopoly, was broken up into a 'long lines' (i.e. long-distance) operator that retained the name, AT&T, and a number of regional operators referred to as the Baby Bells.

The Telecoms Equipment Suppliers The introduction of competition in telecoms services was facilitated by the presence of a group of globally competing telecoms equipment suppliers. Competing with one another for the procurement of the new telecoms operator entrants, they eased the latter's entry into telecoms services markets. Regulators also helped through regulations requiring the incumbents to give favourable access to their own networks to the new entrants. Although the dominant equipment suppliers tended to remain the major suppliers to the telecoms incumbent operator, they simultaneously competed in other developed and developing countries.

The major equipment suppliers included Lucent from the United States (the former Western Electric, which after the breakup of AT&T took control of Bell Laboratories, the new Belcore Laboratories being established to service the needs of the Baby Bells); NEC, Fujitsu, and Hitachi from Japan; Ericsson from Sweden; Alcatel from France; and Northern Telecom from Canada.

From the 1990s the intense competition between the telecoms equipment providers resulted in a significant shakeout. Some exited the industry, whilst others were taken over and merged. For example, Northern Telecom from Canada and GEC, Plessey, and STC from the United Kingdom exited. Lucent and Alcatel merged, as did Siemens and Nokia, to form Nokia Siemens Networks. More recently, Nokia Siemens Networks acquired Alcatel-Lucent.

From around 2005 new entries from China added considerably to the shakeout turmoil.

The Case of Huawei Huawei and ZTE were the most important of the Chinese new entrants. In view of their significant contribution to the changing dynamics of competition in the global layer 1, the entry and rise of Huawei will be briefly examined.

The evolution of Huawei may be divided up into four periods:

Period 1, pre-1988: the background of founder Ren Zhengfei
Period 2, 1988–1996: learning, like Chairman Mao, in the countryside
Period 3, 1996 to the early 2000s: entering the Chinese metropolitan
market and other emerging countries
Period 4, early 2000s to the present: entering advanced country markets
through alliances and the internationalisation of R&D.

Each of these periods will be discussed briefly.

Period 1, pre-1988: The Background of Founder Ren Zhengfei
The background of Ren Zhengfei, the founder of Huawei, is a particularly important factor shaping the evolution of this company. This is all the more the case since Huawei is not a normally publicly floated, owned, and quoted company. Rather, it is a company, as Huawei's official information puts it, owned by around 20,000 of its 80,000-plus employees. Ren himself is the largest shareholder with just under 2 per cent of the company's shares and, according to *Fortune*, one of the richest 100 or so people in China.

The key formative experience for Huawei emerged when Ren worked after the Second World War as a military engineer in a military research laboratory run by the People's Liberation Army of China. It was here that Ren learned the art of adapting technologies to suit the purposes of the customer-user, in this case the Chinese Army. It was a capability that he was later to deploy in working with commercial telecoms operators, helping them to achieve what they wanted.

Period 2, 1988–1996: Learning, like Chairman Mao, in the Countryside
Huawei was established in 1988 in Shenzhen, on the border with Hong Kong. Shenzhen was designated in 1979 as the first of several Special Economic Zones under the reforms introduced by Deng Xiaoping aimed at experimenting with market capitalism within the

context of a new 'socialism with Chinese characteristics'. Further market-based reforms were introduced from 1986. The Special Economic Zone of Shenzhen was located next to Hong Kong in order to benefit from the knowledge and investment that thrived in this British colony.

Huawei began by selling a PBX local telecoms switch manufactured by a Hong Kong company. Huawei soon began to make its own PBX equipment. However, the fledgling Huawei was still technologically immature and lacked the brand name needed to compete with the much more sophisticated foreign telecoms equipment companies that quickly dominated the reforming Chinese economy.

It was in coping with this strategic positioning dilemma that Ren, as he later acknowledged, turned for leadership to the Chairman. Mao, in leading the Chinese Communist Party, initially based his struggle in the countryside with a base amongst the poor and middle-level peasantry. It was only later, with this base consolidated, that the party turned its attention to the cities. Ren followed in this path, focusing first on telecoms equipment for the rural areas of China, which, with their distinctive problems and requirements, were not so well served by the foreign telecoms equipment companies. In serving rural telecoms needs, Ren and his colleagues in Huawei were able to draw on their own earlier experience in the military, except that this time their technological knowledge was to be deployed in developing solutions for Chinese rural telecoms providers.

Huawei learned fast. The company began selling its own products in 1992. By 1996 Huawei was able to sell equipment to Hutchison Whampoa, the Hong Kong conglomerate. With this experience under its belt, Huawei, like Mao in earlier times, was able to take on the cities.

Period 3, 1996 to the Early 2000s: Entering the Chinese Metropolitan Market and Other Emerging Countries
In 1998 Huawei began to sell equipment for use in China's metropolitan areas. However, Ren and his colleagues realised that this would

require more than the knowledge of Mao's military strategies. With China firmly on the reformist road, links with global multinational corporations were becoming the norm.

One particularly important relationship was forged between Ren and Lou Gerstner, who had masterminded IBM's turnaround from a mainframe computer-based company to one focusing on computer solutions and services. Indeed, somewhat incongruously, Ren credits both Mao and Gerstner as the providers of the inspiration that helped him and his colleagues to shape the evolution of Huawei. But other companies, such as PwC, also provided inputs that helped Huawei to develop its managerial and organisational capabilities in tandem with its symbiotic interactions with its customer-users, suppliers, partners, and competitors.

But, despite its growing strength, Huawei was still little match for the most sophisticated of the foreign telecoms equipment providers, European, Japanese, and American. It was these providers that China's telecoms operators – such as China Telecom and China Mobile – preferred. Ren's solution was to focus on other emerging countries. However, rather than a second-best option, this strategy allowed Huawei to reap the extremely powerful benefits of *learning-by-exporting* that had already stimulated the development and growth of Japanese and later South Korean and Taiwanese ICT companies such as NEC and Fujitsu, Samsung and LG, and TSMC, UMC, and Acer.

The export market is a particularly important 'university' for learning and innovation. Unlike the home market where a company may have privileged access because of its contacts and connections (commercial as well as political), in the export market a company has to be tough in order to survive. The reason, simply, especially in the largest, fastest-growing markets, is that a company is forced to compete with the best in the world in order to win orders. Adapting to this environment involves new relationships with symbiotic counterparts – customer-users, suppliers, partners, and competitors. It is these relationships that breed new and improved distinctive competencies (including the ability to innovate in order to better 'live with' counterparts). In turn, these competencies allowed Huawei to consolidate its global strategic positioning.

Period 4, Early 2000s to the Present: Entering Advanced Country Markets through Alliances and the Internationalisation of R&D
From the early 2000s Huawei was strong enough to establish win-win relationships with some of the best companies in the world. In addition to fixed and mobile telecoms operators, Huawei was also able to establish alliances with important partners in the ICT sector. A further element in Huawei's strategy was the internationalisation of its R&D activities.

Huawei's entry into Western markets was spearheaded by the strategically significant relationship that the company formed with BT, the incumbent telecoms operator in the United Kingdom. This relationship is discussed below.

Revenue from Telecoms Network Equipment for the Three Leading Equipment Suppliers Exhibit 4.4 shows the annual revenue from telecoms network equipment for the three leaders in the global telecoms equipment market, Huawei, Ericsson, and Nokia (including its acquired Alcatel-Lucent). Huawei's outstanding competitive success in the telecoms network equipment segment of layer 1 is evident from Exhibit 4.4.

Exhibit 4.4 *Huawei, Ericsson, and Nokia: Revenue from Telecoms Network Equipment, 2015*

Company	Annual Revenue, 2015	Growth 2014–15
Huawei	$35.80bn	21%
Ericsson	$30.36bn	8%
Nokia*	$30.06bn	–

Source: *telecomlead.com*, accessed 3 December 2016.
* Nokia includes Nokia Siemens Networks and Alcatel Lucent.

The section below on innovation in IIE contains further details on how Huawei innovates, taking the example of its symbiotic relationship with BT in the United Kingdom.

Noncompany Players in the IIE

For-profit companies constitute the engine of the ICT innovation ecosystem. It is these players who primarily are responsible for making innovation, as defined in this book, happen. However, noncompany players also play a crucial role.

The main noncompany players in IIE who influence innovation are the providers of knowledge, finance, and the rules of the game.

Knowledge

Universities are the main noncompany players who provide knowledge in IIE, although government research and standardisation bodies also play a significant role. Universities provide knowledge in two ways. First, they provide the trained people who go on to perform innovation-related functions in companies. Second, they contribute their research, skills, and findings.

Universities, however, are a fundamentally different kind of organisation compared with for-profit companies in terms of their goals, organisational structure, and the motivation of their employees. Effectively aligning company innovators and university researchers can, therefore, be a challenging task.

Finance

The providers of finance for company-based innovation come in different forms. They include private banks, government funding agencies, venture capitalists, angel investors, private equity, crowdfunders, etc. They provide the credit that is often needed to fund innovating firms until they have positive cash flows. Market failures in the market for innovation funding often complicate the relationship between innovating companies and the providers of innovation finance, and ways around these failures are needed to mitigate the difficulties. This issue is discussed in more detail in Chapter 7.

Rules of the Game

Finally, institutions of various kinds also influence companies and their interactions. Nobel laureate Douglass North defines institutions as the set of formal and informal 'rules of the game'. They include regulations, competition law, law of property and contract, etc.

But who creates and changes institutions? North's answer is that it is 'organisations' that do this. They change institutions even as they are shaped by them. Organisations for North include political parties and trade unions. In this way, politics and power relationships enter as crucial determinants of the dynamics and innovation processes in innovation ecosystems. This invites the use of political economy in order to understand the interactions.

These three groups of noncompany players, not shown in Exhibit 4.2, both individually and jointly have a significant impact on the innovation process. They and the processes they drive should, therefore, form an integral part of the conceptualisation of innovation ecosystems.

THE INNOVATION PROCESS IN THE IIE

R&D

One component of the innovation process in IIE is research and development (R&D).

The main R&D engine in IIE is located in layer 1, consisting of the providers of ICT equipment. In my book *The New ICT Ecosystem* (2010), it was estimated that '73 per cent of the total R&D expenditure undertaken by all the companies in all three layers was done by the [ICT equipment providers] in layer 1'. In turn, '11 percent was undertaken by the network operators in layer 2, with 16 percent being done by the companies in layer 3 (the difference is due to rounding)'.[6] In terms of R&D, therefore, it is the layer 1 players who are the drivers of IIE.

However, a very different picture emerges if we look at capital expenditure as another engine of growth in IIE. There it was found that '70 per cent of the total capital expenditure made by companies in all three layers came from network service providers in layer 2. The ... companies in layer 1 provided 26 per cent of total capital expenditure, leaving the companies in layer 3 [i.e. the platform, content, and applications providers] to take care of the remaining 4 per cent.'[7] In terms of capital expenditure, therefore, it is the layer 2 players who are the drivers of IIE.[8]

Further information on R&D and profitability at company level is provided in Exhibit 4.5, in which nine companies have been selected from layer 1 and three each from layers 2 and 3. Data are provided on the overall rank of the companies in the European Commission's data, their total R&D expenditure, R&D intensity, and profitability (profits divided by sales).

A number of illuminating points emerge from Exhibit 4.5 (although the figures are for only one year):

1. There is a significant difference in terms of R&D intensity between layers. Whilst the average for the companies shown for layers 1 and 3 was 9.4 per cent and 10.1 per cent, respectively, that for layer 2, the network operator layer, was only 1.7 per cent. This underlines the point made above, namely that the network operators have increasingly left their R&D (embodied in their ICT equipment) to layer 1 providers.
2. Average R&D per company is far higher in layer 1 than in the other two layers. In layer 1 it is 4,009 million euros, compared with 2,248 million euros for layer 3 and 1,559 million euros for layer 2. Again, this highlights

---

[6] Fransman (2010), p. 61.　　[7] Ibid., p. 59.

[8] Based on data for approximately 200 of the largest ICT companies, 'telecoms equipment' companies are a proxy for layer 1 companies, 'telecoms services' companies are a proxy for layer 2 companies, and 'Internet and e-commerce' companies are a proxy for layer 3 companies.

Exhibit 4.5 *R&D and Profitability of Selected ICT Companies by Layer, 2012*

Layer	Company Name	Overall Rank	R&D Expenditure (2011, Euro mill.)	R&D Intensity (Rank)	Profitability (Rank)
1	Microsoft	2	7,583	13.3 (4)	29.9 (3)
1	Samsung	5	6,858	6.2 (8)	9.4 (7)
1	Nokia	15	4,910	12.7 (5)	−2.8 (14)
1	Sony	18	4,311	6.7 (7)	−1.0 (13)
1	Ericsson	29	3,657	14.4 (2)	7.8 (9)
1	Huawei	41	2,907	18.6 (1)	–
1	Fujitsu	49	2,370	5.3 (9)	2.3 (10)
1	Apple	59	1,877	2.2 (12)	31.2 (2)
1	NEC	70	1,611	5.3 (9)	2.2 (11)
1	**Average, Layer 1**		**4,009**	**9.41**	
2	NTT	47	2,664	2.5 (11)	11.7 (6)
2	Telefonica	103	1,089	1.7 (13)	17.4 (5)
2	AT&T	115	925	1.0 (14)	8.0 (8)
2	**Average, Layer 2**		**1,559**	**1.7**	**12.4**
3	Google	26	3,990	13.6 (3)	32.0 (1)
3	Amazon	67	1,637	4.4 (10)	1.8 (12)
3	eBay	100	1,118	12.4 (6)	20.4 (4)
3	**Average, Layer 3**		**2,248**	**10.1**	**18.1**

Source: Fransman, M., 2014. *Models of Innovation in Global ICT Firms: The Emerging Global Innovation Ecosystems.* JRC Scientific and Policy Reports, EUR 26774 EN. Seville: JRC-IPTS.

Exhibit 4.6 *R&D and Profitability Characteristics of Selected ICT Companies, 2012*

Company Characteristics	Company Names
High R&D intensity, high profitability	Microsoft, Samsung, Ericsson, Huawei,* Google, eBay
High R&D intensity, low profitability	Nokia, Sony, Fujitsu, NEC, Amazon
Low R&D intensity, high profitability	Apple, NTT, Telefonica, AT&T

Source: Fransman, M., 2014. *Models of Innovation in Global ICT Firms: The Emerging Global Innovation Ecosystems*. JRC Scientific and Policy Reports, EUR 26774 EN. Seville: JRC-IPTS.
* This is not a conventional public company and therefore its profitability figure may not be strictly comparable with the other companies mentioned.

    the dependence of network operators on the R&D of the ICT equipment providers.

3. There appears to be little relationship between both absolute expenditure on R&D and R&D intensity, on the one hand, and profitability, on the other. This is summarised in Exhibit 4.6.

    The relationship between R&D intensity and profitability among the first group of companies shown in Exhibit 4.6 is what one would expect if the R&D expenditure succeeds in doing what is aimed at, namely increasing innovation and therefore competitiveness and profitability. However, the second group of companies serve as a reminder that there may well be a slip between R&D cup and profitability lip. It is precisely this that makes R&D a poor measure and predictor of the kind of innovation that increases competitiveness and profitability.[9]

4. The Japanese companies included in Exhibit 4.6 are particularly interesting in that although they are high R&D performers, they have low profitability. Traditionally relatively high R&D spenders, the Japanese companies ran into competitiveness problems as a result of their failure to make sufficient

[9] Fransman (2014), p. 51.

headway in the new products that were generating much of the growth in the evolving ICT ecosystem. Given this failure, R&D was insufficient to provide a solution. In Sony's case, for example, its successful innovation-based products (such as its games consoles) were not enough to compensate for its rapidly declining profit margins from some of its traditional businesses such as televisions and monitors as competitors like Korea's Samsung and LG stole a march. Similarly, Fujitsu and NEC, formerly amongst the world's leading companies in the field of computers, were unable to keep up with the disruption that occurred with the introduction of smartphones and tablet computers. In telecoms equipment they were out-innovated by low-cost competitors, notably Huawei and ZTE from China. The substantial R&D expenditure and capabilities that had long characterised Fujitsu and NEC were of little help. These observations serve to reiterate that R&D expenditure is not sufficient to ensure good company performance.[10]

APPLE IS NOT A HIGH-TECH COMPANY!

5. However, it is perhaps Apple that stands out noticeably in Exhibit 4.6. This becomes clear if we compare Apple with its main competitor in the smartphone market, Samsung. In terms of overall rank in the R&D scoreboard data (including all sectors of the economy) Samsung came in fifth. Apple, on the other hand, came in fifty-ninth. Samsung's total R&D expenditure was 6,858 million euros; Apple's was only 1,877 million euros. In terms of R&D intensity, Samsung's was 6.2; Apple's 2.2.[11] Significantly, however, Apple turned the apple-cart upside down in terms of profitability. Apple's profitability was 31.2 (profits divided by sales); Samsung's 9.4.

Is it therefore justifiable to call Apple a low-tech company? The answer depends on the definition of 'low-tech'. The conventional definition of high-tech is given in terms of R&D intensity. The greater its R&D-intensity, the 'higher-tech' the company. According to this definition, for example, the pharmaceuticals sector with R&D intensity levels amongst the highest in the economy is one of the most 'high-tech'. Compare Apple's 2.2 R&D intensity with Microsoft's 13.3, Sony's 6.7, Ericsson's 14.4,

---

[10] Fransman (2014), pp. 51–2.

[11] Apple's R&D intensity has since inched up, although it remains below 3, still well below all the other layer 1 companies shown in Exhibit 4.6.

Huawei's 18.6 (the highest in Exhibit 4.6), Fujitsu's and NEC's 5.3, Google's 13.6, Amazon's 4.4, and eBay's 12.4. According to these data, and given the definition of 'high-tech' in terms of R&D intensity, therefore, it is completely justifiable to call Apple a low-tech company!

But how has Apple managed to get away with being so 'R&D light'? There are two answers to this question. The first is of particular interest in view of the title of the present book. It is that Apple has succeeded in creating a company-level innovation ecosystem in which many of the R&D-intensive elements included in Apple's products are provided by other companies in Apple's innovation ecosystem, rather than by Apple itself. This includes, for example, the microprocessors in the Apple iPhone, which are made and supplied by Samsung, which, ironically, is simultaneously Apple's main competitor in the smartphone market. Indeed, the iPhone contains almost 2,000 components, many of which are very R&D-intensive products produced by Asian companies from Japan, Korea, Taiwan, and China.

The second answer is that R&D is only one element of innovation. Particularly important for Apple are some of the other elements that, although they are crucial for the innovation and competitiveness of Apple's products, are excluded from the R&D measure. Some of these other elements, all of which are regarded for data purposes as *intangible investments*, are shown in Exhibit 4.7.

As Exhibit 4.7 shows, as important as R&D may be, it is only one of a number of innovation-related intangible investment expenditures. Furthermore, all of them are both complementary and necessary for competition-enhancing innovation to happen. The others, in descending order of importance, are organisational capital (i.e. capital expenditures needed to bring about organisational changes needed to make innovation happen), training, design, software development, branding, and copyright expenditures. Obviously, these other non-R&D innovation-related expenditures have also been extremely important in the Apple case.

It is also worth noting that R&D expenditure was only the fifth most important item of expenditure in absolute terms.

Together with the composition of Apple's innovation ecosystem, therefore, other items of innovation-related intangible investment expenditure help to explain the 'Apple paradox' noted here, namely that Apple is a low-tech company.

Exhibit 4.7 *NESTA Innovation Index: Intangible Innovation-Related Investments (£bn)*

	Kind of Intangible Investment (£bn)	Proportion of Total Intangible Investment
Organisational capital	31	22.5%
Training	27	19.6%
Design	23	16.7%
Software development	22	15.9%
R&D	**16**	**11.6%**
Branding	15	10.9%
Copyrights	4	2.9%
TOTAL	**138**	**100**

Source: NESTA Survey 2008, quoted in Department for Business, Innovation and Skills, 2011, *Innovation and Research Strategy for Growth*, BIS Economics Paper No.15, London: BIS, p. 13.

The Limitations of R&D as a Driver of Innovation and Competitiveness and as an Indicator of Innovation

These observations on R&D in IIE should give reason to pause for thought for any R&D enthusiast, whether company executive or government policymaker. In short, even though R&D may in some cases be necessary for competition-increasing innovation (though even this is not always the case), it is unlikely to be sufficient. There are also other ingredients that need to be added to achieve the desired result.

This should hardly be surprising. After all, R&D is an input into innovation, it is not an output.[12] And as with any input expenditure

---

[12] Patents are another commonly used indicator of innovation. Their principal advantage is that, in contrast to R&D, patents are a measure of output rather than input. However, there are also many disadvantages of this indicator. Most important, it is not the number of patents that matter – the measure usually used – but, rather, the value of patents that matters. However, patent data usually excludes value. This is for good reason. Value often accrues to a patent only after the passage of substantial time. Some patents have no value. Despite these drawbacks, however, both patent and R&D data are frequently used simply because they are available.

item, there is no guarantee that it will achieve the purposes intended in making the expenditure. Furthermore, as shown clearly in Exhibit 4.7, R&D excludes many other elements needed to make competition-increasing innovation happen. This is as true at the company level as it is at the country level.[13]

We conclude, therefore, that going down the 'R&D road' does not take us very far in understanding how competitiveness-increasing innovation happens. There remains, therefore, more work to be done. In the last section we will examine in more detail how competitiveness-increasing innovation, as opposed to R&D, which was discussed in this section, happens in IIE.

How Competitiveness-Increasing Innovation Happens in IIE: The Creation of the Innovation Hypothesis

> Together, [Huawei and BT] work from the inception of an idea, through development and test, to market rollout.
>
> – Nigel Abraham, Solutions Director, Huawei

The Innovation Hypothesis

How does innovation happen in the ICT innovation ecosystem? As will be shown in detail in Chapter 6, the innovation process begins with the creation of an innovation hypothesis. This act of creation involves hypothesising about the kind of innovation that will be made, its characteristics and features, and how it will add value for

---

Other possible measures of innovation referred to here are either unavailable in data form or intrinsically difficult to measure. The downside of their use, however, may be untrue or misleading conclusions.

[13] Many countries, such as China, include amongst their science, technology, and innovation plan objectives the attainment of particular R&D to GDP ratios. However, the caveat that has emerged in the present discussion regarding the limitations of R&D as a measure of competitiveness-increasing innovation is also relevant at the country level. Japan provides reasons for being wary. In many cases the top global performers in terms of measures such as R&D as a proportion of GDP, business expenditure on R&D, and patents, leading Japanese companies in many sectors (with some exceptions, such as automobiles) have over the past decade shown rapid deterioration in their global competitiveness. This is so despite exceptional performance in the R&D and patent areas.

its initially intended customer-users relative to that provided by competitors.

At the moment of its creation, the innovation does not yet exist. Its only existence is in the mind of its creator(s). It is 'the imagined deemed feasible'. The act of creating an innovation hypothesis is an act that creates *novelty*. This novelty is injected into the ecosystem. It produces a fundamental discontinuity with the past.[14]

At its moment of creation, the innovation hypothesis is held with irreducible uncertainty. No probability distributions can be defined or estimated to assist decision-making for the simple reason that the innovation is new; it does not yet exist other than as a hypothesis in the mind of its creator(s).

However, a company's innovator(s) does not know whether the innovation hypothesis is true or not. In order to establish its veracity, its creator(s) will have to test it. As discussed at length in Chapters 6 and 7, the innovation process is largely about the creation, testing, re-creation, and retesting of innovation hypotheses.

The Contribution of Sector Innovation Ecosystems Thinking

What does the ICT innovation ecosystem have to do with the creation of an innovation hypothesis in the ICT sector? The answer is that the ecosystem provides the *context* within which innovation hypotheses are created and tested.

Crucially, however, context does not predict creation. A full knowledge of the context does not allow for the prediction of the innovation hypothesis that will be created or its content. The act of creating an innovation hypothesis is, to repeat, the creation of novelty. This act, therefore, is indeterminate.

---

[14] This is the fundamental difference between human systems and biological or physical systems. Whilst uncertainty exists in all three kinds of systems, it is only in human systems that novelty is produced through the exercise of human creativity and imagination. This generates a fundamental break with the past, a discontinuity, that emerges with the new.

Understanding the Context of the Innovation Hypothesis

In order to understand the context within which a company's innovator(s) is creating and testing innovation hypotheses, it will be helpful for the external observer to get a broader perspective, going beyond the company level. This perspective is that of the sector innovation ecosystem as a whole. The case of the ICT innovation ecosystem, for example, has been partially depicted in Exhibit 4.2.

This perspective provides a broader view of two key *contextual coordinates* that play an important role in shaping (though not determining) innovation hypotheses:

1. The *vertical cooperative symbiotic relationships* between the players in IIE's four layers (shown in Exhibit 4.3). These vertical relationships show the populations of consumer-users in the layers of the ecosystem.
2. The *horizontal competitive symbiotic relationships* between providers in the same layer competing in the same markets for the same customer-users. These horizontal relationships define the populations of potential competitors.

In addition, the ICT innovation ecosystem perspective also provides an understanding of the other noncompany players who interact with the company players, influencing their innovation processes. These noncompany players, as discussed earlier, are the providers of knowledge (such as universities), finance (e.g. venture capitalists), and the makers of the 'rules of the game' (e.g. government regulators). An explanation of innovation hypotheses and innovation processes may also require an understanding of how noncompany players such as these have influenced innovation activities.

Structural conditions, unique to particular layers of the innovation ecosystem, may also be important influences on innovation hypotheses and processes. For example, an important part of the innovation architecture of layer 3 – the platform, content, and applications layer – is the Internet innovation platform.

This platform, which 'stands on' the networks provided by the network operators in layer 2, who in turn get their network elements from providers in layer 1, has created a hotbed of activity in layer 3. It has facilitated low-cost entry, thus encouraging the activities of digital Internet-based entrepreneurs of one kind and another, giving them access to potential customer-users globally and making rapid scale-up possible. It has also provided a potentially low-cost way of testing innovation hypotheses.

In short, the ICT innovation ecosystem perspective can provide an external observer with an in-depth understanding of the wider context within which company-level innovation hypotheses and innovation processes are created. This is illustrated by the vertical cooperative symbiotic relationship between Huawei, from layer 1, and BT, from layer 2.

Huawei and BT

The emergence and history of Huawei, now the world's leading telecoms equipment provider, in layer 1, was briefly discussed earlier. In this section Huawei's cooperative symbiotic relationship with BT, the United Kingdom's incumbent telecoms operator, will be briefly considered.

BT played a key role in Huawei's strategic attempt to broaden its global activities by expanding beyond China and emerging countries. Europe was its main focus of attention and, within Europe, the United Kingdom and BT.

But breaking into BT's equipment procurement network was a particularly daunting challenge. Traditionally, telecoms operators have developed close long-term relationships with their equipment suppliers, as was discussed earlier. Furthermore, some of BT's European equipment suppliers were world leaders and tough competitors. For Huawei the challenge was not easy.

There were several dimensions to the strategic approach to BT that Huawei adopted. The first was to take a longer-term perspective. This meant forgoing quick returns. The second dimension was to focus on understanding BT's main priorities and problems. This understanding, which could only be built up slowly over time, served as the basis for a longer-term trust-based symbiotic relationship. By working increasingly closely with BT, Huawei aimed to develop cost-effective and innovative solutions to BT's problems.

One advantage that Huawei enjoyed derived from its location in Shenzhen, China. Here Huawei was able to benefit from China's global comparative advantage in relatively low-cost skilled labour. But the company could not rely only on a low-price advantage. Quality and new equipment characteristics have always been a key requirement in the telecoms equipment market. This necessitated the ability to innovate in order to compete. The importance of innovation to Huawei was indicated in Exhibit 4.5, which showed that Huawei had the highest R&D intensity of all the companies included in the exhibit with absolute R&D expenditures not far behind Ericsson's, the global leader at the time.

Eventually, Huawei's patience and hard work payed off. In 2005 Huawei was selected by BT as a supplier of switching and routing gear for its broadband network. Some of Huawei's innovations succeeded in adding value for BT relative to Huawei's competitors. Evidence for this comes, for example, from Geoff Pearson, Huawei Platform Manager at BT. Quoted in a BT-published collaboration case study, Pearson referred to Huawei devices that were 'faster', had 'lower whole-life cost', with 'more ports and additional features' compared with those of competitors. 'Huawei produces equipment that's very reliable and comparatively cost effective', said Pearson.

Significantly, the Huawei–BT relationship goes far beyond a seller–buyer collaboration. Essentially, both companies are involved in a cooperative symbiotic relationship in which both are co-innovators. Their cooperation includes the joint creation of new innovation hypotheses that are jointly tested, developed, and taken to market.

Some of this innovation occurs in BT's Adastral Park in Ipswich, England, where 'the two companies have established a joint innovation and collaboration programme. Huawei occupies 2 entire floors, with 40 engineering staff working alongside BT people.'[15] Nigel Abraham, Solutions Director at Huawei, summarises the relationship in the following way: 'Our commitment to BT is total, which is why we have our engineers permanently based at Adastral Park. Together, we work from the inception of an idea, through development and test, to market rollout.'[16]

As this brief study makes clear, the innovation that Huawei and BT make happen – innovation that begins with the joint creation of an initial innovation hypothesis – is intimately shaped by the ICT innovation ecosystem within which it occurs. The Huawei–BT relationship, companies from layer 1 and layer 2, respectively, is an example of a vertical cooperative symbiotic innovation relationship.

Less visibly, however, this vertical relationship also interacts with simultaneous horizontal competitive relationships. The reason is that Huawei's competitors such as Ericsson and Nokia-Alcatel-Lucent are also invisibly present in the Huawei–BT innovation process. Their presence is felt by both Huawei and BT, which have knowledge of the competing equipment that Ericsson and Nokia are offering. This competitive presence inevitably influences the innovation hypotheses that are created by Huawei and BT.

Also less visibly present are some of the other noncompany players in the ICT innovation ecosystem. One example is the British and other universities in which many of the engineers employed by BT and Huawei have been trained and the research and consultancy work that academics at these universities have contributed to the innovation process.

These all-too-brief examples illustrate the innovation ecosystem–wide ramifications that have played a role in shaping the innovation processes undertaken by BT and Huawei as they make innovation happen.

[15] Ibid.   [16] Ibid.

Link to Chapters 6 and 7

Chapter 6 takes further the study of *how* innovation happens through a close examination of four key innovations that, separately and jointly, changed the world. These innovations are the transistor, microprocessor, laser, and optical fibre. Chapter 7 explores *who* makes innovation happen and includes discussions of the role of entrepreneurs and the modern division of innovation labour.

A Concluding Word of Caution Regarding Innovation Ecosystems

It is important to emphasise that an innovation ecosystem is not an empirical entity. It is not possible to see an innovation ecosystem. Like an innovation hypothesis at the moment of its creation, an innovation ecosystem exists only in the mind of its creator. An innovation ecosystem is an analyst's conceptual creation. This has important implications and, as noted in the following chapter, is a potential source of confusion.

The most important implication is that it is necessary to be very careful in using the idea of an innovation ecosystem. The reason is that different people, all using the same words, may be meaning different things. It is therefore necessary to begin by defining what is meant by an innovation ecosystem and to what, empirically, it is referring.

Furthermore, an analyst's construction of an innovation ecosystem is usually intended to serve particular purposes. These purposes need to be made explicit since they shape the form and functioning of the ecosystem being conceived. It is only once the definition and purpose have been clarified that it is possible to have reasonable discussion.

An example will make the dangers clearer. The example relates to the boundaries of the conceived innovation ecosystem. Where should these boundaries be?

In this book an innovation ecosystem has been defined as consisting of a set of interdependent players and processes that, through their interactions, make innovation happen and by so doing coevolve.

But which players and processes? Webs of interdependence extend over ever-wider areas, culminating with the globe itself.

So where should the boundaries for a particular innovation ecosystem be drawn, thus making the decision about which players and processes to include and which to exclude? Different boundaries mean different sets of players and processes. As has already been made clear, there is no definitive single answer to this question. Thus, different analysts are likely to come up with different answers. Hence the necessity to make the definition of innovation ecosystem and the purpose of the exercise explicit and clear at the outset.

Innovation Ecosystems at Global, National, Regional, and Organisational Levels Since an innovation ecosystem is a conceptual construct rather than an empirical entity, it follows that it can be used to refer to very different things. For example, the concept may be used to refer to ICT players and processes at the global, national, regional, and organisational levels. Indeed, precisely this is done in Chapter 9, the chapter on innovation ecosystems and government policy taking the example of China.

CONCLUSION

The aim of this chapter has been to elaborate on the notion of an innovation ecosystem through an analysis of the ICT innovation ecosystem. This analysis reveals the dynamics of change in this sector. Specifically, it illustrates the crucial role played by competitiveness-increasing innovation that, as clearly shown, is the main driver of this dynamics. How this innovation happens; that is, which processes are used, and who makes this innovation happen, are key issues that were considered in this chapter. These two questions are pursued further in Chapters 6 and 7.

5 Interview with Martin Fransman on Innovation Ecosystems*

Anders Henten, *Digiworld Economic Journal*: What do you mean by an 'Innovation Ecosystem'?

Martin Fransman: By an 'Innovation Ecosystem' I mean a group of players and processes who through their symbiotic interactions (both cooperative and competitive) make innovation happen and, by so doing, coevolve over time.

AH: How may the idea of an Innovation Ecosystem be applied?

MF: The key point to bear in mind is that an 'Innovation Ecosystem' is not an observable object. Rather, it is a conceptual construct which serves a particular purpose. This important point requires some elaboration.

As Edith Penrose has pointed out, '"a firm" is by no means an unambiguous clear-cut entity; it is not an observable object physically separable from other objects, and it is difficult to define except with reference to what it does or what is done within it'. She goes on to observe that 'Herein lies a potential source of confusion.'[1]

The same is true of an 'Innovation Ecosystem'. This becomes clear in reflecting on my definition of an Innovation Ecosystem as a group of players who make innovation happen. This raises the question of which players should be included in the ecosystem and which excluded.

This is the question of the appropriate boundary of the Innovation Ecosystem being conceived. How far 'back' is it necessary to go in

---

* Interview with Martin Fransman by Anders Henten, *Digiworld Economic Journal*, No. 102, 2nd Q. 2016, pp. 95–100. Note: Some slight changes have been made to the originally published interview.
[1] Penrose, E. T., 1959. *The Theory of the Growth of the Firm*. Oxford: Basil Blackwell, p. 10.

conceiving of an Innovation Ecosystem? If we are using the concept of Innovation Ecosystems to understand how innovation happens in the mobile telecommunications sector, for example, where should this boundary be drawn? It may be readily agreed that players such as final consumers, telecoms operators, telecoms equipment suppliers, and regulators should be included in the ecosystem. And for some purposes this definition may suffice.

However, if the purpose is to understand the main determinants of the innovation process in this sector the net should obviously be considerably widened to include, for instance, universities and government research institutes who not only do relevant research but also provide important training. Other players may also merit inclusion in order to achieve the purpose. This example makes it clear that an appropriate conceptualisation of an Innovation Ecosystem depends on the purposes and questions asked in the investigation.

But complications may go even further than this. For example, even if different analysts can agree on the purposes and questions they may differ regarding which players should necessarily be included. In view of problems such as these it is necessary to exercise more caution than is usually done in defining an innovation ecosystem. At the very least it is important to make explicitly clear the purposes and questions that are being pursued as well as the reasons for particular boundary decisions.

AH: What in your view is the difference between an 'Innovation System' and an 'Innovation Ecosystem' and why did you choose to use the latter concept in your work?

MF: The literature on innovation in this area tends to fall into two groups. The Innovation System Group, which is more homogeneous, is made up primarily of heterodox economists such as Chris Freeman, Dick Nelson, and Stan Metcalfe. They all acknowledge intellectual inspiration from the work of Joseph Schumpeter. Having originally trained as economists they all came to believe that the various approaches to economic growth adopted by mainstream economics do not provide a sufficiently robust explanation of how economic growth happens and why different countries often exhibit different growth patterns. They also share a common belief that innovation is the most important driver of economic growth and that mainstream economics does not have an adequate understanding of how innovation happens and who makes it happen.

The concept of an 'Innovation System', originally proposed by Chris Freeman in his book on Japan,[2] is put forward as an alternative way of explaining growth. Central to this concept, and explicit in their definitions of 'innovation system', is the role played by institutions understood not only in the Douglass North sense of rules of the game but also as nonfirm determinants that help (and perhaps hinder) innovation and therefore economic growth.

The Business Ecosystem literature, in contrast, is far more heterogeneous. It tends to come from scholars with a background in business studies. A notable example is the iconic book by Iansiti and Levien from Harvard Business School, *The Keystone Advantage: What the New Dynamics of Business Ecosystems Mean for Strategy, Innovation, and Sustainability*. A central concern in this literature is the cooperative networks created by complementary businesses which both individually and jointly create value for customers. The common belief (whether tacit or explicit) is that the truth lies in the constellation of businesses, rather than in individual businesses taken alone. This has important implications for dealing with topics such as business strategy and sustainability.

In contrast, my own use of the terms 'ecosystem' and 'innovation ecosystem' is inspired not so much by business behaviour as by the example of biological ecosystems with their populations of interacting organisms and species. As Alfred Marshall, the nineteenth-century economist said, 'The Mecca of the economist lies in economic biology rather than in economic dynamics.'[3] This analogy, however, should not

---

[2] Freeman, C., 1987. *Technology Policy and Economic Performance: Lessons from Japan.* London: Pinter.

[3] Marshall, A., 1962. *Principles of Economics.* London: Macmillan, p. xii.

be pushed too far and I insist that the basic unit that makes up the 'players' in my ecosystem are purposive and conscious individuals whose decisions and actions imply necessary complications such as beliefs, mistakes, and expectations which are not predetermined in any meaningful sense of this word. Whilst there is significant overlap between my 'innovation ecosystem' and the concepts of Innovation System and Business Ecosystem perhaps the main difference is the emphasis I give to the dilemmas involved in interacting individuals, albeit in populations, understanding and acting in the uncertain world that is ours.

AH: Can the concept of Innovation Ecosystem contribute to our understanding of leadership in an area such as mobile telecommunications?

MF: The first problem in answering this question is to agree on what should be understood in this context by 'leadership'. Both countries and companies may lead, the former, for example, in performance of infrastructure and services, and the latter, for instance, in terms of indicators such as revenue growth, market capitalisation, and market share.

Having agreed on who leads, the next problem is to explain why this leader has been able to lead. It is here that the concept of an Innovation Ecosystem as defined earlier potentially becomes useful.

Let us take several examples to illustrate. The first example is the lead by 'Europe' in 2G mobile. Not only were the main European telecoms operators able to introduce world-leading 2G mobile infrastructure and services, the key European mobile equipment providers, notably Ericsson and Nokia, were able to become globally dominant players.

Why did this happen? Whilst the answer to this question clearly necessitates that we understand the strengths (and also weaknesses) of these two groups of company players there were other important determinants without which their global leadership would have been, if not impossible, then far less likely. These include, notably, the prior establishment of an agreed Nordic mobile set of standards and systems initially meant to facilitate intercountry mobile communications within the Nordic region as well as the establishment and functioning of a set of European institutions that enabled the emergence of GSM standards.

These events required the interventions of other players, including policymakers, regulators, and researchers. By following this kind of reasoning we will be able to identify both the relevant players and the ecosystem of symbiotic interactions that facilitated the eventual global success of GSM.

The second example is the remarkable rise of Huawei as a leading player not only in telecoms equipment but also, more recently, in smartphones. Once again, a key part of the explanation must involve an account of the emerging capability inside this company to successfully innovate. This success was dramatically illustrated by the successful entry of this company as a supplier to some of Europe's major telecoms operators in the face of very strong and long-standing competition from the key European telecoms equipment providers. Crucially, this entry depended not only on a Chinese comparative advantage-based cost benefit but also on the ability of Huawei to address some of the important problems expressed by the operators.

But reflection soon reveals that there is more to this success story than only what happened within Huawei. Also significant was Huawei's membership of the Chinese Innovation Ecosystem. Although at first a Chinese outsider that depended as much on other emerging countries as it did on the poorer Chinese regions for sale of its equipment, Huawei, with adept leadership, soon developed sufficiently strong capabilities to become a domestic supplier of growing importance able to both contribute to and benefit from the rapid growth of China and its telecoms infrastructure.

Fleshing this story out requires an account of the key players (including, for instance, Chinese universities and other organisations) in the Chinese Innovation Ecosystem whose interactions made important contributions.

The third example is the central role of the US in smartphone developments. Here too a discussion is needed of the key telecoms operators and equipment providers as well as other important players such as policymakers, regulators, university and other research organisations. But also of crucial importance is the direction taken by the evolution of the mobile telecoms sector itself.

More specifically, it is also important to understand the convergence of the mobile telephone and the computing subsectors that, until the advent of the smartphone with its own operating system, were largely distinct. This convergence gave a huge opportunity to the US that had always dominated the field of computing from its origins. Once the phone became in effect a computer that added many other functionalities, US players, incumbents and new entrants, were able to leverage the superior computing capabilities that they and their ecosystem possessed in this area. This was also a significant contributor to US dominance.

As these three examples illustrate, the idea of Innovation Ecosystems can make a significant contribution to our ability to understand and explain these cases of leadership. However, the conceptual caveats mentioned in the answer to the first question must be kept in mind in deploying this idea.

AH: Does the idea of Innovation Ecosystems have any positive implications for a European attempt to regain global leadership in the field of mobile telecommunications?

MF: We must be careful not to slip into the voluntaristic error, i.e. 'Create the correct Innovation Ecosystem and all will be well!' The reason is that there are always some given constraints that remain binding. Examples are the historically inherited stock of capabilities, whether one's own or those of competitors; the given institutional framework; etc.

One relevant example is the demise of Nokia as one of the global mobile industry's foremost pioneers and leaders. From my personal discussions with some of Nokia's most important leaders I have no doubt that in its last years the company and its key decision-makers had an excellent understanding of what here is called the idea of an Innovation Ecosystem. Indeed, many of the company's key documents, both private and public, were formulated using the terminology of Innovation Ecosystems.

There is every reason to suppose that this made both thinking and strategy formulation in Nokia better than it would have been without these conceptualisations. However, the fact of the matter, sadly and regretfully, was that Nokia was significantly constrained by its historical path-dependence. More specifically, the company was substantially impeded by the Symbian operating system that it had inherited from the pre-computerised smartphone past. Not only did this operating system have defects from the point of view of application development, a key requirement for competitiveness, relative to the operating systems of the main competitors it suffered important shortcomings. No amount of perceptive Ecosystems thinking could, in the time required by competition, suffice to stay the company's threat of execution at the hands of unforgiving market forces. The same goes for the company's new leaders brought in to try and stay this execution.

The Nokia example has important implications for policy-making that uses the concept of Innovation Ecosystems. The main lesson, to repeat, is to avoid voluntaristic errors by coming to better understand what can, and what cannot, be changed by purposeful action.

AH: How useful is the idea of Company Innovation Ecosystems?

MF: Paradoxically, very little scholarly work has been done on how innovation happens, and who makes it happen, within purposefully created Company Innovation Ecosystems. Even the book by Iansiti and Levien referred to earlier, despite the word 'innovation' in its subtitle, does not delve into these questions, preferring to devote only a little attention to the incentive to create organisational innovation that benefits the business network/ecosystem as a whole. Accordingly, these questions unfortunately remain unaddressed.

The 'open innovation' literature does not do justice to these questions either. Although the issue of innovation players outside the focal firm is explicitly addressed, the questions of how all the players in the company's Innovation Ecosystem make innovation happen and who can and should make it happen are not discussed. Yet these questions are crucial for any company or other organisation wanting to improve performance through innovation. What kind of guidance can be given to the leaders of companies who would like to make use of the idea of Company Innovation Ecosystems to improve their performance? This question is currently occupying a good deal of my attention.

6   How Does Innovation Happen?

An Ex Ante Perspective

Chapter 2 of this book analyses the contribution made by some of the major authors who have developed the 'national systems of innovation' approach. They argue that it is companies that are the driving force behind innovation. Companies, however, are assisted (and sometimes frustrated) by other players. The latter include those who provide *knowledge* (e.g. universities, government research institutes, and training organisations), *finance* (e.g. banks, venture capitalists, peer-to-peer funders), and *institutional 'rules of the game'* (e.g. legal frameworks such as the laws of competition, contract, intellectual property, and regulation). The system concept is used in this literature to bring together all these components of the innovation process that jointly shape innovation outcomes.

Also examined in Chapter 2 is some key examples of the 'business ecosystems' approach. This approach focuses far more exclusively on companies and their interactions in business networks, sometimes also referred to as business ecosystems. In contrast to the national systems of innovation approach, the business ecosystems perspective pays far less attention to noncompany players and influences. Perhaps the main contribution of the business ecosystems approach has been the important insight that, frequently, large companies do not innovate alone but work closely with other complementary companies in business ecosystems. As was shown, a special concern of these analysts has been with the strategies and strategic options available to companies positioned in different strategic locations in these ecosystems. A related concern has been with the complexities that arise when companies in ecosystems have to take into account not only their own actions, but also the intended actions of other companies whose complementary activities are necessary for them to achieve their purposes.

Chapter 3 discusses my own efforts to understand the organisational structure and dynamics of what I called the ICT ecosystem (which includes the computer hardware and software, telecommunications, semiconductor, Internet, and media subsectors). I emphasised the importance of the symbiotic relationships between the different players in the ICT ecosystem where innovation emerges from the knowledge that players derive through living together about the wants and needs of complementary players who are also their customers. Value-adding innovation is a profit-motivated supply-side response to an understanding of these wants and needs. The relationship between telecoms operators and their equipment providers, the latter doing the bulk of the total R&D undertaken by both parties, served as an example.

All these approaches, I think it is fair to say, have contributed to a better and broader understanding of 'how innovation happens'. However, it can also be argued that it is worth paying more attention than is usually done to the innovation decision-making process itself in order to develop an even deeper understanding of how innovation happens.

Most of the literature just referred to (my own contributions included) have tended, implicitly if not explicitly, to take an ex post perspective. By this I mean 'looking backwards' in time to understand and explain how innovation happened within the various contexts examined. This perspective has the benefit of hindsight since it is possible, with sufficient information, to know the past. However, decision-making in real time – which is what the ex ante perspective refers to – essentially involves 'looking forward' into an unknowable future. It is from this perspective that innovation decisions at any point in time are made.

There are two reasons why it is important to also have an ex ante perspective complementing the ex post perspective. The first, as just noted, is that actual innovation decisions are necessarily always made from an ex ante position. It is therefore necessary to understand this perspective to understand how innovation decisions are made. The second, related reason is that the ex ante perspective introduces several complications that must also be taken into account to fully understand how innovation happens.

THE EX ANTE INNOVATION DECISION

To understand the essentials of ex ante innovation-making let us imagine, albeit in a somewhat stylised way, the processes through which an innovation decision-maker goes and the issues that have to be confronted in making the innovation decision.

The innovation decision-maker (operating alone or in cooperation and interaction with other decision-makers) necessarily operates within what George Shackle called the 'moment-in-being'.[1] The decision-maker brings their past experience (including knowledge and learning) and current beliefs into this moment-in-being. This experience and beliefs will influence how they see and understand the surrounding environment. It is on this basis that the decision-maker comes up with an innovation idea, that is, an idea intended to lead to a new product or service, new process or technology, new way of organising people and things, or new market, way of marketing, or business model (following Schumpeter's definition of innovation discussed in Chapter 2).

The first problem that the innovator confronts is that these products etc. are *new*. They do not yet exist. Therefore, there is no information about them. How then does the innovator come up with the innovation idea?

The answer is that the innovator *imagines* the innovation. In the words of Brian Loasby,[2] the innovation is 'the imagined deemed

---

[1] Shackle, G. L. S., 1972. *Epistemics and Economics: A Critique of Economic Doctrines.* Cambridge: Cambridge University Press.

[2] Loasby, B., 1996. 'The imagined deemed possible', in E. Helmstadter and Perlman, M. (eds.), *Behavioral Norms, Technological Progress and Economic Dynamics.* Ann Arbor, MI: University of Michigan Press, pp. 17–31. In my view 'feasible' is preferable

possible', or as we will say, 'the imagined deemed feasible' since innovations are usually intended for particular users. A crucial moment in the evolution of humankind occurred with the emergence of the ability to imagine, since this capability allowed first the imagination of a new world and then efforts to realise this world.[3]

The second problem is that the imagined innovation may or may not be feasible. It is only with the *passage of time* that is possible to establish which of these alternatives is true. But in the moment-in-being that time has not yet elapsed. The inevitable result is that *uncertainty* surrounds the innovation idea at its birth. Following Frank Knight,[4] this uncertainty must be distinguished from risk. In the case of risk, it is possible to derive probability distributions from existing data that will facilitate the making of a decision, as is done, for example, by the insurance industry. In sharp contrast, in the case of the ex ante innovation idea, probability distributions cannot be deduced since the innovation exists only in imagination. The inevitable result is that innovation decision-making is necessarily far more complicated than in case where the decision-maker is dealing with risk.

So how does a decision-maker make an innovation decision? The answer is that it is done on the basis of *expectations*. But these expectations are essentially subjective. They depend on the judgments, feelings, or hunches of the decision-maker who is denied the comfort of being reassured by the presence of a degree of objectivity in the expectation, although of course there will be objective information available

---

since innovation is aimed at achieving particular purposes. The innovation hypothesis, therefore, specifies what will be done to try and achieve these purposes, rather than what is possible.

[3] Harari makes this important point, although some reviewers have criticised his argument that the ability to imagine was a random event resulting from genetic mutation, preferring to see it as an evolved event emerging from previous antecedents. Harari, Y. N., 2011. *Sapiens: A Brief History of Humankind*. London: Harvill Secker.

[4] Following Frank Knight, uncertain outcomes exist when probability distributions (which determine risk) cannot be derived. Knight, F., 1921. *Risk, Uncertainty and Profit*, Boston, MA: Houghton Mifflin.

about many elements of the circumstances within which the expectations have been formulated.

A further inevitable consequence of the existence of this uncertainty is that different actors, within the same situation, are likely to come up with different subjective expectations. This follows since there is no reason why they are likely to come to the same conclusions unless this is purely by chance. In the case where actors come to contradictory conclusions, with the passage of time some will turn out to be correct, while others will be incorrect.

From an ex post perspective, accordingly, some will be in error and will have made a mistake. Looking backwards, they will have made an incorrect decision. For this reason, it does not make sense to think of innovation decision-making as an exercise in maximisation or optimisation. It is simply not possible to establish, ex ante, what the optimal decision is. This poses special problems for economic theory where decisions are usually treated as maximising or optimising, albeit probabilistically. We conclude, therefore, that the likelihood of mistakes and errors must be an essential component of the account of how innovation happens. This follows logically from the ex ante perspective.

In view of the uncertainty that surrounds the innovation decision, in this chapter the term 'innovation *hypothesis*' will be used to replace 'innovation idea'. The word 'hypothesis' emphasises that the innovation proposition is held with uncertainty.

Clearly, however, such a proposition does not provide a satisfactory basis for further decisions regarding the allocation of resources in support of the proposition. It will therefore be necessary to take steps to investigate whether or not there are grounds for supporting the proposition. This requires *testing* the hypothesis. A key part of the 'how innovation happens' story, therefore, involves the various tests that are devised to establish the veracity of the hypothesis.

But testing does not always resolve the uncertainty since the results of tests are not always unambiguous. Alternative interpretations of the results may be possible; that is, test results may be subject to *'interpretive ambiguity'*. In the light of such ambiguity different actors may come to different conclusions about the implications of the results. Under such circumstances the decision-making process remains complicated with no definitive indication of what should be done to make the innovation successful.

An innovation hypothesis will typically go through many tests usually starting, after the innovator has finally formulated it to their satisfaction, with attempts to persuade others of the value of the hypothesis. In capitalist societies, however, the ultimate test occurs in the market for the product or service concerned since it is here that the value of the innovation to those intended to buy it will ultimately be determined. The judgment of the market will finally reveal whether the innovation hypothesis and the product or service in which it is embodied does add value for their buyers (bearing in mind that, as with beauty, value resides in the eye of the buying beholder). Those innovations that get the 'thumbs-up' from the market will, like the Roman gladiators who preceded them, be rewarded, whilst those who do not will be punished. The reward will take the form of increased revenue, profits, etc.[5]

But the ex ante story of how innovation happens does not end with selection by the market. The reason is that the information yielded by innovation hypothesis testing, both pre-market and in-market testing, will provide fruit for further innovation hypothesis formulation and testing. In the more suggestive words of John Hicks, the testing of the original innovation hypothesis and interpretation of the results will lead to the birth of further innovation hypotheses, the 'children' of the initial hypothesis.[6] And the children too will have to

---

[5] Clearly, the innovation process will be fundamentally different in other types of society such as hunter-gatherer or feudal societies. Whilst in these societies the creation of innovation hypotheses may be similar to what happens in a capitalist society, the process of selecting from amongst the created hypotheses will be very different, leading to very different outcomes.

[6] John Hicks in his Nobel Prize address refers to 'secondary inventions, "children" of the original invention ... great inventions will give great and long-lasting Impulses [caused by innovation, which is the mainspring of economic growth], because they have many "children"'. www.nobelprize.org/nobel_prizes/economic-sciences/laureates/1972/hicks-lecture.html.

go through similar processes to those of their parents. It is in this way that over time innovation happens, generating the novelty that feeds the capitalist system and causes its restlessness.

It is important to remember, however, that the process of how innovation happens just described is neither mechanical nor deterministic. The reason is that the information yielded by the testing of the grandfather innovation hypothesis, coupled with the ever-present possibility of further imagined novelty, logically implies the existence of continuing uncertainty.

Before leaving this general discussion of how ex ante innovation happens, a word about policy is in order. Understandably, policymakers with an interest in making innovation happen, all too aware of the complications surrounding the innovation process discussed in this section, will want to try through their interventions to aid the innovation process. Their actions are likely to include various measures to compensate innovators for some of the unavoidable difficulties that they have no alternative but to go through. And the incentives and other measures that they take may provide some relief to the innovator. However, policymakers will be significantly constrained in their efforts by the complications discussed here that are an inherent part of the innovation process flowing from the irreducible uncertainty that always surrounds this process.

THE EX ANTE PERSPECTIVE ON HOW INNOVATION HAPPENS: NINE PROPOSITIONS

To make clearer the discussion in the last section of how innovation happens, the main points will be summarised in the form of the following nine propositions.

P1: Innovation is an intentional, purposeful activity. The innovation process begins with the creation of an *innovation hypothesis*. The hypothesis specifies what kinds of innovations will be made to try and achieve the purposes chosen.

P2: Particularly important in creating the hypothesis is the set of assumptions that the innovator makes about who will buy and/or use the innovation and what they need and want. Accordingly, the *innovator–buyer–user relationship* is central to how innovation happens.

P3: The formulation of the innovation hypothesis involves *'the imagined deemed feasible'*. The intended innovations are imagined; they do not yet exist; they are novel.

P4: The hypothesis is held with *uncertainty*. It embodies explicit and/or implicit *subjective expectations*. The hypothesis may, or may not, be true.

P5: To attempt to establish the veracity of the hypothesis, it must be *tested*. Although in a capitalist economy *the market is the ultimate judge,* there are many other tests that arise from the conception of the hypothesis to its testing in the market.

P6: All of these *tests provide information feedback* that may be used to accept the hypothesis, reject it, reformulate it, or construct new hypotheses, the 'children' of the original hypothesis.

P7: It is inherent in the innovation process that it carries the possibility of *ignorance, error, and mistake.*

P8: It follows, therefore, that *innovation is not ex ante predictable.*[7] By implication, models or arguments that explicitly or implicitly assume that innovation is ex ante predictable are incorrect.

P9: The providers of knowledge, finance, and institutional 'rules of the game' significantly influence how innovation happens. These providers are, therefore, a crucial part of the *innovation ecosystem* within which innovation happens.

HOW INNOVATION HAPPENS: THE EMERGENCE OF FOUR INNOVATIONS THAT CHANGED THE WORLD

These nine propositions will now be explored further within the context of the emergence of four key innovations that individually and collectively changed the world. The four innovations are: the transistor, microprocessor, laser, and optical fibre. In combination with other related products and processes, these innovations form

---

[7] Neither is innovation probabilistically predictable following the statement given in the previous note.

the backbone of the information and communications systems that underlie the vast majority of economic and social activity.

It is not suggested that these innovations are representative of the way in which all innovation happens.[8] To some extent, each innovation and its generative processes are unique. However, it is proposed that in a general way most innovation tends to follow a similar pattern. To illustrate this, the somewhat contrasting case of Viagra is examined towards the end of the chapter.

The attempt to reconstruct how innovation happened requires an important caveat. The reason is that such an attempt is very much at the mercy of currently available narratives and information. The relationship of these narratives to the truth of what actually happened must always be treated with caution since it is never possible to be in possession of all the relevant facts. This unavoidable problem and the constraints that it implies are well known to historians. Here we have no option but to note it and to move on as best we can but constantly bearing the limitations in mind.

THE TRANSISTOR

What Is a Transistor?

A transistor is a semiconductor device that controls the movement of electrons.[9] It can be used to amplify or switch electronic signals. A semiconductor is a material with properties in between insulators and conductors. The transistor is the basic building block of electronic

---

[8] All the innovations examined in this chapter succeeded. It would also be helpful to examine the innovation processes in the case of intended innovations that were unsuccessful. A case in point is the Concorde supersonic plane, which is examined later in this book. However, the suggestion is that in unsuccessful cases similar processes occur as with successful innovations except that, as stated in proposition 6, the hypothesis-testing process eventually results in a rejection of the hypothesis. In the case of Concorde, rejection happened only after the passage of significant time and the expenditure of substantial resources.

[9] This section draws on the analysis of the global telecommunications switching industry in Fransman, M., 1995. *Japan's Computer and Communications Industry.* Oxford: Oxford University Press.

devices. The first microprocessor, for example, discussed later in this chapter, contained more than 3,000 transistors.

The transistor was first conceived of by Julius Lilienfeld in 1926. However, it was in Bell Laboratories, the central research laboratory of the US telecoms operator AT&T, that the first operating transistor was created in 1947 by William Shockley, John Bardeen, and Walter Brattain. In 1956 they won the Nobel Prize in physics 'for their researches in semiconductors and their discovery of the transistor effect'. At the time, AT&T was the United States' monopoly telecoms operator. It was privately owned but publicly regulated. But what were the circumstances surrounding this creation of innovation knowledge, and, specifically, what role was played by the users of such knowledge?

Context

To understand how the transistor happened, it is necessary to understand the context within which it was created. The development of the telephone network in the United States provided that context.

In January 1877, Alexander Graham Bell was granted the patent for the telephone. Shortly thereafter, in July 1877, the Bell Telephone Company was established by investors and Gardiner Hubbard, Bell's friend and benefactor who was also to become his father-in-law. The company was established with the specific purpose of commercialising Bell's phone patents.

In 1893 and 1894, Bell's two key patents expired, raising the prospect of increasing competition. In 1899 American Telephone and Telegraph (AT&T) came into existence, consolidating several related companies and acquisitions. Under the leadership of Theodore Vail, the decision was made to develop transcontinental telephone services as part of the solution to the competition problem.

However, this objective was seriously limited by technical constraints. Long-distance communications depended on the amplification of signals that were transferred from one switch to another. The need to improve amplification motivated the innovation hypothesis created by Lee de Forest. In 1906 he was granted the patent for what became known as the vacuum tube, which he imagined would provide the solution to the amplification problem. As the vacuum tube was tested and used, so its capabilities improved. In 1913 AT&T purchased de Forest's patent and further improved it.[10]

The vacuum tube, however, had its own limitations. Specifically, it was an unreliable device that used too much power and generated excessive heat. As Thomas Hughes has pointed out in his study of the evolution of electricity systems, *Networks of Power*,[11] a significant bottleneck in a technological system in commercial use generates incentives that signal the possibility of reward (both pecuniary and nonpecuniary) for those able to alleviate the constraint. These incentives may trigger the formation of a symbiotic relationship between the users of knowledge and the potential creators of knowledge.

In the case of the transistor, the user and the creators were under the same legal roof. The users were the divisions of AT&T in charge of constructing, running, and repairing telecommunications networks. The creators were in the company's central research laboratories, Bell Labs.

Transistor Innovation Hypotheses in Bell Labs

It is one thing for the bottlenecks in a system to generate incentives but quite another to come up with innovations that might provide feasible solutions. The latter requires an inquiring mind capable of interpreting the existence and significance of the signalling incentives and imagining an innovation intended to give a solution. A mind that did precisely this was that of Mervin J. Kelly, at the time Director of Research at Bell Labs.

---

[10] www.pbs.org/transistor/album1/.

[11] Hughes, T. P., 1993. *Networks of Power: Electrification in Western Society, 1880–1930*. Baltimore, MD: Johns Hopkins University Press.

Kelly recognised that a superior device that could replace the vacuum tube would significantly improve the performance of the telecoms network. More than this, the innovation hypothesis that he imagined involved the use of semiconductors.

It was in pursuit of this hypothesis that Kelly in 1936 employed one William Shockley. In 1932 Shockley had completed his PhD thesis on the behaviour of electrons in a crystalline structure. Shockley later referred to 'Kelly's stimulus for new devices useful in [the] telephone business' as an important influence on his own research that led to the transistor.[12] In effect, Shockley was recruited to help test and develop Kelly's innovation hypothesis that became Shockley's own. As the head of the team tasked with developing a solid-state semiconductor switch and amplifier, Shockley in turn recruited two further researchers. Walter Brattain, who worked in Bell Labs, was an experimental physicist, whilst John Bardeen was a theoretical physicist from the University of Minnesota.

However, it was not only the vacuum tube used in signal transmissions that influenced the innovation hypothesis that eventually led to the transistor. Telecoms switching also drove the hypothesis.

Amos Joel, one of the fathers of modern switching who has written a classic text on the interaction between telecommunications and computer innovations, who also worked at Bell Labs, has elaborated on the desire to bring about improvements in both telecoms transmissions and switching that served to orient the research that led to the transistor. Joel notes that Kelly, who was later to become president of Bell Labs, 'was very much aware of the promising prospects of solid-state physics and of research on semiconductors. Even more than the need for the "crystal amplifier" intended to replace the vacuum tube in transmission equipment, Kelly envisaged an electronic device in which a semiconductor would replace the relay as the basic element in automatic telephone exchanges.' Joel, accordingly, concludes that 'electronic switching, even

---

[12] Shockley, W., 1950. *Electronics and Holes in Semiconductors, with Applications to Transistor Electronics*. New York, NY: Van Nostrand.

before World War II, had been one of the main objectives ... of Bell Labs research on semiconductors'.[13]

As this account makes clear, the symbiotic interactions between the creators and the users of the innovation were crucial in the processes leading to the invention of the transistor. However, as already noted, in the case of the transistor the creators and users were in the same company, that is, AT&T, under the same legal roof.

Testing the Innovation Hypothesis

In the spring of 1945, drawing on the first patent for the field-effect transistor principle applied for by Julius Lilienfeld in October 1925, as well as on device research done during the Second World War in radar applications, Shockley designed his first semiconductor amplifier. However, in testing it was found not to work. Shockley's set of hypotheses embodied in the device had to be rejected. Shockley asked Bardeen and Brattain to explore why the device failed. [14]

Children of the Initial Innovation Hypothesis

Shockley's request sparked a close working relationship between Bardeen and Brattain that often excluded Shockley himself, causing rivalrous tensions. But the feedback generated by the testing of Shockley's failed device together with the further research done by Bardeen and Brattain eventually resulted in more robust innovation hypotheses. Their point-contact germanium transistor was demonstrated at Bell Labs on 23 December 1947, the date that is usually given for the invention of the transistor. Bell Labs announced the invention of the transistor on 30 June 1948.

---

[13] Chapuis, R. J. and Joel, A. E., 1990. *100 Years of Telephone Switching*, vol. II: *Electronics, Computers and Telephone Switching: A Book of Technological History, 1960–1985.* Amsterdam: North Holland, p. 28.

[14] A fascinating and detailed account of the development of the transistor, which includes descriptions of the rivalrous relationship between Shockley, on the one hand, and Bardeen and Brattain, on the other, is found in Riordon, M. and Hoddeson, L., 1998. *Crystal Fire: The Invention of the Transistor and Birth of the Information Age.* New York, NY: W. W. Norton.

Significantly, however, the Bell Labs team were not the only show in town. In August 1948 two German physicists, Herbert Matare and Heinrich Welker, employed in France by the company Compagnie des Freins et Signaux Westinghouse, applied for a patent for their own amplifier that they had developed.

Shockley went on to develop further innovation hypotheses relating to the transistor. In 1950 he developed a very different type of solid-state amplifier, the bipolar function transistor, which worked on principles distinct from Bardeen and Brattain's point-contact transistor and addressed many of the weaknesses of the latter. 'This is the device which is most commonly referred to as ... a "transistor" today.'[15]

On 1 October 1951, the first commercial production of the point-contact transistor began in Western Electric, AT&T's in-house telecoms equipment-producing subsidiary. This brought to fruition a further series of innovations that took place after the invention of the transistor, also children of the initial innovation hypotheses. These innovations, and others that followed them, occurred as preparations were made for the scale-up, mass production, and commercialisation of the transistor. Although usually unmentioned in most narratives of the innovation of the transistor, these often incremental innovations had a very significant cumulative impact on the price, quality, and characteristics of the ever-evolving transistor, greatly increasing its value.

In 1956 the Nobel Prize was awarded to Shockley, Bardeen, and Brattain.

Grandchildren of the Initial Innovation Hypothesis

One strand of additional rounds of innovation, involving novel innovation hypotheses, began when the Japanese consumer electronics company Sony became a user of the transistor.[16]

---

[15] https://en.wikipedia.org/wiki/History_of_the_transistor.

[16] This section comes from my analysis of the growth of the Japanese consumer electronics industry in Fransman, M., 1999. *Visions of Innovation*. Oxford: Oxford University Press.

Sony appeared as an inauspicious user of this new and important technology. Sony was a tiny company founded in Tokyo in 1946 by a group of electrical engineers, trained in leading Japanese universities and experienced in practical electronic systems through their activities in the Japanese Army during the war. Sony's first successful commercial product was a rice cooker, but the company soon turned to radios.

Two of Sony's founders were Akio Morita and Masaru Ibuka. In his autobiography, Morita recalls that 'in 1948 we had both read about the work of William Shockley and others at Bell Laboratories in the *Bell Laboratory Record*, and we had been curious about their discoveries ever since. That year small articles began to appear in the American press and elsewhere about the device invented at Bell Labs called the transistor, and in Ibuka's trip [to the United States] he first learned that a license for this marvellous gadget might soon be available.'

At the time, the transistor was out of Sony's technological league. As Morita admits, 'This solid-state device was something completely new to our experience.' Furthermore, we 'didn't know then just what we would make with the transistor if we got the technology'. But they decided to make the creative leap and experiment with the transistor because they were 'excited by the technological breakthrough it represented'. This innovation decision was supported by the capabilities that existed at the time in the fledgling start-up: 'our company now had about one hundred and twenty employees, about a third of them graduate engineers [trained in the engineering faculties of Japanese universities] – electronic, metallurgical, chemical, mechanical – and developing the transistor for our use would be a job that would challenge the skills of all of them.'

At first the enthusiasm of Morita and Ibuka was severely tested. Under the terms of its regulation, the understanding was that as a publicly regulated monopoly AT&T would make its intellectual property relatively openly available. In the case of the transistor, it was AT&T's equipment subsidiary, Western Electric, that held the patent.

Ibuka tried to arrange an interview with Western Electric's patent license manager 'but was told the man was too busy to see him'. Later, using a Japanese contact, Sony was able to negotiate access to the transistor patent. But this was not the end of their woes. Morita recalls that 'when I finally signed the patent agreement a year later, the people at Western Electric told me that if we wanted to use the transistor in consumer items, the hearing aid was the only product we should expect to make with it'. As noted earlier, the transistor was created for use in telecommunications equipment and was not suited, so its developers thought, for use in consumer electronic products. However, research had been already done in hearing aids, since Alexander Graham Bell, whose patent for the phone founded AT&T, was originally involved in teaching the deaf.

But Sony decided to press on nevertheless and see if they could adapt the transistor for use in radios. In order to produce a transistorised radio, however, it was necessary to develop a transistor with a higher frequency than the transistor originally invented in Bell Labs. In the attempt to achieve a higher frequency, Sony's engineers reversed the polarity of their transistor and experimented with different materials.

The original Bell Labs transistor used a germanium slab (which provided the negative pole) that was 'sandwiched' between two pieces of indium alloyed to the germanium (which provided the positive pole). It was therefore a 'positive-negative-positive' device. Reasoning that negative electrons move faster than positive ones, the project team attempted to increase the frequency of the transistor by reversing its polarity – that is, by producing a 'negative-positive-negative' device. The problem was to find appropriate materials.

Eventually, through a process of trial and error, a Sony engineer developed a phosphorus doping method that achieved the desired result, a method that researchers had already tried at Bell Laboratories but without success. This worked, and Sony later went on to develop one of the world's first transistorised radios.

But the innovative role of this use of the transistor did not stop there. It was also through Sony's transistor research – particularly that using phosphorus – that a Sony physicist, Leo Esaki, discovered and described the diode tunnelling effect, i.e. how subatomic particles can move in waves through a seemingly impenetrable barrier. For this research, Esaki was awarded a Nobel Prize in 1973.

In 1960 Sony introduced the world's first all-transistor TV. The technology soon spread to other Japanese consumer electronics companies, helping them to successfully challenge their US rivals.

Further Consequences

In order to pursue the commercial value of the transistor, Shockley left Bell Labs and in 1956 established a company, Shockley Semiconductor Laboratory, in Palo Alto, California, recruiting a number of highly talented scientists and engineers. This was the first company in what is now known as Silicon Valley to be involved with semiconductors. Reportedly as a partial result of Shockley's controversial management style, some of these employees left to form Fairchild Semiconductor. Two of these, Bob Noyce and Gordon Moore, later formed Intel Corporation. It was in Intel that the first microprocessor was created, as later discussed further.

The Broader Innovation Ecosystem

The account given so far of how the transistor happened is an ex ante narrative that focuses largely on the actors most immediately involved in the innovation of the transistor. However, as Proposition 9 reminds us, other players and influences also played a crucial role.

One example is universities. In making their decision in various 'moments-in-being',[17] these actors drew on the knowledge and experience that they had previously acquired in universities. Without this knowledge and experience, the transistor obviously could not have happened. A more complete understanding of how the transistor happened, therefore, must include an account of the set of

---

[17] See earlier in this chapter for a discussion of the meaning of Shackle's concept of the 'moment-in-being'.

circumstances that led to the existence of these universities and the education they provided that endowed these actors with the resources they drew on in coming up with and testing their innovation hypotheses.

Similarly, other innovation ecosystem components also played a role in shaping the emergence of the transistor. These include the financing of the human and material resources that went into the innovation. Funding issues typically do not feature in most accounts of this and other innovations. Furthermore, it was not only the 'stars' who populate the conventional narratives who were significant but also the less-visible such as the lab technicians who also played an important role. The same is true of the technologies, instruments, and materials – the fruits of other often unrelated innovation hypotheses and processes – that were also crucial determinants of the innovation of the transistor.

Institutional 'rules of the game' were also important. For instance, although regulated, AT&T and Bell Labs were monopoly suppliers of telecoms services in the United States. This probably contributed to the resources at their command. It may be no accident that Bell Labs was the most famous of all industrial research laboratories, contributing no less than six Nobel Prize winners. The endowments of human, material, and financial resources that Bell Labs enjoyed, partly the result of its regulated monopoly status, no doubt played an important facilitating role in the innovation of the transistor in Bell Labs.

This all-too-abbreviated list of 'other innovation ecosystem factors' contributing to how the transistor happened makes us aware of just how complex all innovation processes are. If we may justifiably be accused of 'simplification' in our narratives of how innovation happens, we may derive some comfort from the equally justifiable need to avoid too much complexity in order to distinguish 'the wood from the trees'. Reasonable though this may be, however, it is necessary constantly to be aware of the multiplicity of determinants that make innovation happen.

THE MICROPROCESSOR

What Is a Microprocessor?

A microprocessor, or 'computer-on-a-chip', may be defined as a computer central processing unit that is contained on one or a few integrated circuit chips, using large-scale integration (LSI) technology.[18]

The first microprocessor was invented in Intel, a semiconductor company that until then had specialised in memory chips. The year before Intel had invented the world's first dynamic random-access memory (DRAM) chip.

Context

Intel was established by Robert Noyce and Gordon Moore in July 1968 after they left Fairchild Semiconductor. Memory chips constituted Intel's main source of revenue until the early 1980s. Thereafter the company turned to microprocessors, as the memory chip market was increasingly taken over by Japanese companies.

In late 1968 Noyce went to Japan to seek customers. There he visited Sharp, a major producer of calculators. Sharp, however, had already contracted with chip suppliers but offered to introduce Noyce to the president of another Japanese calculator producer, Nippon Calculating Machine Corporation (often known as Busicom after their product brand name).

At the time Busicom had begun to design a chip set intended for use in desktop calculators and other business machines (with some of the chips needing between 3,000 and 5,000 transistors each). They were interested in Intel making the chips using its metal-oxide semiconductor technology.

---

[18] *Chambers Science and Technology Dictionary*, Cambridge: Chambers. Amongst the sources used for this subsection are Malone, M. S., 2014. *The Intel Trinity*. New York, NY: Harper Collins; Berlin, L., 2006. *The Man behind the Microchip*. Oxford: Oxford University Press; Grove, A. S., 1996. *Only the Paranoid Survive*. London: Profile Books; Miller, M., 2014. *The Birth of the Microprocessor*. http:// uk.pcmag.com/opinion/38270/opinion/the-birth-of-the-microprocessor.

In April 1969 Busicom and Intel signed a contract. This stipulated that Intel would be paid $100,000 for the chip set plus $50 for each set made. Busicom guaranteed that it would buy at least 60,000 of the sets.

In 1968, the year Intel was established, Marcian Edward (Ted) Hoff had been employed by Intel. He had a background in computing. Part of his brief was to create products that would get customers to change from older memories to Intel's new memory chips. Hoff was assigned to the Busicom project.

Busicom's main design engineer working on the project was Masatoshi Shima. He and his team proposed the design of between nine and twelve LSI chips. However, having already signed the contract in April 1969, these design intentions created problems. The reason was that the complexity of the intended chip set meant that it was unlikely that the project could be completed on the basis of the prices agreed.

The Microprocessor Innovation Hypothesis

Given the agreed price constraints and perhaps also influenced by his brief to create chips that made ample use of Intel's memory capabilities, Hoff came up with the hypothesis that he could significantly simplify the design of the chip set. Instead of nine to twelve chips he hypothesised that he could use four. This would include a read-only memory (ROM) chip for the programming, a random-access memory (RAM) chip for data, an input–output register to feed data into the main processor and take it out, and a four-bit central processing logic unit. Furthermore, he proposed that their functions could all be integrated into a single chip.

Having come up with this hypothesis and had it approved by Noyce, however, Hoff could not implement it by himself since he was not a design engineer. Additional design skills were accordingly needed. For these he turned to Stanley Mazor, a software engineer who would report to him. Shima and his team in Busicom would also interact with them.

Implementing Hoff's hypothesis, however, whilst reducing the cost of the chip set relative to that of Busicom's initially intended set, did not solve the contracted price problem. Hoff's proposed microprocessor would still cost more than had been agreed. Accordingly, in August 1969 Noyce contacted Busicom's president, Yoshia Kojima, saying that there was 'no possibility that we could manufacture these units for $50 per kit even for the simplest kit'.[19] He suggested the actual cost would be around $300. At a meeting between the two companies in October 1969, Busicom agreed to Intel's design and in February 1970 a formal contract was finalised.

Intel had Hoff's concept for the chips as well as his block diagrams stipulating how they would be required to work, but they did not have 'the actual designs of the chips, the technical details of how the transistors would fit together and could be manufactured'.[20] Since in the interim Hoff and Mazor had been assigned to other work, Intel hired Federico Faggin in April 1970 to become leader of the Busicom project. Faggin had been employed by Fairchild Semiconductor where he had made his own breakthrough, developing silicon gate technology (SGT). He would use this technology with the Busicom microprocessor.

In March 1971, Faggin and Intel delivered the first units of Intel 4004, the first general-purpose programmable commercial microprocessor, to Busicom.

Uncertainty and Unpredictability

However, even as they finally received the Intel 4004, fortunes had changed for Busicom. The reason was a downturn in the calculator market. Facing financial pressures, Busicom asked Intel whether they could renegotiate their contract. In return for a refund of the $60,000 Busicom had finally paid Intel (apart from the per-unit payment and

[19] Miller, M., 2014. *The Birth of the Microprocessor*. http://uk.pcmag.com/opinion/38270/opinion/the-birth-of-the-microprocessor.
[20] Ibid.

down from the $100,000 that Busicom had originally agreed in April 1969), Busicom would relinquish the sole property rights that it had acquired to the microprocessor.

The discussions that took place in Intel in this 'moment-in-being' illustrates starkly the ex ante uncertainty that always surrounds innovation, including in this case the birth of a breakthrough innovation that would go on to change the world. Hoff later recalled the discussion he had with the people in Intel's marketing department when he suggested that Intel should gain possession of the intellectual property rights to the Intel 4004 in order to commercialise it more widely. He got the following reply: 'Look, they only sell about 20,000 minicomputers each year. And we're late to the market, and you'd be lucky to get 10 percent of it. That's 2,000 chips a year ... It's just not worth the headaches of support and everything for a market of only 2,000 chips.'[21]

The Children of the Initial Innovation Hypothesis

It is certainly true that in the moment-in-being the Intel 4004 appeared as a relatively weak and insignificant device with limited processing capability and memory. This was particularly the case compared with some of the other devices Intel was producing at the time for the US military.

Fortunately for Intel, the views of the marketing department did not prevail, and Faggin, Hoff, and Mazor were able to persuade the company's management to reclaim the property rights to the 4004. The passage of time, however, supported the judgment that the 4004 was of limited value to Intel.

Crucially, however, these facts did not take into account the children of Hoff's initial innovation hypothesis. These children, and in time their children, would grow in strength, contributing to the ever-increasing performance of subsequent generations of microprocessors. Indeed, every three years since Intel produced its X86 family

---

[21] Quoted in Miller (2014).

of microprocessors in 1979, their performance increased four to five times. This trajectory became known as Moore's law after Gordon Moore, with Noyce a founder of Intel, who first formulated it.

From an ex post point of view, with the benefit of hindsight, we now know that the microprocessor grew to become mighty, so strong that in time it would destroy mainframe and mini computers, and even desktop and laptop computers, largely replacing them with today's smartphones. However, as we have seen, this outcome was not apparent to those making decisions in the ex ante moments-in-being examined here. This serves to emphasise how important it is to distinguish between these two fundamentally different perspectives. This is particularly so since innovation decisions are always, unavoidably, made ex ante. This has obviously important implications for the understanding of how innovation happens, as emphasised in this chapter.

WHAT IS A LASER?

A laser is an optical amplifier, that is, a device that strengthens light waves. Lasers have three important properties: they emit a *monochromatic* (i.e. of a single colour or wavelength) beam of *coherent* light (i.e. light waves that are precisely in phase with one another), and the light is *collimated* (i.e. the laser light beams are very narrow and can be concentrated on one tiny spot).

'Because the laser light is monochromatic, coherent, and collimated, all of its energy is focused to produce a small point of intense power. This focused power makes laser light useful for cutting and welding. It also makes it possible to control laser light very precisely.'[22] Since laser light does not disperse, it can be sent over very long distances, for example, into space.

To make a laser 'you need to get some excited atoms. Excited atoms emit photons [i.e. light]. This in turn stimulates other atoms to emit photons. To make a powerful laser you can trap the atoms

---

[22] http://spaceplace.nasa.gov/laser/en/.

between two mirrors. This bounces the photons back and forth, increasing the stimulation of other atoms.'[23] The word laser is an acronym for 'light amplification by stimulated emission of radiation'.

Context

Unlike the transistor or microprocessor, whose origins, as shown earlier in this chapter, may be traced back to the wants and needs of particular users, the laser had its origins in theoretical physics. More precisely, it was Albert Einstein who, in a paper published in 1917 that drew on earlier work by Max Planck, established the theoretical principles on which lasers are based. In this paper Einstein 'introduced the concept of stimulated emission where a photon interacts with an excited molecule or atom and causes the emission of a second photon having the same frequency, phase, polarization and direction'.[24] As Charles H. Townes, who won a Nobel Prize in 1964 for his work on the laser and its predecessor, the maser, notes in his Nobel Prize lecture, 'A review of [Einstein's] conclusions almost immediately suggests a way in which atoms or molecules can in fact amplify.'[25] However, the advent of the first working laser, as we shall see, had to wait until 1960.

By the early 1950s a good deal of research had been done by theoretical physicists on stimulated emission.[26] One of the most prominent researchers at this time was Townes, who in 1954 at Columbia University was one of the inventors of the maser. Townes saw the laser as an extension of the maser principle. In 1957 Townes and his brother-in-law, Arthur Schawlow, who had joined Bell Laboratories, began research on an infrared laser.[27]

---

[23] www.planet-science.com/categories/over-11s/technology/2012/01/what-is-a-laser.aspx.

[24] http://laserfest.org/lasers/history/early.cfm.

[25] Townes, C. H., 1965. 'Production of coherent radiation by atoms and molecules', 1964 Nobel Lecture, *IEEE Spectrum*, p. 31.

[26] For a list of some of the main contributors and their publications, see https://en.wikipedia.org/wiki/Laser.

[27] Townes had worked at Bell Labs from 1933 until 1947 when he moved to Columbia University where his brother-in-law to be was based. Schawlow moved to Bell Labs in 1951.

In 1958 Townes and Schawlow published a seminal paper in *Physical Review* in which 'they described the various conditions required to generate coherent radiation in the optical part of the electromagnetic spectrum'.[28] This spelled out the theoretical rationale for laser action. The article also provided the basis for a patent application for the laser made by Bell Labs.

The *Physical Review* article unleased 'a furious competition ... to build the first working laser involving institutions such as Bell Labs, Hughes Research Labs, RCA Labs, Lincoln Labs, IBM, Westinghouse, and Siemens'.[29] In the event, on 16 May 1960, Theodore Maiman, working at Hughes Research Laboratories in California, succeeded in producing the first working laser, generating 'the first coherent light in the form of a burst of deep red light from a small ruby crystal'.[30] In 1964 Townes shared the Nobel Prize with Russians Nicolay Gennadiyevich Basov and Aleksandr Mikhailovich Prokhorov for having developed the maser/laser principle, and in the same year Bell Labs was awarded the patent for the laser.

When Was the Initial Innovation Hypothesis Made?

When was the initial innovation hypothesis regarding the laser made? In order to answer this question, it is necessary to remind ourselves what is meant in the present book by the 'innovation hypothesis'. As discussed at the beginning of this chapter, innovation decision-making begins with the formulation of an innovation hypothesis. This hypothesis stipulates what needs to be done in order to produce an innovation in the form of a new product or service, a new process or technology, a new way of organising people and/or things, or a new market, way of marketing, or business model. The hypothesis also stipulates, explicitly or implicitly, who the consumers and users of

---

[28] www.laserlab-europe.net/events-1/light2015/light-links/when-lasers-first-saw-the-light-of-day.

[29] http://laserfest.org/lasers/history/early.cfm.   [30] Ibid.

the innovation will be and how their wants and needs will be met by the innovation.

In the case of the laser, when was such an innovation hypothesis first put forward? Townes, perhaps the most self-reflective of all the major contributors to the laser, makes some important observations that are relevant in tackling this question.

According to Townes, there are often human activities in innovation ecosystems that precede the making of innovations. These activities are undertaken by other kinds of players in the ecosystem, embedded in different types of institutions, who play a different role from the innovators of the ecosystem. These are scientists who are motivated largely by curiosity, in sharp contrast to innovators, who are driven mainly by the desire to create new products etc. to meet the wants and needs of particular consumers and users. In Townes's own words:

> Many of today's practical technologies result from basic science
> done years to decades before. The people involved, motivated
> mainly by curiosity, often have little idea as to where their research
> will lead. Our ability to forecast the practical payoffs from
> fundamental exploration of the nature of things (and, similarly, to
> know which of today's avenues are technological dead ends) is poor.
> This springs from a simple truth: new ideas discovered in the
> process of research are really new.[31]

In the case of the laser, Townes asks:

> What research planner, wanting a more intense light, would have
> started by studying [the interaction of] molecules with
> microwaves? What industrialist, looking for new cutting and
> welding devices, or what doctor, wanting a new surgical tool as the
> laser has turned out to be, would have urged the study of

---

[31] Townes, C. H., 1999. *How the Laser Happened: Adventures of a Scientist*. New York, NY: Oxford University Press, p. 4.

microwave spectroscopy [the study of interactions between radio waves and microwaves, on the one hand, and molecules, on the other]? The whole field of quantum electronics is almost a textbook example of broadly applicable technology growing unexpectedly out of basic research.[32]

'The truth is', Townes says, 'none of us who worked on the first lasers imagined how many uses there might eventually be [for the laser]'.[33]

Townes continues: 'for several years after the laser's invention, colleagues used to tease me about it, saying, "That's a great idea, but it's a solution looking for a problem."'[34]

But is the distinction between 'scientists', driven purely by 'curiosity', as opposed to the promise of practical and commercial application, and 'innovating technologists', whose sole motivation is such application, as clear-cut and watertight as Townes is suggesting? Whilst such a distinction may indeed contain an important element of truth, surely there are areas, or 'shades of grey', where there is a degree of overlap between the motivations and preoccupations of these two important sets of players in innovation ecosystems. Indeed, in other writings Townes himself suggests that this is the case.

Writing in 1984, more than a decade before the last quotation, Townes also recalls that 'A favourite quip which many will remember was "the laser is a solution looking for a problem".' However, significantly, he continues, 'While an enthusiast myself, and *aware of the potential for high precision measurements, monochromaticity, directivity, and the high concentration of energy that optical masers would provide*, I missed many potent aspects. The area of medical applications is one that did not occur to me initially as promising' (emphasis added).[35]

Here Townes acknowledges that he was 'aware' of some potentially important practical and commercial applications of masers and

---

[32] Ibid. [33] Ibid. [34] Ibid.
[35] Townes, C. H., 1984. 'Ideas and stumbling blocks in quantum electronics'. *IEEE Journal of Quantum Electronics*, QE-/20/6, 549.

lasers. This awareness, accordingly, must have coexisted in his consciousness together with the 'curiosity' that he suggests provided his prime motivation. Both factors are likely to have encouraged him to persevere in this field since both pushed in the same direction. It is not necessary for Townes to have foreseen *all* the future applications of the laser for the possibility of several important applications of which he was aware to have played some role, even if a role subordinated to that of curiosity, in driving his enthusiasm for his work in this area.

Furthermore, elsewhere Townes admits that around 1955, *well before* the invention of the first working laser by Maiman in 1960, there was a significant amount of commercial interest in this field. In other words, already circa 1955 the maser and embryonic laser were seen as potentially significant solutions to important preexisting problems. In Townes's words:

> we [i.e. Townes and Schawlow] published in August 1955, a longer and more detailed paper on the maser in *The Physical Review*, which gave more complete information to other physicists of its intriguing properties. As interest spread, we found ourselves with a steady stream of visitors. The Jet Propulsion Laboratory in Pasadena [California], especially keen on experimenting with this new device, sent Walter Higa to spend some time with us. We also got into a regular interaction with people at Varian Associates Inc., near the Stanford campus in Palo Alto, who wanted to build commercial masers.[36]

Further evidence of strong practical and commercial interest in the potential of the laser as a solution to substantial problems, even before it had come into existence as a working device, comes from Maiman. In his Japan Prize lecture given in Tokyo in 1987 (Maiman was never

---

[36] www.acamedia.info/sciences/J_G/references/Townes_How_the_Laser_
Happened.pdf.

awarded a Nobel Prize and neither was he given patents relating to the laser), Maiman recalled that

> around 1958 [i.e. two years before he produced the first working laser] ... a number of scientists started to think about making coherent light. They knew that if coherent light could be achieved they could use it to convey 10,000 times more information than with any existing electromagnetic signal such as microwaves.[37]

This means that several years before the production of the first working laser by Maiman, there were already a large number of innovation hypotheses in existence featuring the laser. As Maiman notes, these hypotheses also existed in the substantial field of telecommunications where, as will be shown in detail in the following subsection on optical fibre, the laser would come to play a key role.

On the basis of this evidence, therefore, it is reasonable to conclude that Townes's colleagues were wrong when they suggested, in his own words, 'for several years after the laser's invention [the laser was] "a great idea, but it's a solution looking for a problem"'. To the contrary, the evidence is clear that by circa 1955, at the latest, 'innovation hypotheses' in the sense defined in this book were a key driver of the development and the eventual production of the laser.

Before leaving this issue, one last point is worth making regarding Townes's over-sharp distinction between science/curiosity, on the one hand, preceding innovation/commercial application, on the other. This point relates to the important role that technological innovations, and the innovation hypotheses that gave birth to them, play in facilitating scientific advance. It is a point that Townes himself has pointed to. 'In many cases', he notes, 'it is not just new [scientific] insight, but new tools or technology that open up more penetrating [scientific] exploration than was previously possible.'[38]

---

[37] Maiman, T., 1987. 'The laser: its origins, applications and future'. *Japan Prize 1987* (official brochure), Tokyo, pp. 15–16. I had the good fortune to attend this lecture.
[38] Townes (1999), p. 190.

We conclude, therefore, that although it was primarily theoretical concerns in the field of physics that drove work on the principles that would be used to produce working lasers, by around 1955, at the latest, the development of innovation hypotheses as defined in this chapter played an important role in driving the innovation of working lasers. This motivating force contributed to Maiman's creation of the first working laser on 16 May 1960 as his account quoted above makes clear.

Uncertainty, Unpredictability, and Mistakes

Uncertainty and unpredictability, as referred to in Proposition 4 discussed at the beginning of this chapter, surrounded the innovation of the laser. This uncertainty is evident in the initial response of the Bell Labs patent office to the suggestion that the 1958 article on the laser written by Townes and Schawlow, and later published in *Physical Review*, should form the basis for a patent application. As Townes later recalled, 'Bell's patent department at first refused to patent our [laser] because, it was explained, optical waves had never been of any importance to communications and hence the invention had little bearing on Bell system interests.'[39]

Locked into a set of assumptions and beliefs based on the technologies that at the time provided the basis for telecoms services (such as copper cabling), these patent officers in their particular 'moment-in-being' failed to see the radical technical changes that would take place in their markets with the introduction of lasers and optical fibre (as documented in the following subsection). Ironically, as Maiman later pointed out (documented above), at precisely the same time many scientists in this field, existing in their very different subjective moments-in-being, were highly aware of the significant breakthrough and some of the related payoffs that would follow from

---

[39] Quoted in Rosenberg, N., 1994. *Exploring the Black Box: Technology, Economics and History*. Cambridge: Cambridge University Press.

the advent of viable lasers. In the event, however, the Bell Labs patent office relented and a patent application was made in 1958 for the laser.

However, no one foresaw the extraordinary events that would later take place after Bell Labs was granted the patent in 1964. In 1977, after the Bell Labs patent for the laser had expired, a US patent for the optical pumping of lasers was given to a former Columbia University PhD student. How did this unpredictable event occur?

At the same time that Townes and Schawlow were doing their work, a PhD student, Gordon Gould, was independently doing his research in the same field (although he was never awarded a PhD). As a result of this research Gould wondered how the maser principle could be applied in the optical area. He collected his thoughts in a research notebook of some one hundred pages that he titled, 'Some rough calculations on the feasibility of laser light amplification by stimulated emission of radiation'. In this way he was the first to coin the term 'laser'.

Thinking that his calculations may have some future value, he went to the owner of a sweet shop (a friend of his wife's) and on 16 November 1957 got the shop owner's seal on the first nine pages of the research notes. Based on this notebook, Gould later claimed that he had been the first to propose optical pumping to excite a maser. This was an idea that at one stage he discussed with Townes. In his book on the laser,[40] Townes acknowledges that the meeting took place but insists that he did not get any of his ideas from the discussion.

In Townes's words:

> Because Gould believed he needed to actually build a laser in order to get a patent, he abandoned his PhD research and joined the private company TRG in order to pursue this goal. Ironically, TRG got a million dollars from the U.S. government for their project, but since they envisaged military applications the project was declared

---

[40] Townes (1999), p. 190.

classified. Gould, who had been a member of the Communist Political Association, was therefore not allowed to enter the lab where his colleagues were trying to build a laser based on his ideas. TRG subsequently lost the race to both Maiman and Bell/Columbia.[41]

Since his authorised and dated notebook pre-dated the article of Townes and Schawlow, Gould spent almost three decades contesting the Bell Labs laser patent. In 1977 he finally succeeded when the US Patent Office gave him a laser patent after Bell's patent had expired. 'Ironically, due to the growing volume of laser applications, Gould made a lot more money from his delayed patent than he ever could have, had he been given the patent when he filed it. In the nineties, Gould's patents were worth 7 million dollars a year, whereas Bell Labs made only about a million in total in 17 years.'[42]

Mistakes also played a key role in the innovation of the laser. One such mistake was to have a negative (though fortunately short-term) effect on Maiman's research on the laser. At this time Maiman was researching the possibility of using ruby lasers. In his Japan Prize lecture,[43] Maiman recalled that

> At this very moment one of the authors of the 1958 *Physical Review* article [i.e. the Schawlow and Townes article] announced at a professional meeting that ruby would never work. At the industrial laboratory where I was employed [i.e. Hughes] my project was not popular and I received little support. But now as a result of these comments it was even more difficult for me to proceed.[44]

However, Maiman bravely took the bold decision to defy his firm's hierarchy: 'Nevertheless, I was so highly motivated by what I was doing I insisted on proceeding with my project, despite growing criticism from the administrators of the laboratory.'[45] On 16 May 1960,

---

[41] www.laserlab-europe.net/events-1/light2015/light-links/when-lasers-first-saw-the-light-of-day.
[42] Ibid.   [43] Maiman (1987).   [44] Ibid., p. 16.   [45] Ibid.

Maiman succeeded in generating 'the first coherent light in the form of a burst of deep red light from a small ruby crystal'.[46]

Innovation Ecosystem Effects

Townes has raised an intriguing thought. 'As I see it', he wrote, 'lasers might well have been invented during ... [the period] 1925–40' following Einstein's famous 1917 article, referred to earlier.[47]

This presents an important puzzle. If Townes is correct that the laser could have been invented some two decades earlier, why was it not? Townes tackles this question, and his conjectures raise interesting issues about the structure and organisation of the providers of research knowledge in the broader innovation ecosystem that existed at the time.

Townes offers two reasons. The first is the fragmentation of knowledge that existed between the two communities of practitioners who created and implemented the knowledge that eventually found its way into the laser. Physicists made up the first community, while electrical engineers were the second. In Townes's words:

> I believe that whatever unnecessary delay occurred was in part because quantum electronics lies between two fields, physics and electrical engineering. In spite of the closeness of these two fields, the necessary quantum mechanical ideas were generally not known or appreciated by electrical engineers, while physicists who understood well the needed aspects of quantum mechanics were often not adequately acquainted with pertinent ideas of electrical engineering.[48]

In short, these two communities of potentially complementary knowledge creators were unable to benefit from the symbiotic interchanges that would have occurred had they become the users of each other's knowledge.

---

[46] Ibid.   [47] Townes (1984).   [48] Ibid., p. 547.

Townes's second reason provides part of the explanation regarding why these two communities did not interact more closely. His second reason for the delay in the invention of the laser was the lack of practical applications foreseen at the time. 'In addition to conceptual stumbling blocks which affected the course of quantum electronics', he notes, 'in the early days there was also a limited appreciation of the potential of this field'.[49]

Townes's comments serve to highlight the importance of the broader innovation ecosystem within which the innovation processes that eventually led to the innovation of the laser took place (as is emphasised in Proposition 9 at the beginning of this chapter).

OPTICAL FIBRE

What Is Optical Fibre?

'An optical fiber (or optical fibre) is a flexible, transparent fiber made by drawing glass (silica) or plastic to a diameter slightly thicker than that of a human hair. Optical fibers are used most often as a means to transmit light between the two ends of the fiber and find wide usage in fiber-optic communications, where they permit transmission over longer distances and at higher bandwidths (data rates) than wire cables. Fibers are used instead of metal wires because signals travel along them with lesser amounts of loss; in addition, fibers are also immune to electromagnetic interference, a problem from which metal wires suffer excessively.'[50]

Context

To understand how optical fibre happened, it is helpful to understand the environment in this area that existed in the mid-1960s.

---

[49] Ibid., p. 549.
[50] https://en.wikipedia.org/wiki/Optical_fiber. This subsection draws on Fransman, M., 1995. *Japan's Computer and Communications Industry.* Oxford: Oxford University Press.

At this time a serious bottleneck existed in the communications system. The demand for telephones (voice communications) and new data services – such as data transmission, fax, and video – had increased significantly. Furthermore, the development of new electronic switches had greatly increased the potential capacity of the system. However, a significant bottleneck, which held back both capacity and the speed of communications, was the dominant transmissions technology based on copper cable.

This bottleneck generated signals that indicated that significant profit could potentially be made by those able to create innovations that would alleviate the constraint. The signals, in turn, provided incentives.

There were two broad, competing, innovation hypotheses – that constituted uncertain search paths – that emerged in the attempt to tackle this bottleneck. The first was to create waveguides that guided electromagnetic signals that carried the voice and data.[51] The second approach was to send light signals through glass.

Those initially treading these paths were based in the research laboratories of telecoms operators (such as companies like AT&T and BT) and telecoms cable providers (for example, Standard Telephone and Cable and Sumitomo Electric). The operators were the potential consumer-users of these new transmissions technologies, incentivised to switch from copper cable to the superior alternatives.

Amongst those searching for an optical fibre–based solution were two researchers in ITT's Standard Telephone Laboratories in the United Kingdom.[52] One was Dr Charles Kao (who later became known as the 'father' of optical fibre and was awarded the Nobel Prize

---

[51] These were known as millimetre waveguides.

[52] Standard Telephone Laboratories was the research laboratory of Standard Telephone and Cables. The latter was a British telecoms equipment company that was founded in London in 1883 under the name International Western Electric, an agent for Western Electric (the American company that was the main provider of telecoms equipment to its parent, ATT). From 1925 to 1982 Standard Telephone Laboratories was owned by ITT of the United States, and in 1991 it was bought by the Canadian telecoms equipment company Nortel.

in Physics in 2009 for 'ground-breaking achievements concerning the transmission of light in fibres for optical communication').[53] Beginning their research in 1963 Kao and Hockham published a seminal paper in 1966 summarising the state of the art in the optical fibre field.[54]

Crucially, in their 1966 paper Kao and Hockham established the minimum 'threshold target' that optical fibre would have to achieve in order to become competitive with the prevailing dominant technology, namely copper cable. (This emphasises the important role played in the optical fibre story by competition between technologies.)

Specifically, in order to become competitive, optical fibre would have to achieve an attenuation rate (i.e. light-loss rate) of at least 20 decibels per kilometre, i.e. 20 dB/km. (A decibel is a measure of the fraction of the signal that makes its way through a communication system. With a 20 dB/km attenuation rate, 1 per cent of the light entering an optical fibre would emerge after one kilometre.)

Kao and Hockham showed that quartz glass was the most suitable material for optical fibre transmission. They argued that it was impurities in the glass that accounted for the high attenuation rate. With some of the impurities removed, they suggested, the 20 dB/km threshold could be breached and optical fibre could become the superior technology.

By the mid-1960s it was also known (from research done in the 1950s) that it was necessary for cladding (i.e. a layer covering the quartz glass) with a *lower* refractive index to surround the glass core. It was the refractive index differential that reflected light back into the glass fibre, reducing light loss.

Kao and Hockham's paper, therefore, suggested an innovation hypothesis search path with the following characteristics: use quartz

[53] Nobel Foundation (2009), *The Nobel Prize in Physics 2009*. 6 October.

[54] Kao, C. and Hockham, G. A., 1966. 'Dielectric-fibre surface waveguides for optical frequencies'. *Proceedings of the IEEE*, 113, 1151–8. This paper subsequently became a key reference establishing the temporal state of the art in several crucial patent legal trials.

glass, find ways of reducing the impurities in the core, and add cladding with a lower refractive index. Experimentation along this search
path together with the empirical results that emerged would eventually, hopefully, lead to an optical fibre with an attenuation rate below
20 dB/km.

However, as things would later turn out, although unrecognised
at the time by the major players following the optical fibre path, there
was other knowledge available in the innovation ecosystem of the late
1960s that would come to play a crucial role in the mission to significantly lower the attenuation rate of optical fibre.

Since 1954 it was known that the introduction of a dopant (in
this case, fluorine) could reduce the refractive index of multicompo-
nent glasses. In 1967, a patent was awarded for a method for reducing
the index of a silica fibre through the addition of a dopant. And in
1968 another patent was granted for *increasing* the index of a fibre
core through the introduction of a dopant.[55]

Significantly, however, the 1967 patent was given not to a telecoms operator or a telecom equipment company but to a company that
was, until then, operating in an entirely different neck of the woods – a
glass company, Corning, whose stock of knowledge had been accumulated in response to very different industrial conditions.[56]

In the United Kingdom, in the mid-1960s, the Post Office (the
communications part of which later became British Telecom) began
research on optical fibre for communications purposes. It was this
research interest that brought the researchers into contact with a
visiting scientist from Corning. He took some of the ideas that were
generated by his visit back to Corning, which resulted in the establishment in the company of a research team that began work on
developing low-loss optical fibre for communications. It was this
team that was awarded the 1967 patent.

[55] District Court, S.D., 1987. *Corning v. Sumitomo Electric USA Inc.*, 21 December
1987, 1545–71. New York.
[56] Duke, D. A., 1983. *A History of Optical Communications*, Special Report,
Telecommunication Products Department. New York, NY: Corning Glass Works.

As things evolved, Corning, drawing on its specific stock of knowledge that had been shaped by its specific past, brought some crucial knowledge assets to bear on the optical fibre search process. Most counterintuitively, it altered the direction of research with the new innovation hypothesis that what was needed was *not*, as had hitherto been thought, the *reduction* of impurities in the optical fibre in the attempt to reduce attenuation rates. Instead, what was needed was the *increase* of impurities through the introduction of a dopant that would *raise* the refractive index of the core, thus increasing the differential of core and cladding and, accordingly, reducing attenuation.

Furthermore, Corning's experience had taught the company which kind of glass would be suitable (fused silica) and which kind of dopant would produce the required results. Equally importantly, the company also had experience with the manufacturing processes that would prove to be effective, further reducing the attenuation rate.

In May 1970, Corning applied for the first patent that would result in an optical fibre that would break the 20dB/km threshold. In autumn of that year Corning took an optical fibre (based on the knowledge referred to in this patent application) for testing to Bell Laboratories, part of the telecoms operator AT&T. A loss rate of 17 dB/km was confirmed. In May 1972 this patent was granted. The threshold target identified by Kao and Hockham in 1966, therefore, had been decisively broken, making optical fibre the superior communications transmissions technology.

One might be forgiven for assuming that on becoming the superior technology its creators would immediately bask in a windfall of profits. This, however, was not to happen. Obstacles such as the fixed investments that had already been made in copper cable, together with the reliable maturity of the manufacturing methods and associated technologies in copper cable, constrained rapid and significant investment in optical fibre. Indeed, it was only in 1983 that Corning first turned a profit on its optical fibre sales, and that only after a multitude of additional innovations that significantly reduced attenuation rates, and manufacturing costs, much further.

Coevolution of Optical Fibre and the Laser

As Maiman noted, before he created the first working laser there was already acknowledgement of the potentially important role that lasers could play in greatly increasing communications transmissions rates. This is precisely what happened with lasers becoming the light source for optical transmissions systems. New optical fibres were developed with minimum attenuation rates at particular wavelengths. This required lasers that produced light at these wavelengths. In this way, lasers and optical fibre became part of the same technological system establishing coevolutionary processes between these two technologies and their evolving innovation hypotheses.

'Indeed, in 1970, the same year that Corning's researchers broke the 20 dB/km barrier, Hayashi and Panish achieved the first continuous wave operation of a semiconductor laser at room temperature. Several years later, with the demonstration that optical fibres with zero dispersion could be produced which operated at 1.55 micrometres, new semiconductor lasers were developed at this wavelength. In 1979, Yasuharu Suematsu and his colleagues at the Tokyo Institute of Technology reported a continuous-room-temperature semiconductor laser at 1.55 micrometres using a mixture of indium, gallium, arsenic, and phosphorus.'[57] The grandchildren, and even the great-grandchildren, of the parent laser innovation hypotheses were doing their work.

INNOVATION PROPOSITIONS AND THE FOUR TECHNOLOGIES THAT CHANGED THE WORLD

The detailed studies of the transistor, microprocessor, laser, and optical fibre and the innovation processes through which these innovations went provide empirical evidence for the nine innovation propositions discussed at the beginning of this chapter. However, there is one possible exception. Is innovation always intentional, as is stated

---

[57] Fransman, M., 1995. *Japan's Computer and Communications Industry*. Oxford: Oxford University Press.

in Proposition 1? Or are there cases where innovation just happens without intent? In order to examine these questions, the case of Viagra is discussed in the next subsection.

VIAGRA

What Is Viagra?

Viagra is a medication that is used for erectile dysfunction.

Context

It has been suggested that some innovations such as Viagra happen unintentionally, by chance. One report, for instance, gives ten examples of products, including Viagra, that 'were invented by accident'.[58]

But is this an accurate description of how Viagra happened? The main purpose of this subsection is to examine in detail the innovation processes that led to the advent of Viagra. This discussion is intended as a further contribution to the main theme of the present chapter, namely an exploration of how innovation happens.

The Initial Innovation Hypothesis

The original innovation hypothesis that eventually led to the advent of Viagra had nothing to do with erectile dysfunction. Rather, it had to do with the treatment of angina (heart-related chest pains, a symptom of ischaemic heart disease) and hypertension (high blood pressure).

The original innovation hypothesis, innovation hypothesis 1 (IH1), was formulated in 1989 by two chemists working in the laboratories of the pharmaceutical company Pfizer, in Kent, United Kingdom, Peter Dunn and Albert Wood. IH1 was based on their imagined belief that a particular compound, sildenafil citrate, would be useful in the treatment of angina and high blood pressure. In order to test this

---

[58] 'From Velcro to Viagra: 10 products that were invented by accident', www.historyextra.com/article/feature/velcro-viagra-10-products-were-invented-accident.

hypothesis, they developed a process for synthesising sildenafil citrate.[59] It is the names of Dunn and Wood that appear in the patent application for this process (WOWO9849166A1) filed by Pfizer.[60]

In 1991, pursuing the testing of IH1, Andrew Bell, David Brown, and Nicholas Terrett (who was team leader), also of Pfizer's Kent laboratories, found evidence that sildenafil did have some positive effects relating to the treatment of angina. Terrett is named in the 1991 patent for which Pfizer applied for the use of sildenafil in the treatment of heart conditions.[61]

Further testing of IH1, however, was needed in order to make sure that the drug was effective outside the laboratory setting and safe for human consumption. Clinical trials were also a regulatory requirement. It was the information feedback flows generated in these clinical trials that led to a rejection of IH1 as well as the formulation of a new innovation hypothesis, IH2, the 'child' (in Hicks's terminology, see above) of the original innovation hypothesis.

Innovation Hypothesis 2, Child of the Original Innovation Hypothesis

The clinical trials were undertaken under the direction of Ian Osterloh. However, these trials were disappointing since they revealed that sildenafil had little if any effect on angina, the target ailment. This meant a rejection of IH1. However, some of the male patients taking part in the trial reported an unexpected side-effect of sildenafil – they experienced erections.

This feedback flow of information, unexpected though it was, had to be interpreted by an enquiring human mind. Causation and the possibility of using the caused effect in safe medication aimed at erectile dysfunction required far more than casual observation. Viagra certainly did not happen 'by accident'. It required a new innovation hypothesis (the 'imagined deemed feasible' – see Proposition 3) and, as

---

[59] http://edition.cnn.com/2013/03/27/health/viagra-anniversary-timeline/.
[60] www.sildenafilakaviagra.com/history-of-viagra.   [61] Ibid.

with all innovation hypotheses, the rigorous testing of the hypothesis in order to establish that the drug was indeed feasible. And this would take time.

In 1994, in researching further the effect of sildenafil on erections, Nicholas Terrett and Peter Ellis from Pfizer found that the drug was effective in enhancing the flow of blood to the penis, the cause of an erection. Sildenafil increases the muscle-relaxing effectiveness of nitric oxide, a chemical that is released when a person is sexually stimulated. This and other related research led Pfizer to undertake clinical trials of sildenafil as a potential cure for erectile dysfunction, providing the evidence needed to test IH2 and establish whether a drug for this purpose was feasible.[62]

These clinical trials and the information they generated established that the drug was indeed feasible, and in 1996 Pfizer applied for a sildenafil patent in the United States. In March 1998 the US Food and Drug Administration approved the use of the drug.[63] In 1998, sales of Viagra increased Pfizer's second-quarter profit margin by 38 per cent. In 1999, annual sales of Viagra exceeded $1 billion.[64]

Conclusion

As the evidence provided here shows, far from being an exception to the general propositions being put forward in this chapter about how innovation happens, the innovation processes followed in the Viagra case were similar to those of the transistor, microprocessor, laser, and optical fibre. Viagra was not 'invented by accident'. Its innovation process began with the formulation of an innovation hypothesis, IH1, the imagined deemed feasible. The information generated in the testing of IH1 led to both the rejection of this hypothesis and the formulation of a new innovation hypothesis, IH2, the child of the original hypothesis (see Proposition 6). In the innovation of the other

---

[62] Ibid.

[63] http://edition.cnn.com/2013/03/27/health/viagra-anniversary-timeline/.

[64] www.sildenafilakaviagra.com/history-of-viagra.

four products there were many instances, as shown in the case studies in this chapter, where, similarly, innovation hypotheses were rejected by testing and were replaced by new hypotheses. It was the testing of IH2 that eventually resulted in Viagra, the iconic drug for erectile dysfunction. The case of Viagra, therefore, is, in essential respects as far as the innovation process is concerned, similar to those of these other four products.

CONCLUSION

The main aim of this chapter has been to examine how value-increasing innovation happens. The examination has been based on a detailed analysis of how innovation happened in the case of four innovations that both individually and collectively literally changed the way in which the world works, namely the transistor, micropro-cessor, laser, and optical fibre. The similar case of Viagra is also examined.

It is not suggested that these cases are representative of all instances where innovation happens. It is accepted that to a signifi-cant extent all cases of innovation happening are sui generis. In Chapter 10 the case of Concorde is briefly discussed. Unlike the cases considered in this chapter, Concorde is a case of commercial failure. However, here too the nine propositions proposed at the beginning of this chapter hold. In the case of Concorde, in contrast to the other cases, the innovation hypotheses put forward failed to be validated by market selection, the ultimate arbiter of the fate of such hypotheses. The fact that it took so long for the hypotheses to be rejected and the considerable loss that followed is the tragedy of Concorde.

Finally, a few words are needed to relate the present chapter to the broader concern of this book, namely the conceptualisation and use of innovation ecosystems. One of the main conclusions of Chap-ter 3 – the chapter dealing with the two clusters of literature that take a systems view of innovation, the innovation systems and business ecosystems literatures – was that both these approaches do not give as much attentions as is desirable to the question of how innovation happens; that is, the processes that are needed to make value-adding innovation happen.

It is this issue that has been the focus of attention in the present chapter. Based on an analysis of how innovators make their innovation decisions, necessarily from an ex ante perspective, this chapter has highlighted the importance of nine innovation propositions. The chapter's main conclusion is that the incorporation of these nine propositions into the conceptualisation of innovation ecosystems would constitute a significant advance, facilitating a deeper understanding of the innovation process. By so doing, the innovation process that lies at the heart of innovation ecosystems will be seen as the unfolding process that it is, riddled with uncertainties, interpretive ambiguities, ignorance, subjective expectations that at times turn out to be true and at other times false, mistakes, and errors. This is the name of the innovation game.

In the following chapter another issue that also does not receive the attention it deserves in the conceptualisation of innovation ecosystems is examined, namely *who* makes innovation happen.

7 Who Makes Innovation Happen? Is the Entrepreneur Becoming Obsolete?

Creating an Organisation-Level Innovation Ecosystem

In the last chapter we explored *how* innovation happens. This enquiry was based on a close examination of four key technologies that together and combined in systems have changed the world: the transistor, microprocessor, laser, and optical fibre. The enquiry yielded nine propositions about how innovation happens.

In this chapter the question of *who* makes innovation happen is examined. Innovation does not happen automatically. It must be made to happen by people. But who are these people? The conventional answer to this question is that it is entrepreneurs who make innovation happen. This was the original view expressed by Joseph Schumpeter, and indeed he did a great deal to propagate this idea.

The chapter begins with a brief characterisation of the popular notion of the classical, iconic entrepreneur. The ideas of Schumpeter are then examined in detail, discussing his arguments about the function of entrepreneurs, their motivations, and the reasons for their existence. The discussion then proceeds to Schumpeter's distinction between the role of the entrepreneur and the qualitatively different role of three other players in the innovation process: managers, the providers of funds for innovation, and inventors. Schumpeter's distinction between entrepreneurs and inventors, however, is found to be wanting and a reformulation is proposed.

Intriguingly, after championing the role of the entrepreneur, Schumpeter came up with the surprising notion that the entrepreneur is becoming 'obsolete' in the modern, large-scale capitalist economy. He suggested that there were three reasons for this fundamental change: the routinisation of innovation and the replacement of the entrepreneur by teams of innovators; the increase in what he called 'provability', which he suggested leaves little room for the entrepreneur; and the reduction in resistance to innovation, which also undermines one of the entrepreneur's key functions. These three reasons are examined closely and are rejected.

Empirically, however, it is clear that Schumpeter's observation that innovation teams have come to play a more significant role in innovation is correct. This raises an important, broader question: How is the innovation process changing and what are the causes of this change?

To understand the reasons for the change in the innovation process, as this chapter demonstrates in detail, it is necessary to understand the wider process of the division of labour and, in the present case, the division of innovation labour. For this understanding, however, it is necessary to begin with the work of two economists who preceded Schumpeter, namely Adam Smith and Alfred Marshall, and one of Schumpeter's contemporaries, Friedrich Hayek.

With a firmer conceptual understanding of the process of the division of labour and the complications that accompany it providing a foundation, the discussion in this chapter proceeds to examine in greater detail the contemporary division of innovation labour. This discussion begins with a close analysis of a current iconic book on innovation that has made a significant impact in many countries, Eric Ries's *The Lean Startup: How Constant Innovation Creates Radically Successful Businesses*. Both the strengths and the limitations of this influential book are investigated.

This leads to the final section in this chapter, a detailed analysis of the specialised *functions* of innovation that have emerged in the contemporary division of innovation labour and that have to be performed if innovation is to happen. Tying the discussion of this chapter in with the overall theme of the present book, the crucial notion of an organisation's innovation ecosystem, embodying all the players and processes that together make innovation in that organisation happen, is developed in order to establish who should make innovation happen.

So, has the entrepreneur become obsolete? The answer to this question is provided in the last part of this chapter.

INTRODUCTION

In the last chapter we asked how innovation happens and we examined nine propositions relating to the innovation process. In this chapter we ask: Who makes innovation happen and how should an organisation-level innovation ecosystem be created?

THE ENTREPRENEUR AS PERSON WHO MAKES INNOVATION HAPPEN

Following Joseph Schumpeter, it is the entrepreneur as a person who makes innovation happen.[1] But what does he mean by 'innovation'? Schumpeter's answer is that innovation refers to one or more of the following: new or improved products and/or services, new or improved processes and/or technologies, new or improved ways of organising things and people, and new or improved markets, ways of marketing, and business models. Schumpeter's definition of innovation has been adopted by all the international organisations responsible for defining and collecting data on innovation.

The Classical, Iconic Entrepreneur

Entrepreneurs are often portrayed as almost heroic figures. To begin with, they see opportunities that others do not. Not only that, they

---

[1] Whether innovation can be created and carried out by a 'machine' rather than a person is an intriguing question. Although this question is not examined in detail here, several comments are offered in this chapter.

pursue their visions of opportunity with an energy and insight that others seldom show. They battle against the odds, surmounting challenges and defying the probabilities that clearly show that the great majority of entrepreneurial enterprises fail.

What motivates this unusual behaviour? Schumpeter points to three such motivations. The first is 'the dream and the will to found a private kingdom, usually, though not necessarily, also a dynasty'. Included in this dream is the desire for power and independence. But as Schumpeter wryly notes, 'The sensation of power and independence loses nothing by the fact that both are largely illusions.'[2]

The second motivation is 'the will to conquer: the impulse to fight, to prove oneself superior to others, to succeed for the sake, not of the fruits of success, but of success itself. From this aspect, economic action becomes akin to sport – there are financial races, or rather boxing-matches.' Schumpeter reiterates that it is success itself that is the goal rather than the material benefits that success brings: 'The financial result is a secondary consideration, or, at all events, mainly valued as an index of success and as a symptom of victory, the displaying of which very often is more important as a motive of large expenditure than the wish for the consumers' goods themselves.'[3]

Third, 'there is the joy of creating, of getting things done, or simply of exercising one's energy and ingenuity'. This joy, Schumpeter points out, is in fact anti-hedonistic since its realisation usually comes with more pain than pleasure: The entrepreneur 'seeks out difficulties, changes in order to change, delights in ventures. This group of motives is the most distinctly anti-hedonistic of the three.'[4]

The Distinctiveness of the Entrepreneurial Function

In discussing the role of the entrepreneur Schumpeter distinguishes the role of other players who are also intimately involved in the innovation process.

---

[2] Schumpeter, *Theory of Economic Development*, p. 93.   [3] Ibid.
[4] Ibid, pp. 93–4.

The first of these is the primary 'risk-taker'.[5] Whilst the entrepreneur also faces uncertainty and will bear some of the costs of failure, the main bearer of these costs is the player(s) that puts up most of the money needed to enable the entrepreneurial enterprise to survive until positive net cash flows are realised. Unless they have funded this start-up period themselves the main loser in the case of failure will be the other provider(s) of money, those whom Schumpeter called the 'capitalists', not the entrepreneur.

Second, Schumpeter distinguishes between the entrepreneur and the manager. Managers play an essential role in the entrepreneurial enterprise. Whilst it is possible for an entrepreneur also to be a manager, the roles and capabilities that each require are fundamentally different. Accordingly, these two roles are usually performed by different people. The manager, essentially, uses existing knowledge, processes, and tools to try and run an efficient organisation. In strong contrast, the entrepreneur is devoted to the creation of the new. As Schumpeter illuminatingly put it, these two roles are as different as creating a road, on the one hand, and walking along it, on the other.

Far more problematical, however, is Schumpeter's third distinction between the inventor and the entrepreneur. Again, Schumpeter argues that these two roles, although both are essential and in rare cases may be undertaken by the same person, are fundamentally different. For Schumpeter, the inventor's role is, essentially, to create new ideas. But Schumpeter's perspective was that of the economist, and his main focus was on the effects on economic variables such as output, prices, and employment. Ideas per se, however, produce no economic effects. It is only when they are implemented, applied and used that they have an economic effect. In Schumpeter's view the entrepreneur's main function is, in his words, to 'carry out' the created ideas.

---

[5] Strictly speaking, here we are referring not to risk but to uncertainty. In the case of risk, probability distributions can be determined to aid decision-making. However, this is not the case, by definition, with uncertainty. Typically, entrepreneurial decisions, dealing as they do with novelty, involve uncertainty rather than risk.

In *Business Cycles*, published in 1939, Schumpeter states:

> Although most innovations can be traced to some conquest in the
> realm of either theoretical or practical knowledge, there are many
> which cannot. Innovation is possible without anything we should
> identify as invention and invention does not necessarily induce
> innovation, but produces of itself no economically relevant effect at
> all ...
>
> [E]ven where innovation consists in giving effect, by business
> action, to a particular invention which has either emerged
> autonomously or has been made specially in response to a given
> business situation, the making of the invention and the carrying
> out of the corresponding innovation are two entirely different
> things. They often have been performed by the same person; but
> this is merely a chance coincidence which does not affect the
> validity of the distinction.[6]

In similar vein, writing in *Capitalism, Socialism and Democracy*,
published in 1943, Schumpeter says:

> the function of entrepreneurs is to reform or revolutionise the
> pattern of production by exploiting an invention or, more generally,
> an untried technological possibility for producing a new
> commodity or producing an old one in a new way, by opening up a
> new source of supply of materials or a new outlet for products, by
> reorganising an industry and so on ... To undertake such new
> things is difficult and constitutes a distinct economic function ...
> because they lie outside of the routine tasks which everybody
> understands ...
>
> [T]he entrepreneurial function ... does not essentially consist in
> either inventing anything or otherwise creating the conditions
> which the enterprise exploits. It consists in getting things done.[7]

---

[6] *Business Cycles*, pp. 59–60.   [7] *Capitalism, Socialism and Democracy*, p. 132.

But this Schumpeterian perspective presents problems. The main problem is that the distinction between 'creating ideas' and 'carrying them out' is too sharp. In practice, there is usually a blurring and fusion of these two processes. Whilst the creation of ideas does not necessarily also require the carrying-out of them, it is far more likely that the 'carrying-out' necessitates the generation of further new ideas about what may work, how performance may be enhanced, etc. These are precisely the string of innovation hypotheses discussed in the last chapter that were embodied in the nine propositions about how innovation happens.

Indeed, it is possible that Schumpeter himself came to a similar conclusion. In a paper published in 1947, four years after *Capitalism, Socialism and Democracy* was published, he draws the important distinction between 'adaptive responses' and 'creative responses' and states:

> [C]reative response means, in the economic sphere, simply the combination of existing productive resources in new ways or for new purposes, and … this function defines the economic type that we call the entrepreneur.[8]

Clearly, coming up with such 'new combinations' involves the creative act of imagining them in the first instance (i.e. 'the imagined deemed feasible' discussed in the previous chapter). Obviously, this goes beyond merely 'carrying-out' and 'getting things done'.

However, it is also possible that Schumpeter was not aware of the significant departure that these words imply from the views he expressed earlier in *Business Cycles* and *Capitalism, Socialism and Democracy* as quoted above. For it appears that he has not commented on the implications for his earlier ideas of his insistence in 1947 that the 'creative response' is an essential component of the role of the entrepreneur.

---

[8] Schumpeter, J. A., 1947b. 'Theoretical problems: theoretical problems of economic growth'. *The Journal of Economic History*, 7: 1–9.

Further problems are created by Schumpeter's statement in his 1947 paper that 'creative response means ... the combination of existing productive resources'. Schumpeter had long equated his idea of 'new combinations' with innovation. In his *Theory of Economic Development*, first published in 1934, for example, he refers collectively to the different types of innovation that he identifies as 'new combinations'.[9] But 'new combinations' implies that the novelty resides in the combination itself and not in the elements being combined. However, this is far too restrictive since innovation often relates to the elements themselves (for example, in the case of new materials).

It seems reasonable to conclude, therefore, that Schumpeter's distinction between invention and innovation and his notion of 'new combinations' are at best not particularly helpful and at worst confusing, muddying the waters in the analysis of both how innovation happens and who makes it happen.

Nevertheless, Schumpeter does highlight a further important component of the entrepreneurial role. This is the part that the entrepreneur plays in overcoming resistance to the reallocation of resources (material and human) away from existing pursuits and towards the new entrepreneurial endeavours. In Schumpeter's words,

> the environment resists [innovation] in many ways that vary, according to social conditions, from simple refusal either to finance or to buy a new thing, to physical attack on the man who tries to produce it. To act with confidence beyond the range of familiar beacons and to overcome that resistance requires aptitudes that are present in only a small fraction of the population and that define the entrepreneurial type as well as the entrepreneurial function.[10]

In the following section we explore in further detail the entrepreneur's role in overcoming the resistance to innovation.

[9] *Theory of Economic Development*, p. 66.
[10] *Capitalism, Socialism and Democracy*, p. 132.

The Entrepreneur's Function in Overcoming Resistance to Innovation

The entrepreneur's role is not only to innovate but also to overcome the frictions that are an inherent part of the innovation process and result in resistance to innovation. In this section we examine the market for entrepreneurial ideas where these frictions are evident.

In the market for entrepreneurial ideas, it is entrepreneurs who are the main suppliers. For these ideas to be realised and implemented, however, there must be a variety of 'takers' or demanders of these ideas. They include customers of the resulting products and/or services, the providers of money who will fund the entrepreneurial enterprise until it becomes financially self-sufficient, employees who agree to provide their labour to the enterprise, partners who are willing to buy into the ideas, and suppliers who are happy to provide their products and/or services as inputs into the enterprise.

However, it is by no means certain that these counterparties will be willing to provide what the entrepreneur requires to successfully implement the entrepreneurial idea. Indeed, there are many reasons why this is unlikely to happen automatically or at low cost. The result is resistance to innovation. It is the entrepreneur who, as we shall see, is well placed to overcome this resistance.

It is helpful to identify the following five causes of friction in the market for entrepreneurial ideas. Individually and in combination they result in resistance. They are:

- Uncertainty
- Asymmetric information
- The possibility of opportunism
- Conflict of interest
- Inertia.

The future is irreducibly uncertain. Although the entrepreneurial idea may make sense in the entrepreneur's moment-in-being, there is no guarantee that in the future the idea will meet the entrepreneur's expectations. Furthermore, no assistance can be provided by probabilities since, as noted earlier, these cannot be calculated in this case, unlike in the case of risk. The takers of the entrepreneur's ideas in the market for entrepreneurial ideas will, therefore, also have to accept this uncertainty. This, all other things equal, will be a deterrent to taking.

Different problems are presented by asymmetric information. Here the problem is not one of uncertainty. Rather, it is one of the distribution of existing information. Almost always the entrepreneur will have more information about the idea itself and the various factors that may contribute to its success or frustration. Typically, the potential takers will have significantly less information.

The difficulties are compounded by the possibility of opportunism. This possibility exists when the potential taker cannot ask the entrepreneur to 'tell the truth, the whole truth, and nothing but the truth' and be certain that the entrepreneur is telling the truth in giving the answer. Where this condition exists, the potential taker cannot be sure that the entrepreneur is not being opportunistic. Opportunism ranges from being downright fraudulent to merely 'spinning' the entrepreneurial narrative.

Where there is a conflict of interest, the resistance results not from the first three points but from the fact that the potential taker does not have a self-interest in taking. Indeed, they may have an interest in actively opposing the entrepreneurial idea because of the threat it poses.

Finally, the friction may come from inertia, that is, the cost of doing what is needed if the entrepreneurial idea is to be taken relative to not doing anything at all. Even if the first four points present no problem for the entrepreneurial idea, inertia may stymie its being taken.

The entrepreneur is well placed, indeed usually best placed, to mitigate all five causes of friction. Not only is the idea the entrepreneur's, who is best informed about it. It is also the entrepreneur who is best motivated to deal with these potential problems (i.e. the entrepreneur has the will to deal with them) and who is best incentivised to deal with them (i.e. the entrepreneur will be the greatest beneficiary). An important implication of the present discussion is that even if it is possible for innovation to happen, without the entrepreneur as the person who makes it happen, it may still be essential for an entrepreneur to be the person to overcome the frictions that inevitably may frustrate the implementation of the entrepreneurial idea.

But is it possible for innovation to happen without the entrepreneur as person? This question is explored in the following section.

Is the Entrepreneur Becoming Obsolete?

Intriguingly, it is precisely this that Schumpeter suggests has happened. Schumpeter begins chapter 12 of *Capitalism, Socialism and Democracy* with a section titled 'The Obsolescence of the Entrepreneurial Function'. The reasons that he gives for this surprising statement will be explored in this section.

Schumpeter gives three reasons for his conclusion that the entrepreneurial function is becoming obsolete. The first is increasing routinisation. In Schumpeter's words: 'it is much easier now than it has been in the past to do things that lie outside familiar routine – innovation itself is being reduced to routine.'[11] As a result of the routinisation of the innovation process, 'Technological progress is increasingly becoming the business of teams of trained specialists [i.e. rather than the business of entrepreneurs].'[12]

But is this argument true? According to the *Oxford English Dictionary*, routine means 'a sequence of actions regularly followed'. However, innovation, by definition, refers to the creation of the new. Surely, if all past actions are followed, including patterns of thought, past outcomes will be repeated and innovation will not happen. To put this another way, no amount of routinisation is guaranteed to produce a successful new product, process, etc. Accordingly, innovation must involve a break with past routines if it is to happen. Therefore, it is not possible for 'innovation' to be reduced to routine

---

[11] Schumpeter, *Capitalism, Socialism and Democracy*, p. 132.　　[12] Ibid.

if it is to be innovation (which produces a rupture with the past by the creation of novelty).

Schumpeter's second reason is that innovation is becoming more 'provable' and therefore predictable. 'The entrepreneurial performance involves ... the ability to perceive new opportunities that cannot be proved at the moment at which action has to be taken ... But the range of the provable expands, and action upon flashes or hunches is increasingly replaced by action that is based upon "figuring out".'[13] Schumpeter continues: 'So far as this is so, the element of personal intuition and force would be less essential than it was: it could be expected to yield its place to the teamwork of specialists: in other words, improvement could be expected to become more and more automatic.'[14]

Significantly, however, for Schumpeter this is essentially an empirical argument, for he adds: 'But this [argument] is at present only an impression. It is for the historian to establish or to refute it.'[15]

Schumpeter's second argument has highly significant implications. For to the extent that he is correct in asserting that 'innovation hypotheses' are becoming more predictable, they are not hypotheses that have to be tested in order to be refuted or validated but statements of fact. And if they are statements of fact, they are amenable to automation, as Schumpeter suggests. In such a world, innovation will indeed pass from the person called the entrepreneur to 'machines'.

But can an 'innovation hypothesis' ever be ex ante predictable? By definition, an innovation hypothesis refers to the new. But the new does not yet exist. Its only existence is in the imagination of the innovator. But if it does not yet exist, how can provable predictions be made about its existence? Surely, innovation ex ante is inherently uncertain. No probabilities can be derived ex ante regarding its future existence or effects. In this case, both the future existence and the

---

[13] Schumpeter, J. A., 1947a. 'The creative response in economic history'. *The Journal of Economic History*, 7(2): 157.
[14] Ibid. [15] Ibid.

consequences of the innovation cannot be predicted. If this is true, then Schumpeter's assertion that innovation is becoming more 'provable' must be wrong.

It is, however, conceivable that there are some areas where ex ante prediction has become possible. But innovation would not be possible in these areas. For if outcomes are ex ante predictable, they cannot yield future novelty. For novelty implies a discontinuous rupture with the past. Where ex ante prediction is possible, there is continuity of the past.

However, even if more areas are becoming predictable, therefore precluding innovation, this does not imply that there is no longer a role for the entrepreneur, who accordingly becomes obsolete and dies. As long as other areas remain ex ante unpredictable, there will be a continuing role for the entrepreneur as defined by Schumpeter. Indeed, ironically, earlier in his 1947 article just quoted, this is precisely what Schumpeter suggests.

Here Schumpeter makes the distinction between an 'adaptive response' and a 'creative response'. 'Whenever ... an industry reacts to [a change] ... within its existing practice we may speak of the development as an *adaptive response*.' However, 'whenever ... an industry [does] ... something that is outside of the range of existing practice we may speak of *creative response*'. But whilst creative response 'from the standpoint of the observer who is in full possession of all relevant facts ... can always be understood *ex post* ... it can practically never be understood *ex ante*, that is to say it cannot be predicted by applying the ordinary rules of inference from the pre-existing facts'.

Schumpeter concludes, 'Accordingly, a study of creative response in business becomes coterminous with a study of entrepreneurship. The mechanisms of economic change in capitalist society pivot on entrepreneurial activity.'[16]

It is reasonable to argue, therefore, that Schumpeter's first two reasons fail to make a convincing case that the entrepreneur is

---

[16] Ibid., p. 150, emphasis in original.

becoming obsolete in the modern economy. The two reasons that he gives for suggesting that this is happening – increasing routinisation and predictability – whilst no doubt occurring to some extent in reality, do not provide a sufficient basis for the proposition that the entrepreneur and the entrepreneurial function are becoming obsolete.

Schumpeter also provides a third reason for the increasing obsolescence of the entrepreneur. He argues that resistance to innovation is decreasing:

> personality and will power must count for less in environments which have become accustomed to economic change – best instanced by an incessant stream of new consumers' and producers' goods – and which, instead of resisting, accept it as a matter of course. The resistance which comes from interests threatened by an innovation in the production process is not likely to die out as long as the capitalist order persists ... But every other kind of resistance – the resistance, in particular, of consumers and producers to a new kind of thing because it is new – has well-nigh vanished already.[17]

The argument that resistance to innovation, apart from that based on conflict of interest, has all but disappeared is also not convincing. As was shown in the last but one section dealing with the role of the entrepreneur in overcoming resistance to innovation, there are four other reasons for such resistance. These are uncertainty, asymmetric information, the possibility of opportunism, and inertia. There is little reason to believe that these have declined in significance. As pointed out there, entrepreneurs are particularly well situated to mitigate these causes of resistance to innovation as a result of their motivation and incentive. Resistance to innovation, therefore, remains a reason for the continuing role of the entrepreneur and the entrepreneurial function.

[17] Schumpeter, *Capitalism, Socialism and Democracy*, pp. 132–3.

It may be concluded, therefore, that even though some areas of economic activity might have become more predictable, thus obviating the role of the entrepreneur and the entrepreneurial function, the rest of economic activity is sufficiently large and growing so as to sustain the continuing important role of both these factors.

But is the process of innovation itself changing and, furthermore, changing in such a way as to undermine the role of the entrepreneur as a person who makes innovation happen? This question is examined in the following section.

SPECIALISATION AND THE FUNCTIONS OF ENTREPRENEURSHIP

In order to understand the change that is occurring in the function of entrepreneurship, which is to make innovation happen, the place to look is not routinisation and neither is it provability. Instead, it is specialisation. Rather than to Schumpeter, we have to look to much earlier economists, namely Adam Smith and Alfred Marshall, and, later, Friedrich Hayek.

In 1776 Adam Smith published his now-famous book, *An Inquiry into the Nature and Causes of the Wealth of Nations.*[18] As the title makes clear, Smith was concerned to explain why countries become wealthy. His answer was that the main reason is the process of specialisation, which he referred to as the division of labour.

To illustrate the benefits of specialisation, Smith takes the example of 'a very trifling manufacture', the 'trade of the pin-maker'.[19] Smith notes that 'a workman not educated to this business (which the division of labour has rendered a district trade), nor acquainted with the use of the machinery employed in it (to the invention of which the same division of labour has probably given

---

[18] Smith, A., 2010. *An Inquiry into the Nature and Causes of the Wealth of Nations.* London: J. M. Dent & Sons.

[19] Ibid., pp. 4–5.

occasion), could scarce ... make one pin in a day, and certainly could not make twenty'.

However, 'in the way in which this business is now carried on ... one man draws out the wire, another straights it, a third cuts it, a fourth points it, a fifth grinds it at the top for receiving the head; to make the head requires two or three distinct operations; to put it on is a peculiar business, to whiten the pins is another; it is even a trade by itself to put them into the paper; and the important business of making a pin is, in this manner, divided into about eighteen distinct operations'.[20]

What impact has this division of labour had on productivity? Taking the example of a small and poor pin-making firm 'indifferently accommodated with the necessary machinery' and employing ten people, Smith notes that an output of 'upwards of forty-eight thousand pins in a day'[21] was achieved.

Writing in his book *Principles of Economics*, published in 1890, Alfred Marshall, the Cambridge University economist, whilst drawing on Adam Smith, takes the specialisation argument significantly further. Combining the insights of Adam Smith and Charles Darwin, Marshall proposed a 'general rule' that expressed the 'fundamental unity of action' between the laws of the physical and social worlds:

> This central unity is set forth in the general rule, to which there are not very many exceptions, that the development of the organism, whether social or physical, involves an *increasing subdivision of functions* between its separate parts on the one hand, and on the other a more intimate connection between them.[22]

So far, this is pure Smith. But Marshall goes significantly further when he adds: 'Each part gets to be less and less self-sufficient, to depend for its well-being more and more on other parts, so that any disorder in

---

[20] Ibid., p. 5.   [21] Ibid.

[22] Marshall, A., 1969. *Principles of Economics*. London: Macmillan, pp. 200–1, emphasis added.

any part of a highly-developed organism will affect other parts also. This increased subdivision of functions, or "differentiation", as it is called, manifests itself with regard to industry in such forms as the division of labour, and the development of specialized skill, knowledge and machinery.'

As this quotation makes clear, Marshall's contribution is to point out that there is a sting in the division of labour's tail. Although, as Smith demonstrated, the division of labour leads to increased productivity, the opposite side of the same coin is the increased vulnerability to which the system is subjected. In short, the performance of the system as a whole depends on the performance of each of its interdependent parts. Failure or underperformance of one of these parts will have a significant impact on the performance of the whole. Accordingly, the benefits of the division of labour are purchased at the cost of an increased vulnerability of the system.

Marshall was well aware of this cost. In the quotation, he notes that the 'increased subdivision of functions' has been applied in the areas of 'skill, knowledge, and machinery'. Indeed, he goes so far as to argue that 'Knowledge is our most powerful engine of production.' However, in the following sentence he goes on to qualify this statement by noting that 'organisation' is necessary in order to harness the benefits of increasing knowledge. As he very simply put it: 'Organisation aids knowledge.'[23]

It is to another economist to whom we must turn to get a firmer grip on the problem that the division of labour creates by fragmenting knowledge whilst at the same time requiring its integration if that knowledge is to be organised in a useful way. That economist is Friedrich Hayek.

It was Hayek who drew attention to some of the difficulties that arise in attempting to integrate segmented knowledge. Writing in 1945, Hayek argued that 'the problem of what is the best way of utilizing knowledge dispersed among all the people is ... one of the

[23] Ibid., p. 115.

main problems ... of designing an efficient economic system'. Indeed, he went further, stating, 'The economic problem of society ... is a problem of the utilization of knowledge which is not given to anyone in its totality.'[24]

Hayek felt that this problem has some resolution at the level of both the economy as a whole and in the decision-making of an individual: 'in a system in which the knowledge of the relevant facts is dispersed among many people, prices can act to co-ordinate the separate actions of different people in the same way as subjective values help the individual to co-ordinate the parts of his plan'.[25]

Crucially, however, and particularly unfortunate from the point of view of the concerns of the present book, Hayek does not go on to discuss how this problem may be resolved within an organisation. As we shall see in the following section, which deals with the division of innovation labour in the modern large company, the problem is crucial.

The Division of Innovation Labour in the Modern Large Corporation

In modern large companies, there is a well-defined division of innovation labour. A categorisation of the division that exists in many companies contains the following divisions:

1. Research
2. Development
3. Production
4. Marketing and sales.

These divisions are shown in Exhibit 7.1, which provides a stylised account[26] of the division of innovation labour in many contemporary

---

[24] Hayek, F. A., 1945. 'The use of knowledge in society'. *American Economic Review*, 35(4): 519–30.

[25] Ibid., p. 25.

[26] Of course, there is in reality significant variation regarding the precise division of innovation labour in different companies as well as in the way in which these divisions and what happens within them are organised. For the purposes of the present discussion, however, these differences do not matter.

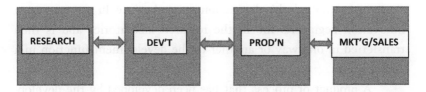

EXHIBIT 7.1 The Division of Innovation Labour in Many Modern Large Companies

large companies. Four main functions are identified. Going from upstream down, these functions are research, development, production, and marketing/sales.

Research often takes place in central research laboratories. Frequently, these laboratories are separated, physically and organisationally, from the business units into which the rest of the multidivisional, multiproduct company is divided. A reason for this separation is to reinforce the longer time horizon of the research function compared with that of development. As some Japanese companies put it, whilst research deals with 'the day after tomorrow', development is for 'tomorrow'.

By separating research laboratories from the rest of the company's activities, the intention is that researchers will be less influenced by today's processes and technologies, today's customers, and today's markets. Instead, their focus will be on what might become possible the day after tomorrow. A further distinction in research is between research that is oriented towards the achievement of specified commercial goals and so-called basic research, which has no such goals.

Whilst some of the development function may also be located in the central research laboratories, a good deal of this function is usually situated in the business units. This proximity allows developers to respond to the demands of the business unit for short- to medium-term improvements in products and processes.

In general, therefore, while research tends to 'push' innovation, development is more often 'pulled' by the demands of current customers, although this distinction is not absolute. In many cases an innovation begins its life in the research laboratories and is then transferred in one way or another to the development function in a business unit.

A product or process that has been developed by the development function (including its design) is then transferred in one way or another to the production function. Here it is turned into the final product or process, which is either passed to the marketing and sales function for sale to external customers or passed to internal users within the company.

Problems Arising from This Division of Innovation Labour

Some of the problems arising from this division of innovation labour were anticipated by Marshall and Hayek. The dependence of each specialised part of the innovation process on all the other parts noted by Marshall may cause problems. For example, highly skilled researchers trained in the PhD programmes of good universities may not connect very effectively with their colleagues in the development function, thus depriving the company of the research-push engine of innovation. Design and development specialists may not take fully into account the wants and needs of the production people or customers, both external and internal.

Hayek's 'problem of the utilization of knowledge which is not given to anyone in its totality', clearly, may cause difficulties in this division of innovation labour. For instance, the needs, wants, and problems of customers, with which the marketing and sales people may be most familiar since it is they who have most contact with customers, may not be sufficiently shared with those involved in the other functions, causing a misalignment of their outputs with customer requirements.

Marshall may be correct in his observation that 'Knowledge is our most powerful engine of production' and, we may add, of productivity, profitability, and growth. His statement that 'Organisation aids knowledge' may also be true. However, what should be done to more effectively organise the production and use of knowledge is by no means obvious. Furthermore, it is apparent that companies differ considerably in the solutions to these problems that they have devised.

In general, therefore, it seems reasonable to conclude that although the division of labour may greatly enhance the prospect of significant benefit, it simultaneously creates serious challenges that have to be dealt with if the benefits are to be realised. Neither is it possible to 'optimise' this all-too-human innovation system.

Where Is the Entrepreneur?

To return to Schumpeter's discussion of the obsolescence of the entrepreneur, where are the entrepreneurs in this division of innovation labour? The answer is: They have disappeared. They have metamorphosed into the research, development, production, and marketing/sales functions. The entrepreneur as 'person who makes innovation happen' is no more, in this division of innovation labour.

Having said this, however, although the entrepreneur as person who makes innovation happen has died, the entrepreneurship function (or, more accurately, functions that together make innovation happen) is alive and well. In short: the entrepreneur is dead; long live entrepreneurship!

It is important to note, though, that the present discussion has focused on the division of innovation labour in the modern large company. This does not preclude the entrepreneur's continued existence in other parts of the economy. In these parts the entrepreneur's reign may continue in the realm of entrepreneurial companies. There is also the possibility that the entrepreneur may be found in the interstices of the modern large company, even one characterised by the division of innovation labour that we have discussed here. This possibility will be further examined later in this chapter.

Subdivision of Innovation According to How Innovation Happens

Exhibit 7.1 shows how innovation labour is divided in many large companies. However, this is based on what people do, e.g. research, development, production, marketing, and sales. It is not based on how innovation happens. In this section a stylised 'subdivision of innovation functions' is provided, to use Marshall's words, based on how innovation happens. This categorisation is based on the nine propositions about how innovation happens developed in Chapter 6 that draw on the study in that chapter of the transistor, microprocessor, laser, and optical fibre.

According to this categorisation, innovation may be divided into the following four functions:

1. Creating innovation hypotheses
2. Selecting innovation hypotheses
3. Testing and developing the selected hypotheses into product/service
4. Marketing and selling the developed product/service.

These four innovation functions are depicted in Exhibit 7.2.

It will be recalled from the discussion earlier in this chapter that Schumpeter suggested that the role of the entrepreneur is to 'carry out innovation' rather than to make the invention upon which innovation is often based. We took issue with his distinction between invention and innovation, arguing that innovation also involves creating a new idea, specifically a new innovation hypothesis. Our argument is reflected in the first function, creating the innovation hypothesis.

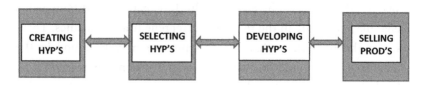

EXHIBIT 7.2 Subdivision of Innovation According to How Innovation Happens

The remaining three functions may, following Schumpeter, be thought of as 'carrying out' the innovation hypothesis.

The Difference between the Categorisations in Exhibits 7.1 and 7.2

To repeat, the categorisation shown in Exhibit 7.1 is based on what different people do in many modern large companies, i.e. research, development, etc. However, in Exhibit 7.2 the categorisation is based on the functions that must be performed in making innovation happen. But an important aim in most modern large companies is to make innovation happen, and this purpose underlies the division of innovation labour into research, production, etc. So, what is the relationship between these two categorisations?

The answer is that the four innovation functions shown in Exhibit 7.2 (creating innovation hypotheses, etc.) must also be performed collectively by those who do research, development, etc. However, who does the four Exhibit 7.2 functions, how they do them, and how they coordinate amongst one another in doing them often differs from company to company and from case to case in each company.

Microsoft, for example, has chosen to locate research in university-like research laboratories in different parts of the world. For example, computer research is located in its Cambridge laboratory in the midst of the buildings of Cambridge University. These researchers have a significant degree of autonomy in doing their work. Google, on the other hand, has selected to embed its researchers in customer-facing so-called engineering units. In both cases, however, researchers are expected to come up with innovation hypotheses that will benefit the mother company.

It is relevant to ask of the modern large company with the kind of division of innovation labour shown in Exhibit 7.1: Who does the functions referred to in Exhibit 7.2, how are they performed, and what are the challenges that are faced in performing them? This question is relevant because it relates precisely to the difficulties that both

Marshall and Hayek referred to regarding the division of labour in organising the creation of knowledge and innovation.

THE LEAN STARTUP, BY ERIC RIES

To examine further many of the issues raised in this chapter, we will discuss in detail the book by Eric Ries, *The Lean Startup: How Constant Innovation Creates Radically Successful Businesses.*[27] There are several reasons for choosing to do this.

The first is that the book relates very closely to the concerns of this chapter. Second, the book has become an iconic best-seller. Not only has it sold widely in significant numbers in many countries of the world, it also has many enthusiastic adherents who have set up online communities to further propagate the messages of the book. The third and most important reason is that, going by the enthusiasm generated, there appears to be evidence that the innovation methods proposed do actually work. Finally, despite the book's title, Ries claims that its lessons are just as relevant for large companies as they are for start-ups and, indeed, that they are also relevant for organisations in the nonfirm sector such as government departments.

What are the innovation methods proposed in the book? What implications do they have for the present discussions? Most specifically, what implications do they have for the two main questions posed in this chapter: Who makes innovation happen? Has the entrepreneur become obsolete?

Eric Ries

Ries is a Silicon Valley entrepreneur and software product developer. He was cofounder and chief technology officer of a Silicon Valley software company called IMVU, which he established in 2004 with Will Harvey. His experiences in this company and the lessons he learned led him to write his book, *The Lean Startup*.

---

[27] Ries, E., 2011. *The Lean Startup: How Constant Innovation Creates Radically Successful Businesses*. Penguin.

An important early influence whilst he was at IMVU was an academic, Steve Blank, who was also an early investor in IMVU. Blank insisted that the company's executives attended his class on entrepreneurship at the University of California, Berkeley. Blank had developed his idea of rapid customer feedback that he called 'customer development'. These ideas would have a significant impact on Ries's thinking. Also important was Ries's reflections on the reasons for his own failings and those of others in their attempts to successfully develop software products.

Ries's experiences at IMVU have been written up and used as case studies in business schools, including the Graduate School of Business at Stanford University and Harvard Business School where Ries has served as an entrepreneur in residence. Ries's ideas, as noted, have stimulated the establishment of communities around the world interested in applying the principles of *The Lean Startup*. Lean Startup meetings are held in ninety-four cities in seventeen countries.[28]

The Prism through Which Ries Views Innovation

In examining Ries's work, it is important to understand the background from which he has come. This, understandably, has coloured the way he sees innovation and the concerns on which he has focused. As Ries himself has put it, 'I am one of those people who grew up programming computers, and so my journey to thinking about entrepreneurship and management has taken a circuitous path.'

More specifically, he has 'always worked on the product development side of [his] industry; [his] partners and bosses were managers or marketers, and [his] peers worked in engineering and operations'.[29] Significantly, his thinking has been shaped by the development of online digital software products, and this, as will be seen, has some important implications.

---

[28] *theleanstartup.com* (accessed 8 November 2016).   [29] *The Lean Startup*, p. 5.

Definition of Start-Up and Entrepreneur

Ries defines a start-up as 'a human institution designed to create new products and services under conditions of extreme uncertainty'.[30] This uncertainty has very important implications. The reason is that it implies that 'Startups do not yet know who their customer is or what their product should be.'[31] From this starting point Ries assumes that 'The goal of a startup is to figure out the right thing to build – the things customers want and will pay for – as quickly as possible.'

This starting point also leads to Ries's definition of an entrepreneur: 'Anyone who is creating a new product or business under conditions of extreme uncertainty is an entrepreneur whether he or she knows it or not.' Entrepreneurs, furthermore, are to be found not only in for-profit firms. They are also to be found 'working in a government agency, a venture-backed company, a non-profit, or a decidedly for-profit company with financial investors'.[32] Similarly, they are to be found not only in small start-ups but also in large, established companies.

Definition of Product and Innovation

Ries defines a product as 'one that encompasses any source of value for the people who become customers'. Unusually, however, a product is defined broadly to include aspects that go beyond the artefact itself: 'Anything those customers experience from their interaction with a company should be considered part of that company's product.'[33]

Innovation is also defined broadly to include 'novel scientific discoveries, repurposing an existing technology for a new use, devising a new business model that unlocks value that was hidden, or simply bringing a product or service to a new location or a previously underserved set of customers.'[34]

---

[30] Ibid., pp. 8 and 27.   [31] Ibid., p. 9.   [32] Ibid., p. 27.   [33] Ibid., p. 28.   [34] Ibid.

Why Lean?

From the outset, Ries makes clear why he uses the term 'lean'. The concept comes from the Japanese notion of just-in-time manufacture. More specifically, he explains that in attempting to deal with the problems of new product development in his start-up software companies, he was inspired by the writings of key Toyota engineers such as Taiichi Ohno.

In the early 1950s, with Toyota under severe financial pressures and facing opposition from its own workforce, Ohno attempted to tackle areas of significant inefficiency in his company. In the first instance he introduced several piecemeal organisational changes that had their own knock-on effects. Eventually, these incremental improvements had substantial cumulative effects, resulting in the just-in-time system that revolutionised the dominant manufacturing paradigm, not only in Japan but worldwide.[35]

For Ries, however, the main message that emerges from this Toyota story is the need to eliminate waste. Applying this thinking in *The Lean Startup*, Ries argues that any new product development activity that does not add, immediately and directly and on the basis of experimental evidence, to product value should be regarded as 'waste' and eliminated. By 'lean' product development he means development that does not involve such waste.

The Lean Startup *Innovation Process*

How does an entrepreneur so defined – whether in a start-up, an established large company, or a government department – go about innovating? In this section we will answer this question by examining the *Lean Startup* innovation process.

---

[35] For a brief account of the origins of Toyota's *kanban* and just-in-time systems, see Fransman, M., 1994. 'Knowledge segmentation–integration in theory and in Japanese companies', in Granstrand, O. (ed.), *Economics of Technology*. Amsterdam: North-Holland, pp. 172–5.

Step 1: Vision

The *Lean Startup* innovation process begins with what Ries calls vision. It is its vision that gives the organisation direction: 'Startups ... have a true north, a destination in mind: creating a thriving and world-changing business. I call that a startup's *vision*.'[36]

In innovating, 'The first step would be to break down the grand vision into its component parts. The two most important assumptions entrepreneurs make are what I call the value hypothesis and the growth hypothesis.'

According to Ries, the '*value hypothesis* tests whether a product or service really delivers value to customers once they are using it'. It is the '*growth hypothesis* which tests how new customers will discover a product or service ... how will it spread ... from initial early adopters to mass adoption'.[37] Later Ries refers to these two hypotheses as '*leap-of-faith* assumptions', the 'riskiest elements of a startup's plan, the parts on which everything depends'.[38]

Step 2: Strategy

To 'achieve' their vision, 'startups employ a *strategy*'. This strategy 'includes a business model, a product road map, a point of view about partners and competitors, and ideas about who the customers will be'.[39]

Step 3: Product

'The *product* is the end result of this strategy.'[40] The problem, however, is that 'Most of the time customers don't know what they want in advance.'[41] This leads the argument to Step 4.

---

[36] *The Lean Startup*, p. 22, emphasis in original. Page 23 contains one of Ries's few diagrams. Without a heading, the diagram shows a triangle with the bottom layer labelled 'vision'. The middle layer is called 'strategy' and the top layer 'product'.
[37] Ibid., p. 61.   [38] Ibid., p. 76.   [39] Ibid., p. 22.   [40] Ibid.   [41] Ibid., p. 49.

Step 4: *Testing through Experimenting*

For Ries it is crucial that 'the goal of a startup's early efforts be to test them [i.e. the leap of faith value and growth hypotheses and the product] as quickly as possible'. This in turn leads to two challenges. 'The first challenge for an entrepreneur is to build an organisation that can test these assumptions systematically. The second challenge, as in all entrepreneurial situations, is to perform that rigorous testing without losing sight of the company's overall vision.'[42]

Summarising the approach advocated in the *Lean Startup* model, Ries states that in this approach 'every product, every feature, every marketing campaign – everything a startup does – is understood to be an experiment designed to achieve validated learning'.[43]

Indeed, Ries takes this even further, arguing that an experiment is also a product: 'In the Lean Startup model, an experiment is more than just a theoretical inquiry; it is also a first product. If this or any other experiment is successful, it allows the manager to get started with his or her campaign: enlisting early adopters, adding ... to each further experiment or iteration, and eventually starting to build a product. By the time that product is ready to be distributed widely, it will already have established customers.'[44]

It is important to note that this implies that there is a feedback interaction between steps 3 and 4. With the passage of time and the process of experimentation, testing, and iteration, the final product and its customers emerge. This is apparent in one of the key concepts in *The Lean Startup*, the *Build-Measure-Learn* feedback loop.

As Ries explains, 'a startup is a catalyst that transforms ideas into products. As customers interact with those products, they generate feedback and data. The feedback is both qualitative (such as what they like and don't like) and quantitative (such as how many people use it and find it valuable) ... the products a startup builds are really experiments; the learning about how to build a sustainable business is the outcome of those experiments'.[45]

---

[42] Ibid., p. 81.   [43] Ibid., p. 55.   [44] Ibid., pp. 63–4.   [45] Ibid., p. 75.

This is visualised as a three-step process. 'This Build-Measure-Learn feedback loop is at the core of the Lean Startup model.'[46] However – and this is where the 'lean' dimension enters the argument – 'build' must not be done in a wasteful way. 'Building' requires that only the minimum necessary to experiment and test should be done. This is expressed in another of *The Lean Startup*'s key concepts: the *minimum viable product*:

> Once clear on [the] leap-of-faith assumptions, the first step is to enter the Build phase as quickly as possible with a minimum viable product (MVP). The MVP is that version of the product that enables a full turn of the Build-Measure-Learn loop with a minimum amount of effort and the least amount of development time.

Ries continues:

> The minimum viable product lacks many features that may prove essential later on. However, in some ways, creating a MVP requires extra work: we must be able to measure its impact. For example, it is inadequate to build a prototype that is evaluated solely for internal quality by engineers and designers. We also need to get it in front of potential customers to gauge their reactions. We may even need to try selling them the prototype.[47]

Step 5: Persevere or Pivot

The final step, having reflected on the experimental testing feedback, involves deciding whether to 'persevere or to pivot'. 'Every entrepreneur eventually faces an overriding challenge in developing a successful product: deciding when to pivot and when to persevere. Everything that has been discussed so far is a prelude to a seemingly simple question: are we making sufficient progress to believe that our original strategic hypothesis is correct, or do we need to make a major change?'

[46] Ibid., p. 76.   [47] Ibid., pp. 76–7.

Ries defines a pivot as 'a structured course correction designed to test a new fundamental hypothesis about the product, strategy, and engine of growth'. This challenging decision, he emphasises, cannot be simply routinised or automated: 'There is no way to remove the human element – vision, intuition, judgment – from the practice of entrepreneurship.'[48]

With a pivot the whole process begins again, entering a second round.

Who Makes Innovation Happen in the Lean Startup Model?

Here Ries is less clear. More specifically, he is not clear whether 'entrepreneur' refers to a *person* or to a set of *functions*. If the latter, is someone who performs at least one of the functions an entrepreneur? And if this is the case, since there are so many functions involved in the total process of innovation, then the question is: Who is *not* an entrepreneur? If the definition of entrepreneur is so wide as to include all the functions necessary for innovation – including coming up with ideas, selecting them, testing and developing them, and marketing and selling them – then surely the concept has lost its conventional purpose of designating a subgroup in the economy who possess the rare set of skills needed to make innovation happen. In this case, it seems, we are referring not to a person who makes innovation happen but to a set of entrepreneurial functions that are necessary to make it happen.

To illustrate this lack of clarity, when Ries refers to making the challenging decision on whether to persevere or pivot (as just quoted under step 5 above), it is clear that he has the entrepreneur as person in mind. It is this person who exercises 'vision, intuition, judgment'. However, as noted earlier, he defines an entrepreneur as 'Anyone who is creating a new product or business under conditions of extreme uncertainty'.[49] But what if a person is involved in only one of several

---

[48] Ibid., p. 149.   [49] Ibid., p. 27.

functions that jointly are necessary to make innovation happen? Is that person an entrepreneur?

Muddying the conceptual waters further, elsewhere he refers to 'the entrepreneurial *prerequisites*', which include 'proper team structure, good personnel, a strong vision for the future, and an appetite for risk taking'.[50] He continues: 'Thus when I use the term *entrepreneur* I am referring to the whole startup ecosystem.'[51] Unfortunately, however, he does not clarify what he means by the 'whole startup ecosystem'.

Furthermore, Ries argues that a 'comprehensive theory of entrepreneurship should address all the functions of an early-stage venture'. These functions include 'vision and concept, product development, marketing and sales, scaling up, partnerships and distribution, and structure and organisational design. It has to provide a method for measuring progress in the context of extreme uncertainty.' Such a theory of entrepreneurship 'can give entrepreneurs clear guidance on how to make the many trade-off decisions they face'.[52]

But what he does not make clear is which of these functions should be the responsibility of the entrepreneur as person who makes innovation happen and which can be left to others involved in the innovation process. Surely, all of these functions cannot be the responsibility of the entrepreneur as person and neither can all of the people involved in these functions be called entrepreneurs. The second part of his statement makes it clear that it is entrepreneurs who make 'the many trade-off decisions' involved in innovation, presumably as opposed to the others who, although they perform innovation functions, are not involved in these trade-off decisions. But how labour should be divided – to pursue the theme of specialisation and division of labour in innovation discussed earlier – between the entrepreneur and these others is not made clear.

Ries also distinguishes between the role of the 'product development team' and the 'business leadership team'.[53] But once again

---

[50] Ibid., p. 26.   [51] Ibid., p. 27.   [52] Ibid., p. 19.   [53] Ibid., pp. 164 and 201.

there is no clarification regarding whether there is a division of labour between the activities of these teams and those of the entrepreneur.

Accordingly, as these quotations clearly suggest, we have no option but to conclude that whilst *The Lean Startup* is exceptionally clear about *what* needs to be done to develop new products and services, it is very unclear about *who* should do it. Little light is thrown, therefore, on the Schumpeterian question of whether the entrepreneur as person who makes innovation happen has become obsolete and has been replaced by a set of entrepreneurial functions undertaken individually and jointly by numerous people organised through a division of labour that gives each of them responsibility for only a small part of the total process.

The Strengths of The Lean Startup

It is not at all surprising that *The Lean Startup* has been given the attention it has. As our discussion of the *Lean Startup* innovation process clearly demonstrates, the argument is concise and clearly laid out and the recommendations are both practical and implementable. Furthermore, the proof of the pudding is in the eating. Many practitioners have tasted and liked what they tasted, coming back for more.

Having said this, however, the *Lean Startup* model has some serious limitations. Enthusiasm with the argument of the *Lean Startup* model should not blind readers to its shortcomings. Some of these will now be discussed.

The Limitations of The Lean Startup

The main limitation of *The Lean Startup* is its overly narrow focus on new product development in the software industry. True, this narrow focus is also the book's strength. What it does it does extremely well. Neither is this focus surprising. As we have made clear, Ries himself has emphasised that he comes to the questions of innovation and entrepreneurship primarily through the role that he has played as a new software product developer.

The main problem with the book lies in what it does not do. This could be overlooked in a book with a title to do with new product development. The subtitle of *The Lean Startup*, however, promises far more: 'How Constant Innovation Creates Radically Successful Businesses.' As we have pointed out, Ries argues that his model applies not only to software-based start-ups, but also to large, established, for-profit companies, the whole of the nonfirm sector including government departments, and also start-ups more generally.

Specifically, the book's subtitle promises a solution to the innovation problem in general, not only to the problem of new product development. But 'innovation', as the present book shows, is about many complex issues that collectively go far beyond new product development.

In the next section we will examine some of these issues.

WHO NEEDS TO DO WHAT? CREATING AN ORGANISATION'S INNOVATION ECOSYSTEM AND DIVISION OF LABOUR TO MAKE INNOVATION HAPPEN

An innovation ecosystem may be defined as a set of players and processes that, through their interactions, make innovation happen and thus coevolve. Earlier in the present book this concept of innovation ecosystems was applied at a more aggregated level, namely at the level of countries as a whole and also at sector level, specifically the ICT sector. Here we will be concerned with innovation ecosystems at the level of the individual organisation, whether for-profit companies, large or small, or nonprofit organisations, including government departments.

This section draws on the discussion of specialisation and the division of innovation labour that was examined earlier in the present chapter. It also makes use of the insights and conclusions of the previous chapter, which analysed how innovation happens based on the examination of the cases of the transistor, microprocessor, laser, and optical fibre.

The process that will be followed is to examine, in chronological order, the functions that must be carried out in making innovation happen. The case where this involves the establishment of a new firm will also be considered.

Coming up with an Innovation Hypothesis

As the last chapter demonstrated, innovation starts with an innovation hypothesis. This hypothesis puts forward an initial set of propositions regarding what the innovation involves and how it will add value for the initially intended consumer-users. Following Schumpeter, innovation includes not only new products and services (the focus of *The Lean Startup*) but also new processes and technologies, forms of organisation, markets, ways of marketing, and business models. Those who consume and use the innovation may be either external or internal to the organisation.

The first innovation function involves creating an innovation hypothesis. But how is this done? Where does the hypothesis come from? Whose role is it to create innovation hypotheses? What circumstances are needed to create conditions conducive to generating innovation hypotheses? These questions need to be asked and answered by an organisation wanting to make innovation happen.

Underlying these questions is the assumption, examined in detail in the last chapter, that an innovation hypothesis is an indeterminate act of creation. It is indeterminate in the sense that the hypothesis that will be created cannot be predicted from the antecedent set of conditions that precede it. In Schumpeter's words, discussed earlier, it is a 'creative response' rather than an adaptive response. It is the innovation hypothesis that injects novelty into the organisation and, if it is new to the world, also into the economy.

Coming up with an innovation hypothesis is included in step 1 in the *Lean Startup* model, which deals with what Ries terms 'vision'. However, he neither asks nor answers the questions just posed. His vision falls like manna from heaven, exogenous to the *Lean Startup* model, and becomes its starting driving force.

Testing and Implementing the Innovation Hypothesis and Formulating Strategy

Following closely on the heels of the innovation hypothesis come questions about how the hypothesis should be both tested and implemented. As was stressed in the last chapter, uncertainty is inherent in the notion of hypothesis. We do not know if it is true. It therefore has to be tested. Testing and implementation are intricately interconnected.

Implementation also involves the development of an initial (soon to be evolving) strategy. This strategy is a statement of purpose, a statement of what will be done to realise the innovator's (and also the organisation's) purposes. If the organisation operates under competitive conditions, that is, competing with rivals for consumer-users, then achieving competitiveness will be a major strategic imperative, though not the only one.

The point about the possibility of competitors arriving on the scene makes it clear we are already, even though at this point implicitly, thinking in terms of an innovation ecosystem that transcends the organisation's boundaries. At this stage the players in this ecosystem already include external customer-users and current competitors (though account should also be taken of potential competitors who may enter the market and compete).

If the innovation hypothesis is being created in an already established organisation, then its creation will have to take account of the priorities and constraints imposed on this innovation process by the organisation in which it is housed. It may be, for example, that overall strategy will not need to be formulated ab initio but will be given by the mother organisation.

In dealing with these issues, however, little guidance is offered by the *Lean Startup* model. As we saw, step 2 in the *Lean Startup* model, 'strategy', is also assumed to be exogenous. It is a driver of the *Lean Startup* innovation process but where it comes from, how it is formulated, what form it takes, how it should be created, etc. is not discussed by the model itself.

Starting the Start-Up

If the decision has been made to implement the innovation hypothesis through the establishment of a new organisation, as is usually the case with an entrepreneurial start-up, then an additional set of issues arise. These were discussed earlier in this chapter through Schumpeter's notion of the 'frictions' that are often confronted by innovations, which in his view provide a traditional justification for the existence of the classical entrepreneur. We broadened Schumpeter's discussion by adding complications caused by factors such as uncertainty, asymmetric information, the possible existence of opportunism, and inertia.

In starting a start-up one of the important and necessary functions, bedevilled by the existence of these complications, is to raise initial money, find managers, and recruit innovation team members. All of these people will need to be persuaded by the initial innovation hypothesis and strategy. This requires a convincing narrative, told by a convincing person (here machines certainly will not do, since that quintessentially human element, trust, is crucial), in a convincing way.

This is another set of crucial issues that the *Lean Startup* model does not examine as a result of its exclusive focus on new product development. The startup in *The Lean Startup* is simply assumed to exist. How it came to be is not part of the *Lean Startup* story.

The function of raising money is immediately complicated by the imperfections in the market for innovation money, imperfections caused by uncertainty, asymmetric information, the possibility of opportunism, etc. Imagine the poor person tasked with this function sitting across the desk from the bank manager/venture capitalist/ angel investor/private equity investor and having to tell, within a very limited time, a sufficiently persuasive narrative in order to be offered the money needed. Little more need be said.

A similar problem arises in convincing managers and potential innovation team members that this start-up, based on this innovation hypothesis and this strategy, is the right thing for them.

The inclusion of money providers, necessary for the starting of the start-up, widens the organisation's innovation ecosystem even further. Money providers become one of the group of players whose joint actions produce innovation. Therefore, the hypotheses to be tested as part of the development process include not only hypotheses about products and consumer-users (the focus of *The Lean Startup*) but also hypotheses relating to the wants, needs, and objectives of money providers without whose money the start-up show cannot get on the road.

Co-Creating Products and Customers through Experimenting, Testing, and Learning

An understanding of the functions that need to be performed to achieve these things is provided by the *Lean Startup* model. It is here that its new product development focus comes into its own.

However, when *The Lean Startup* refers to 'product development', it is often implicitly referring specifically to digital online products. This focus limits its applicability.

The difficulty here is that experimentation and testing is often more easily done with digital online products that can readily and at low cost attract significant numbers of early adopters. This makes practices proposed in *The Lean Startup* such as split testing feasible (where different groups of customers are offered different versions of the same product). When the product is complex and nondigital, however, far more costly to develop even in minimum viable form, and initially capable of attracting only few early adopters, then experimentation and testing become a completely different ball game. Here the *Lean Startup* model is far less useful.

Moreover, as already noted, the focus needs to be broadened to take into account not only the emerging product and the symbiotic relationship between innovators in the organisation and their customers. Attention will also have to be constantly paid to actual and potential competitors and to money providers as already discussed. Thus, to take an example, second and subsequent rounds of funding are crucial for the progress of most start-ups. Hypotheses, explicit and implicit, about these other crucial players in the organisation's innovation ecosystem therefore also need to be tested.

Learning and Evaluating from Feedback

Feedback is continually being generated by the innovators' efforts to implement and test the propositions contained in the innovation hypothesis. By learning from and creatively responding to this feedback, this hypothesis and its propositions are continually being changed, never remaining static but being in a constant process of flux, becoming other than they were.

But this is not an automatic process. It requires human assessment and judgment. This takes place under conditions of uncertainty; that is, frequently it is not clear ex ante what the correct response is. But neither is the process random. It therefore cannot be automated. It is, essentially, a human subjective process that takes place under uncertainty. It is one of the innovation process's most important, but also one of its most difficult, functions. Not just anyone is capable of doing it. It includes the persevere-or-pivot decision that the *Lean Startup* model does a good job explaining.

Including Players from Outside the Organisation

At some stage, the organisation's innovators will have to consciously decide how they will deal with relevant players outside their organisation. We have already discussed the cases of customers and the providers of money.

At a very early stage, innovators will also have to deal with suppliers to the organisation for the simple reason that organisations are never fully self-sufficient and will have to depend on outside suppliers for some inputs. But it is also possible to look at suppliers from an innovation perspective, seeing them not simply as the providers of inputs but also as the possessors of capabilities and resources that may be able to be mobilised by the organisation's innovators to help realise their innovation objectives and ambitions.

Similar considerations also apply to other outsiders, including partners of various kinds, university researchers, government research institutes, and intermediaries who may be important conduits in reaching customers. Key questions arise such as the formulation of subsidiary hypotheses regarding how these outside players might contribute to the organisation's innovation process. These hypotheses also need to be experimented with, tested, and evaluated. This is an important innovation function, raising additional questions about who should have responsibility in this area and how they should do their job. These considerations are not dealt with by the *Lean Startup* model, as a result of its restrictive focus only on new product development.

The inclusion of these kinds of issues makes the organisation's innovation ecosystem more complex. At the same time, it complicates the processes and functions that are needed in order to effectively leverage these potentially valuable outside sources of knowledge, capabilities, and resources.

General Considerations

The specialised innovation functions discussed in this chapter and the division of innovation labour that they imply are by no means comprehensive. Indeed, following Marshall's notion of ever-increasing subdivision of functions, it is to be expected that over time this process of division of labour will continue. New functions will emerge and old functions be subdivided. This continuous process of the division of labour coincides and interacts with the other innovation processes discussed here. Together they are all part and parcel of what it means to be an innovating organisation in a constantly changing world.

Conclusion: So, Is the Entrepreneur Obsolete?

One of the key questions asked in this chapter is: Who makes innovation happen? In answering this question, we first provided a brief sketch of the 'classical, iconic entrepreneur' beloved in many narratives. We then pursued the issue through a discussion of Schumpeter's views on the role of the entrepreneur and the function of entrepreneurship. We also examined the arguments that led him to conclude that the entrepreneur was becoming obsolete in a world of large, regularly innovating companies and consumers. However, we rejected his arguments that 'routinisation' and 'provability' were causing the obsolescence of the entrepreneur.

Instead, we argued that to understand the changes that have been taking place in innovation processes and in the roles played by the people involved in making it happen, it is fruitful to see these changes as part of the broader continuous process of specialisation and the division of labour. To understand this process is greater detail, the contributions of Adam Smith, Alfred Marshall, and Friedrich Hayek were examined. This provided the basis for our own discussion of the division of innovation labour and its various functions in creating an organisation's innovation ecosystem, a discussion that included the contribution of Eric Ries's *The Lean Startup*.

Where does this leave us regarding the question of whether the entrepreneur is becoming, or has become, obsolete? Our conclusion is that this is not the appropriate question to ask. Rather, it is appropriate to ask how the process of the division of innovation labour has led to new specialised innovation functions, many of which have been discussed in this chapter.

Who performs these functions and whether, as in Adam Smith's example of pin manufacture, functions that were performed by one person are now performed by several is an important question to ask and answer. The answer could throw light on the significant issue of whether productivity in the process of innovating is increasing, with significant implications for the growth of companies and countries.

But what the people who perform these functions are to be called, specifically whether they should be designated as 'entrepreneurs' or not, is purely a question of naming. As the great man wrote, 'What's in a name? That which we call a rose / By any other word would smell as sweet.'

It makes little substantive difference if, on the one hand, we reserved the title of 'entrepreneur' for only some of the functions of innovation (and even then, there would inevitably be disagreement regarding where the boundary should be drawn between entrepreneurs and nonentrepreneurs) or, on the other, we referred to all those involved in innovation functions as entrepreneurs. What does matter at any point in time is what functions must be performed if innovation is to happen, who should perform these functions, and how they should do them. These are crucial questions that must be considered in designing an organisation's innovation ecosystem.

8 Innovation Ecosystems and Financial Markets*
The Telecoms Boom and Bust, 1996–2003

An innovation ecosystem has been defined in this book as a collection of interdependent players and processes that, through their interactions, jointly make innovation happen. Over time, through these interactions, the players and processes coevolve. But this ecosystem is not isolated. It interacts in numerous ways with other ecosystems. One of these ecosystems is the financial services ecosystem, which consists of those players and processes who jointly provide financial services.

How do these two kinds of ecosystem interact? The answer is: in a multiplicity of ways. The present chapter focuses on one way, by examining some of the mechanisms through which the attendant beliefs and expectations that accompany innovation are carried over into financial markets. On occasion the transmission is smooth with immediate mutually beneficial consequences. On other occasions the transmission is disruptive, causing significant fallout in both ecosystems and even threatening the economy as a whole.

An example of the latter is the Telecoms Boom and Bust, 1996–2003, which had just such an impact. It is this event, which illustrates the significant financial instability that radical innovation can produce, that is the object of study in this chapter.

BACKGROUND

The reason why innovation is such a potent economic force is that it creates new opportunities. Companies, investors, and consumers, for

* Reprinted from *Journal of Evolutionary Economics*, The telecoms boom and bust 1996–2003 and the role of financial markets, vol. 14, 2004, 369–406, Martin Fransman, © Springer-Verlag 2004, with permission of Springer.

example, are confronted with new possibilities created by innovation. These new opportunities provide incentives to act, to set up new entrepreneurial businesses, to make new investments, to consume new bundles of goods and services. These actions stimulate economies, raising output, including the new goods and services, and generating new demands for employees.

Often, however, perhaps even usually, there is at first a significant lack of clarity regarding the nature of the opportunities that are becoming available as a result of the new innovation. For example, Andy Grove, one of the founders of Intel, the company in which the microprocessor was invented, later confessed that he originally thought that the use of this device would be confined to simple applications such as in traffic lights. As we saw in Chapter 6, on how innovation happens, the laser was described as a solution looking for problems. Theodore Maiman, the inventor of the first working laser, admitted that he had absolutely no idea that the device would make significant contributions in areas as distant as medicine. Thomas Watson, the founder of IBM, originally believed that in the whole of the United States there would be demand for only a handful of mainframe computers. There are many other similar stories.

All these stories have in common the creation, following the emergence of an innovation, of a set of beliefs and associated expectations that eventually, with the passage of time and the exploration of the potential of the innovation, turn out with hindsight to have been fundamentally misguided. In some cases, the mistaken beliefs and expectations, under the influence of correcting flows of feedback information, adapt and facilitate, without much disruption, new paths exploring the potential of the innovation. However, in other cases the beliefs and expectations that turn out to be incorrect have huge disrupting effects.

One area in which such disruption has on occasion arisen is in financial markets. This raises important questions regarding the relationship between innovation and financial markets.

What is the connection between innovation and financial markets? The answer is that innovation often leads to beliefs and expectations regarding opportunities to make above-average profits. These beliefs and expectations are acted upon through the purchase of assets, both real and financial, that the buyer assumes will benefit from the opportunities opened up by the innovation. Investment in the global railways bonanzas of the late nineteenth century is one well-known example.

If these beliefs and expectations are sufficiently strong and widespread, they can lead to a significant increase in the relative price of financial assets such as equities, creating capital gains for shareholders. The gains, in turn, signal to other investors that above-average returns may be earned in this area. Cumulative effects may follow, leading to a self-reinforcing cycle of expectations creation, followed by expectations confirmation, followed by further increases in relative asset prices, etc. This cycle has the makings of a boom and even what Charles Kindleberger, an expert on financial booms and busts, called mania as more and more investors jump in to take advantage of the rising share prices.

In Chapter 6, on how innovation happens, we examined in detail the innovation of the transistor, microprocessor, laser, and optical fibre that both individually and jointly provided the foundation for the creation of systems such as computers, telecoms switches, transmissions equipment, routers, servers, and mobile phones. With the passage of time these metamorphosed into the system of systems commonly known as the Internet. What impact did the advent of the Internet, a cluster of many interdependent innovations, have on financial markets? This is the question addressed in the present chapter.

INTRODUCTION

As the Telecoms Boom and Bust, and its cousin the Dot-Com Boom and Bust, 1996–2003, have painfully reminded us, financial crises are still as much a part of the modern information and communications technologies (ICT)-based economy as they were of previous economies. But why is this the case? Why are we apparently unable to learn lessons from the past and avoid what Charles Kindleberger

(2000) has called 'manias, panics and crashes'? Why is it that our sophisticated stock of information, made readily and relatively cheaply available to us by our investment in ICTs, and our abundant theories and models, have not allowed us to steer clear of these financial excesses?

The aim of this chapter is not to attempt to provide a definitive answer to these important but complex questions. Rather, the more modest aim is to highlight some of the processes and mechanisms that seem to have played a significant role in causing the Telecoms Boom and Bust, 1996–2003. The question of whether anything can be done about these processes and mechanisms in order to try and modify such financial excesses in the future is taken up in the conclusion.

PERIODISING THE TELECOMS BOOM AND BUST, 1996–2003

The analysis in this chapter is based on a periodisation that is shown in Exhibit 8.1. In this section, a brief description is provided of the periodisation as a whole, while in subsequent sections a more detailed analysis is provided of each of the four periods.

Brief Description of the Telecoms Boom and Bust, 1996–2003

In Period I (circa 1995–7) the process leading to the Telecoms Boom and Bust was triggered. The events that provided the trigger were the widespread commercial adoption of the Internet coupled with the prior liberalisation of telecoms markets.[1]

In 1995 it was recognised that the Internet was becoming a mass phenomenon of fundamental importance for the entire economy. But did the Internet create new opportunities for making above-average returns? And if so, who would profit from the Internet? Around these

---

[1] For a more detailed analysis of the advent of the Internet and its implications for the telecommunications industry, see M. Fransman, *Telecoms in the Internet Age: From Boom to Bust to ... ?* (Oxford University Press, 2002), chapter 2.

Exhibit 8.1 *A Periodisation of the Telecoms Boom and Bust,*
1996–2003 Period Description Characteristics

Period	Description	Characteristics
I (circa 1995–7)	Trigger	1. Events in the real economy
		2. The interpretive framework (i.e. the 'story')
		3. Macroeconomic conditions (money supply, interest rates, credit)
		4. Response of the financial markets and the making of paper profits
II (circa 1997 to early 2000)	Mania	1. Financial markets take over
		2. Beauty contests and benchmarking
III (circa early 2000)	Turning point	1. Growing contradiction between financial prices and real performance
		2. Panic
IV (circa early 2000–3)	Bust	1. Realignment of financial and real markets; devaluation of financial assets
		2. Shake-out and consolidation

questions a consensual interpretive framework began to be constructed. This framework would provide 'the story' justifying enthusiasm for the Telecoms Industry as a whole and several parts of it in
particular. Conducive macroeconomic conditions would further fuel
the fires of enthusiasm. This enthusiasm resulted in a sharp rise in the
share price of many telecoms companies, both incumbents and new
entrants.

In Period II (circa 1997 to early 2000) financial markets and their
dynamics became the prime drivers of the process, although they also
had effects on the real markets of the telecoms industry. The sharp
rise in the share price of many telecoms companies was reflected in
stock market indices against which the performance of most fund
managers was benchmarked. This was a specific instance (shaped by
modern routinised practices) of a more general phenomenon in stock

markets that John Maynard Keynes had characterised as a 'beauty contest'. According to this phenomenon, investors such as fund managers select shares not according to their own evaluations of the long-term performance of the companies concerned but in accordance with the way they believe other investors will select the shares. Indeed, as we shall see, as a result of the widespread practice of benchmarking, investors such as fund managers were *forced* to participate in the beauty contest in order to ensure that the performance of their funds kept up with those of competing funds. In this way a financial market dynamic was initiated that pushed the price of telecoms shares further upwards, entirely independently of what was happening in the 'real' telecoms industry.

However, financial markets did influence real markets insofar as the former's enthusiasm for telecoms shares spread – contagion is an appropriate word in this context – influencing real investment in the telecoms industry. In this way investment by telecoms network operators in equipment and other inputs increased to enable them to take advantage of the expected exploding demand for Internet-related services and the associated derived demand for telecoms carrying capacity. Accordingly, the revenue of telecoms equipment supplying companies and others supplying inputs increased, stimulating increases in their share prices too. In turn, this led, via the bench-marking beauty contest process, to further increases in the share prices of the companies supplying the telecoms operators.

However, in Period III a turning point was reached. The reason was the growing contradiction between financial prices and real performance in the telecoms industry, on the part of both telecoms operators and their input suppliers. To a large extent, as will be shown in detail below, lagging real performance in the telecoms industry resulted from changes on the supply side that had not been antici-pated in the consensual interpretive framework that provided the rationale for attractive returns in this industry. However, despite this growing contradiction, in the early part of Period III fund managers continued to invest in the shares of many of the leading telecoms companies. This important paradox will be analysed later. But eventually the pressure behind the dam wall, generated by the growing contradiction, was too great and enough holders of telecoms shares began to desert the cause, resulting in a sustained fall in telecoms share prices over a sufficiently long period to generate panic. Now the causation of the benchmarking processes went into reverse and it became necessary to sell telecoms shares in order to meet performance measures (i.e. in order to minimise negative growth in value).

In Period IV (circa early 2000–3) a major realignment of financial and real markets took place with the substantial devaluation of financial assets related to the telecoms companies (not only equity, but also bonds and other forms of debt). At the same time, much of the capital that hitherto had plugged the gap between growing expenditure on new networks and equipment and supportive business functions, on the one hand, and revenue, on the other, dried up, leaving many companies high and dry. Some exited, some filed for protection and later managed to limp on, but all scaled back drastically. Period IV ended with shake-out and consolidation that, ironically, increased the financial pressure while at the same time easing some of the competitive pressure on the companies that had managed to survive. The process of boom and bust, triggered by the Internet and telecoms liberalisation, had run its course.

PERIOD I: THE TRIGGER – CIRCA 1995–1997

Introduction

Charles Kindleberger (2000), the author of one of the classics on the economics of financial booms and busts, has had the following to say about the initial period that triggers a financial boom. Drawing on the work of Minsky (1975), Kindleberger states that

> events leading up to a crisis start with a 'displacement', some
> exogenous, outside shock to the macroeconomic system. The
> nature of this displacement varies from one speculative boom to
> another ... But whatever the source of the displacement, if it is

sufficiently large and pervasive, it will alter the economic outlook by changing profit opportunities in at least one important sector of the economy. Displacement brings opportunities for profit in some new or existing lines and closes out others. As a result, business firms and individuals with savings or credit seek to take advantage of the former and retreat from the latter. If the new opportunities dominate those that lose, investment and production pick up. A boom is under way.

(p. 14)

As is clear from this quotation (and from the book as a whole), Kindleberger implicitly assumes that the 'changing profit opportunities' that constitute a displacement are unproblematic. These new opportunities emerge and everyone recognises them as opportunities even if not everyone responds with concrete actions.

The Telecoms Boom, however, suggests that the displacement and its effects may not occur as automatically as is implied here. The reason was that there was considerable interpretive ambiguity regarding whether the Internet and telecoms liberalisation would provide profitable opportunities (more accurately, opportunities for above-average returns) for anyone. In order to make the causal link between the Internet and liberalisation, on the one hand, and opportunities for profit, on the other, an interpretive framework was needed, one that would persuade some of those with resources to put their bets on the telecoms industry. In other words, a justifying 'story' was needed. An important element in the present analysis of the Telecoms Boom and Bust, 1996–2003, is the creation of the justifying interpretive framework on which the story was based and the subsequent fate of this framework as the process of the boom unfolded.[2]

---

[2] It is not always the case that a shared justifying interpretive framework is created. In some cases the interpretive ambiguity is so great that it either prevents such a framework from being created or results in the creation of different contradictory frameworks. One such case, prevalent at the time of writing, is the housing market in the United Kingdom. House prices have gone through a period of sharp rises but

The Events That Triggered the Telecoms Boom

The Internet

The Internet had its origins in events that occurred from the late 1950s.[3] However, it was only from the late 1980s that the Internet began to take off as a mass phenomenon with economy-wide implications. Furthermore, it was only from the early to mid-1990s that some key individuals began to recognise that this was happening. Take, for example, Vinton Cerf, often referred to as one of the fathers of the Internet.[4] Cerf has stated that in 1977 he assumed that ARPANET, the earlier project on which the Internet as we know it today was based, 'would probably never get bigger than 128 networks'.[5] According to Cerf, 'We now know that the lift-off point for exponential growth [in the Internet] came around 1988, though it wasn't obvious at the time. I certainly didn't sense it in the early days.'[6] By 1996 the Internet was a network of some 50,000 networks.

Bill Gates, CEO of Microsoft, began to understand the implications of the Internet only in early 1995. On 6 October 1994 Gates wrote an internal memorandum titled 'Sea Change' that spelled out plans for networked computing in Microsoft. However, the system that he proposed was not intended to be Internet-compatible. Gates has stated that 'I wouldn't say it was clear [at this time] that [the

---

professional opinion is sharply divided about whether this 'boom' will be followed by a bust. The divergence of expectations under conditions of Knightian uncertainty may be thought of as a healthy response for the system as a whole since different options are covered and expectations to some extent tend to cancel one another out. In contrast, the Telecoms Boom was the more dangerous precisely because there was, to a significant extent, a consensual vision. When this vision turned out to have significant flaws (as will be seen below) the subsequent panic was all the more damaging.

[3] For details, see Fransman (2002a), pp. 60–70 and references cited therein.

[4] Cerf co-developed the Internet Protocol (IP) with Robert Kahn and made major contributions to the Transmission Control Protocol (TCP). Together, these protocols (TCP/IP) facilitate the connections between networks that make the Internet possible. Cerf later became a vice president in the telecoms operator MCI, the first major new entrant to challenge AT&T after its divestiture and the beginnings of liberalisation in the United States.

[5] Cerf (1996).   [6] Ibid.

Internet] was going to explode over the next couple of years. If you'd asked me then if most TV ads will have URLs [web addresses] in them, I would have laughed.[7] However, on 26 May 1995, Gates issued another internal memorandum, titled 'The Internet Tidal Wave', that finally confirmed his conversion to the belief that the Internet would drive developments in computing.

Telecoms Liberalisation

Earlier, in the mid-1980s, the evolutionary path of the global telecoms industry began to be significantly transformed with the simultaneous advent of telecoms liberalisation in the United States, United Kingdom, and Japan. Liberalisation created more readily identifiable opportunities for new entrants who would compete with the incumbent telecoms operators in these three countries, AT&T, British Telecom, and NTT.

One example from the United States illustrates the new opportunities that were created by liberalisation. In August 1983, US District Judge Harold Greene had given final approval for AT&T's divestiture of its local operations, the Bell Operating Companies. This measure, long opposed by AT&T, opened competition in the US long-distance market for the first time. Two companies – MCI and Sprint – quickly became the major facilities-based competitors to AT&T in the US long-distance telephone market.

One month later, in September 1983, a small group of people in Hattiesburg, Mississippi, decided to establish a small start-up company that would offer discounted long-distance calling, initially in the state of Mississippi. They decided to call the company Long Distance Discount Calling (LDDC).[8] They faced not only the option of building their own network to compete with AT&T – as MCI and Sprint would do – but also the option of becoming a 'reseller', that is, buying capacity from AT&T at a wholesale price (which was low at the time

---

[7] Quoted in Fransman (2002a), p. 67.
[8] The company later changed its name to Long Distance Discount Service (LDDS).

because AT&T had excess capacity) and reselling this capacity to long-distance customers at a price below that currently being charged by AT&T. This start-up would later change its name to WorldCom.

In August 1988 LDDS made its first of many acquisitions when it acquired Telephone Management Corp. This allowed LDDS to expand its services throughout Mississippi into Western Tennessee. In August 1989 LDDS went public through its acquisition of Advantage Companies Inc. By becoming a publicly quoted company, LDDS was able to reap increasing benefit from a virtuous circle that it subsequently exploited to the full: growing earnings leading to growing market capitalisation, leading to further acquisitions (financed principally with LDDS's own shares), leading to further business opportunities, leading to further earnings, etc. In December 1992, LDDS acquired Advanced Telecommunications Corp., allowing the consolidated company to become the fourth-largest US long-distance provider. In December 1993, LDDS had annual revenue of $1.14 billion and operating income of $198.2 million.

Exhibit 8.2 shows the rapidly increasing value of LDDS's shares from the time the company went public to 1993.

The message was clear to all those who wanted to hear it: telecoms liberalisation provided new opportunities for making money. And all this was still in the era of voice telephony, before the burgeoning Internet opened up the additional market for data communications.

Exhibit 8.2 *The Value of $100 Invested in LDDS in 1989*

Value	Date
$100	December 1989
$186	December 1990
$427	December 1991
$1,078	December 1993

Exhibit 8.3 *Funding for the World Telecoms Industry, 1996–2001*

Syndicated bank loans	$890 billion
Private equity and stock markets	$500 billion
Bond markets	$415 billion
Total	$1,805 billion

Macroeconomic Conditions

Without delving into the economic data that would only be an unnecessary distraction here, suffice it to say that macroeconomic conditions in the mid- to late 1990s were conducive to boom-type investments. Although global interest rates were to fall much further after the Telecoms Bust in an effort to revive the stalling world economy, in the mid- to late 1990s financial markets were able and willing to provide the funds that would stoke the Telecoms Boom. Exhibit 8.3 shows the funding for the telecoms industry between 1996 and 2001 that totalled $1,805 billion.[9]

Why did the investors behind these figures make these investments? The short answer is that they believed they would make above-average returns by doing so. But how did they come to this conclusion? The answer to this question is that they came to accept a 'story' about the telecoms industry based on an interpretive framework that provided the rationale for expecting above-average returns in the telecoms industry.

The Consensual Vision That Drove the Telecoms Boom

From around 1996–7 a shared framework began to emerge that purported to provide an accurate interpretation of what was happening in the telecoms industry and who the major winners would be. Stripped

---

[9] *Financial Times*, 5 September 2001.

Exhibit 8.4 *Beliefs Underpinning the Consensual Vision*

Belief 1	The Internet will drive an explosive demand for bandwidth.
Belief 2	New telecoms operators will out-compete the incumbents in providing this bandwidth.
Belief 3	Financial markets will support the fittest new operators.
Belief 4	Technical change will further reinforce the processes referred to in the first three beliefs.

Source: Fransman (2002a), pp. 9–11.

to its essentials, there were four main planks in this Consensual Vision.[10] These are shown in Exhibit 8.4.[11]

Belief 1: Explosive Demand for Bandwidth Will Beneit Telecoms Operators

In 1995 – the same year that Bill Gates finally acknowledged the significance of the Internet – Gates was invited by Warren Buffet, the billionaire investor 'sage of Omaha', to a private meeting for Buffet's investors in Dublin. It was at this meeting that the link between the burgeoning Internet and opportunities for profit in

---

[10] This 'Consensual Vision' has been reconstructed by the present author. It is based on a number of original sources. These include the telecoms reports of financial analysts; the presentational material of telecoms companies; material presented at telecoms conferences, including those focusing on the so-called alternative carriers; analyses of telecoms in the United States and European financial press; and last but not least, personal interviews by the author with several CEOs and other senior managers of leading European and US telecoms companies. In reconstructing this Consensual Vision one focus of attention was the work of Jack Benjamin Grubman and his associates at Salomon Smith Barney. According to *Business Week*, in the second half of the 1990s Grubman 'may have been the most influential person in the telecoms industry' (13 May 2002, p. 42). Between 1998 and 2000 Grubman helped Salomon Smith Barney to raise $53 billion for telecoms companies, more than any other firm on Wall Street. However, after the onset of the Telecoms Bust from March 2000, Grubman's influence quickly crumbled. At least ten of the major telecoms companies he strongly supported – including the most prominent such as WorldCom and Global Crossing – filed for bankruptcy. Grubman was later tried, convicted, and punished for fraudulently misrepresenting the prospects for the companies he publicly supported.

[11] The ensuing discussion is drawn from Fransman (2002a), pp. 9–11.

telecoms was formed in the minds of a number of important US investors. The same connection would soon be made by many others.

At this meeting Gates spoke about his newfound belief in the potential of the Internet. Attending the meeting was Walter Scott Jr, an engineer who had for decades been chairman of Peter Kiewit Sons', a Nebraskan conglomerate that had been primarily involved in construction. Hearing Gates, Scott came to the conclusion that the Internet would become a hugely important phenomenon.[12] Furthermore, he came to understand that the Internet was nothing more than a network of Internet Protocol (IP) networks. This insight led him later to create Level 3, one of a new generation of aggressive new entrant telecoms operators that built their networks on IP technology.

The starting belief in the Consensual Vision, accordingly, was demand-led. The rapid world-wide diffusion of the Internet would generate huge demand for telecoms capacity, which, in turn, would create significant opportunities for above-average profits for those telecoms network operating companies that were sufficiently well placed.

Belief 2: New Telecoms Operators Will Out-Compete the Incumbents in Providing This Bandwidth

But demand is one thing, opportunities for relatively profitable investment another. More specifically, who would be best placed to meet this demand: the incumbents (such as AT&T, BT, Deutsche Telekom, France Telecom, and NTT) or the new entrant telecoms operators? Would demand increase fast enough for both these groups of

---

[12] How did Scott react to Gates's comments? 'From my perspective, if Bill really thought the Internet was important and he needed to understand it, I thought it was important and we needed to understand it. And I thought that because I have a lot of faith and confidence in Bill knowing and understanding a lot more about these things than I do. And with the interest that Bill had in it, I just came back and told [my colleagues] that I thought it was something we now needed to do something about.' The result was a substantial series of investments made by Scott in Internet-related telecoms companies. Author's interview with Scott, Omaha, Nebraska, 2002.

companies to grow rapidly, or would a battle ensue with only one group emerging as victor? It was in answering this question that Grubman and his colleagues at Salomon Brothers made their contribution to shaping the second plank of the Consensual Vision: that the fittest new entrant telecoms operators would enjoy a competitive edge over the incumbents. This contribution came in the form of a number of studies of new entrant telecoms operators that included companies such as WorldCom, Qwest, and Level 3 in the United States, and COLT (City of London Telecommunications) and Energis in Europe.

In turn, this second plank was based on four other crucial assumptions. The first was that the incumbents, though enjoying advantages of economies of scale and scope, existing market domination, financial muscle, and brand recognition, were severely constrained technology-wise by their legacy networks.[13] Second, the technology constraint on incumbents created a window of opportunity for the new entrants who could rapidly deploy the latest technologies that were available on technology markets. In this way they could seize a technological competitive edge in their battle with the incumbents.[14]

Third, it was argued, the new entrants also possessed organisational advantages over their incumbent rivals. While the new entrants were small, focused, flexible, fast, and organizationally flat, their opponents were large, complex, hierarchical, bureaucratic, and prone

---

[13] Legacy networks refer to the incumbents' existing networks that embodied older generations of technology.

[14] In the studies by Salomon Brothers, for example, much was made of the deployment by the new entrants of new technologies such as Sonet/synchronous digital hierarchy (SDH) and self-healing ring architectures that facilitated higher bandwidth and quality of service. Reading the reports of Grubman at the time one was struck by his degree of confidence in interpreting and explaining to his largely nontechnical audience of financial people the implications of new technologies for stock market valuations.

These technical issues must have remained largely a mystery for many of them. As a former employee of AT&T, Grubman seemed well placed to provide such authoritative interpretations.

to inertia. Fourth, while the incumbents were impeded by regulation and universal service obligations, the new entrants could cream-skim. By concentrating investments in only the high-usage parts of the major cities (e.g. financial districts), with relatively small investments and relatively little geographical coverage the new entrants could address the major proportion of the rapidly growing telecoms services markets, such as that for corporate data, the growth of which was quickly outstripping the market for voice services.

These four assumptions led to the crucial conclusion that the new entrants would outperform the incumbents in meeting the explosive demand for bandwidth. In turn, this conclusion led to the third plank in the Consensual Vision.

Belief 3: Financial Markets Will Support the Fittest New Entrants
Financial markets would give significant support to the fittest new entrant telecoms operators relative to the incumbents. To the extent that this expectation was realised in reality, the market value of the assets of these new entrants would rise, resulting in relatively attractive returns to investors.

In turn, this led to the establishment of a positive feedback loop. Financial markets (debt, equity, and bank-lending), accepting the planks in the Consensual Vision, supported the fittest new entrants (such as WorldCom, Qwest, Level 3, Global Crossing, COLT, and Energis). As a result of this support, the market value of these companies rose, particularly after their initial public offerings (IPOs). This led to a self-fulfilling expectation, further fuelling the cycle of self-fulfilling expectations and justifying the 'buy' recommendations of analysts such as Grubman.

Belief 4: Technological Change Will Further Reinforce the Chain of Expectations
Technological change would further reinforce the chain of expectations on which the vision was based, thus adding an endogenous element to the causation. Technological change, stimulated by

demand from the rapidly growing new entrant telecoms operators, would further contribute to their competitive success against the legacy-constrained incumbents. In turn, this would increase the relative attractiveness of these new entrants. As a consequence, their relative share price would rise even further, reinforcing the original expectations. In this way the power of technological change provided further fuel for the positive feedback loops.[15]

Response of the Financial Markets

How did financial markets respond to the growing belief that the Internet together with the earlier telecoms liberalisation was creating new opportunities for above-average returns? Perhaps the simplest way to answer this question is to examine what was happening to the share prices of telecoms operators.[16] This is shown in Exhibits 8.5 and 8.6.

In Exhibit 8.5 the share price of the US incumbent, AT&T, is compared with that of two of its main new entrant competitors, World-Com and Qwest, for the period from mid-1996 to the end of 2001.[17] Several observations emerge from this exhibit. The first is that there was not much difference in the share price movement of AT&T and World-Com until early 1997, when Qwest had its IPO, with WorldCom slightly outperforming AT&T. From this time, however, until early 2000 the new entrants significantly outperformed the incumbent AT&T (except for a brief period at the end of 1997 and early 1998 when AT&T

---

[15] See Shiller (2000), pp. 60–8, for an analysis of the role played by feedback loops in causing speculative financial bubbles.

[16] The fortunes of the telecoms equipment and other input suppliers are derived, as in the case of all capital goods sectors, from the fortunes of their customers, in this case the telecoms operators.

[17] The early history of WorldCom was discussed earlier. In 1985 Bernard Ebbers was made CEO of LDDC/WorldCom. Founded in 1988 by US billionaire Joseph Anschutz (who made his initial money in cattle-ranching, oil, and railroads), Qwest's initial aim was to acquire high-capacity long-distance networks. As with WorldCom, the explosion of the Internet in the mid-1990s provided an additional impetus to the company's growth. Joseph Nacchio, a former disaffected AT&T employee, played an important role in engineering Qwest's growth during the boom years and its acquisition of the Baby Bell, US West. For further details, see Fransman (2002a).

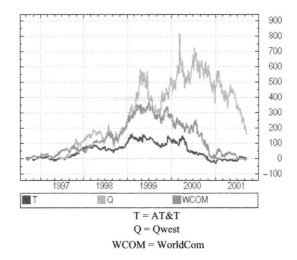

T = AT&T
Q = Qwest
WCOM = WorldCom

EXHIBIT 8.5 US Incumbents and New Entrants: Share Price

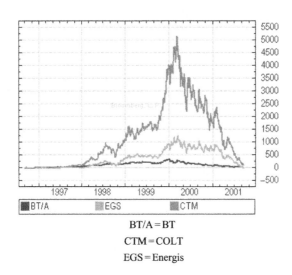

BT/A = BT
CTM = COLT
EGS = Energis

EXHIBIT 8.6 UK Incumbents and New Entrants: Share Price

outperformed WorldCom, though not Qwest). Over this period all the telecoms companies shown performed well in absolute terms. However, Exhibit 8.5 makes clear that the real excitement in terms of share price performance lay in the out-performance by the new entrants.

The divergence in price over this period, with the new entrants outperforming the incumbent, provides indirect evidence in support of the existence of a Consensual Vision consisting of the four beliefs summarised in Exhibit 8.4.

Significantly, almost exactly the same picture emerges for the United Kingdom. This is shown in Exhibit 8.6, which shows the movement in share prices for the UK incumbent, BT, and two of its main new entrant competitors, COLT and Energis.[18] Several important observations may be made on the basis of Exhibit 8.6.

The first is that the divergence of share price between the British incumbent and the two new entrants began more than six months after the same thing happened in the United States. This lag is not surprising. Not only does it mirror the general tendency of the London Stock Exchange to take its cue from Wall Street and Nasdaq, it was also the result of the adoption in the United Kingdom of the Consensual Vision that had its origins in the United States. Indeed, this process of adoption, and the crystallisation of thinking that it implied, can be precisely traced through the activities of Salomon Brothers, Jack Grubman's company. Not surprisingly, Grubman heavily influenced his London colleagues such as Andrew Harrington. Partly through Salomon's publications on British and European telecoms companies, the Consensual Vision took root in the United Kingdom and other parts of Europe.

Second, when the divergence begins in the United Kingdom it is more decisive than in the United States (note the difference in scale on the vertical axis in the two diagrams), probably because the Consensual Vision had already become widely accepted in the United States.

---

[18] COLT was established by the largest American mutual fund, Fidelity. Following initial experience in the United States when Fidelity established its own competitive local exchange carriers (CLECs) in New York and Boston, Fidelity repeated the model in the United Kingdom. Under its first CEO, Paul Chisholm, COLT began its activities in Britain and then expanded them to become a pan-European carrier. Energis was the new telecoms subsidiary of the English electricity company, the National Grid. Its first CEO was Mike Grabiner. For further details, see Fransman (2002a).

The sharp rise in share price particularly of the new entrants had important further repercussions in the stock market as will be shown in the next section.

PERIOD II: MANIA – CIRCA 1997 TO EARLY 2000

Introduction

As Charles Kindleberger (2000) notes in his book *Manias, Panics and Crashes: A History of Financial Crises*, 'The word *mania* ... connotes a loss of touch with reality or rationality, even something close to mass hysteria or insanity' (p. 23). Assuming that something like this characterised the last stage of the Telecoms Boom, it is necessary to ask how such an extreme state of mind, one shared by large numbers of otherwise well-informed and responsible people, came about.

Drawing on the work of Hyman Minsky (1975, 1982), Kindleberger notes that a boom and subsequent mania may be fed by an expansion of bank credit.[19] This is similar to the Austrian theory of the business cycle associated with Friedrich Hayek (discussed later), whereby the boom phase is triggered by a fall in short-term interest rates below their 'natural' equilibrium level (which equates the savings of households with the investment of firms). In turn, this leads to an increase in credit and investment that becomes too great relative to savings, resulting in a mismatch between future output and future spending, which takes the form of over-investment. The problem with these theories as they stand, however, is that they deal only with the cost side of the cost–benefit calculation that any purchaser of assets (real or financial) must make. While expanding and cheaper credit reduces the cost side of the calculation, these costs must be weighed against the accompanying benefits. This raises the question of how these benefits, which will accrue only in the future, are to be calculated.

In tackling this question it is important to distinguish between real markets and financial markets. The present discussion will be confined to the latter, more specifically to stock markets.

---

[19] Kindleberger (2000), p. 14.

The Benefits of Purchasing Telecoms Shares in Period II of the Telecoms Boom and Bust

The potential gain from holding shares may come from two sources: dividends and increases in capital value as the share price rises. As shown in Exhibits 8.1 and 8.2, in the United States from mid-1997 and in the United Kingdom from the end of 1997 the share price particularly of the new entrants rose rapidly. This meant that from 1997 to 1998 significant capital gains were made by the owners of shares in these and similar telecoms companies. Returns from dividends, however, tended to be far lower since the companies had to make large expenditures in developing their expensive networks *well in advance of* the compensating revenues.[20]

Handsome profits, therefore, were made at this stage by those who owned shares in these companies. At this stage one of the mechanisms producing mania, referred to by Kindleberger (2000), begins to take effect:

> As firms or households see others making profits from speculative purchases and resales, they tend to follow: 'Monkey see, monkey do.' In my talks about financial crisis over the last decades, I have polished one line that always gets a nervous laugh: 'There is nothing so disturbing to one's well-being and judgment as to see a friend get rich.' When the number of firms and households indulging in these practices grows large, bringing in segments of the population that are normally aloof from such ventures, speculation for profit leads away from normal, rational behavior to what has been described as 'manias' or 'bubbles'. The word *mania* emphasizes the irrationality; *bubble* foreshadows the bursting.
>
> (p. 15)

---

[20] As an early-comer able to take advantage of AT&T's excess network capacity and corresponding low wholesale price, WorldCom was able to benefit by first becoming an arbitraging reseller of AT&T's capacity. However, the potential for arbitrage was soon squeezed out when wholesale prices rose as AT&T used more of its capacity for data communications and market competition from other new entrants reduced long-distance tariffs. WorldCom then had little option but to buy its own networks.

In this way, Kindleberger suggests that what begins from a 'rational' process of profiting from new opportunities turns, for essentially psychological reasons, into an 'irrational' process involving people purchasing overpriced assets in the mistaken belief that they will in time receive sufficient benefits from these assets to be adequately compensated for bearing the associated costs. In other words, people incorrectly overestimate the benefits of owning these assets.

However, although Kindleberger does not emphasise it, there is a closely related process that also played an important role in the Telecoms Boom and Bust, 1996–2003, but worked in a fundamentally different way.

Beauty Contents and Benchmarking

Keynes on the Stock Market

It is significant that Keynes's oft-quoted comments on the stock market, which he saw as an institution essentially preoccupied with short-term considerations, are made in a chapter titled 'The State of Long-Term Expectation'.[21] Keynes notes that this chapter considers 'some of the factors which determine the prospective yield of an asset'.[22] His somewhat ironic conclusion is that stock markets have very little to do with the calculation of long-term prospective yields of assets.

For Keynes there are two fundamental 'givens' that must be grasped if the workings of the stock market as an institution are to be understood. The first is a paradox. The stock market, a key financial institution in a knowledge economy, is a place where ignorant people trade ownership titles (shares) to the major part of a country's capital stock.

---

[21] The chapter concerned is chapter 12, which is part of Book IV of *The General Theory* titled 'The Inducement to Invest'.

[22] Keynes (1961), p. 147.

Why are these people ignorant? Keynes's answer is clear:

> As a result of the gradual increase in the proportion of the equity in the community's aggregate capital investment which is owned by persons who do not manage and have no special knowledge of the circumstances, either actual or prospective, of the business in question, the element of real knowledge in the valuation of investments by those who own them or contemplate purchasing them has seriously declined.[23]

The result, Keynes notes, is that

> A conventional valuation which is established as the outcome of the mass psychology of a large number of ignorant individuals is liable to change violently as the result of a sudden fluctuation of opinion due to factors which do not really make much difference to the prospective yield ... In abnormal times in particular, ... the market will be subject to waves of optimistic and pessimistic sentiment.[24]

But surely this statement does not take account of the professional fund managers, these days organised into company and even sector specialists? Surely, they have the degree of knowledge and expertise necessary to calculate long-term prospective yields? Keynes himself anticipates this objection:

> It might have been supposed that competition between expert professionals, possessing judgment and knowledge beyond that of the average private investor, would correct the vagaries of the ignorant individual left to himself.[25]

It turns out, however, that professionals such as fund managers cannot perform this function because in fact they are not concerned with the business of making long-term forecasts of the probable yield of an investment:

[23] Ibid., p. 153.   [24] Ibid., p. 154.   [25] Ibid.

It happens, however, that the energies and skill of the professional investor and speculator are mainly occupied otherwise. For most of these people are, in fact, largely concerned, not with making superior long-term forecasts of the probable yield of an investment over its whole life, but with foreseeing changes in the conventional basis of valuation a short time ahead of the general public. They are concerned not with what an investment is really worth to a man who buys it 'for keeps', but with what the market will value it at, under the influence of mass psychology, three months or a year hence.[26]

But why is it that professional investors are not primarily concerned with long-term prospective yields when they make their decisions regarding which shares to buy, hold, and sell? The answer, according to Keynes, is that their preoccupation with short-term performance, and therefore with the short-term effects of mass psychology, is the inevitable result of investment markets organised with a view to so-called liquidity.[27] These markets, Keynes argues, are dominated by 'the fetish of liquidity', that is, 'the doctrine that it is a positive virtue on the part of investment institutions to concentrate their resources upon the holding of "liquid" securities [i.e. securities that can be readily sold for cash]'.[28]

Why are investment markets dominated by the fetish of liquidity? Keynes's answer is that in order to be motivated to make their investments in these markets, individual investors want to feel that they can always withdraw from the market by selling their liquid asset if their sentiment and therefore their commitment changes.[29] However, the liquidity of investment markets has very important consequences. For it means that the short-term preoccupation of the professional investor (as well as the speculator)

---

[26] Ibid., pp. 154–5.   [27] Ibid., p. 155.   [28] Ibid.

[29] Ibid., p. 160. Keynes argues here that investment markets that dealt only in illiquid assets would not be sufficiently attractive to work so long as the option of holding money as an asset existed.

is not the outcome of a wrong-headed propensity ... For it is not sensible to pay 25 for an investment of which you believe the prospective yield to justify a value of 30, if you also believe that the market will value it at 20 three months hence.[30]

This simple proposition has profound implications:

Thus the professional investor is *forced* to concern himself with the anticipation of impending changes, in the news or in the atmosphere, of the kind by which experience shows that the mass psychology of the market is most influenced. This is the inevitable result of investment markets organised with a view to so-called 'liquidity'.[31]

It is this reasoning that leads to Keynes's famous metaphor, comparing the activities of the stock market to a beauty contest in which the contestants choose not the face they think the most beautiful but the face that they think the other contestants will choose as the most beautiful.

Beauty and Benchmarking

In the stock markets at the time of the Telecoms Boom and Bust, 1996–2003, the widespread routinised practice of benchmarking by fund managers turned beauty-contest behaviour into a hard institutional requirement. In order to meet the desire of clients to compare the returns they were getting on their (liquid) investments with those of alternative investments, the practice of benchmarking the performance of particular fund managers against measures such as stock market indices had become widespread.

This, however, institutionalised and made more binding the behavioural responses that Keynes analysed. For it meant that the performance of specific fund managers (and often their remuneration) would be measured by their performance relative to the benchmark,

---

[30] Ibid., p. 155.   [31] Ibid., emphasis added.

that is, relative to the average measure of the judgment of the other players regarding which shares were the most 'beautiful'. Not only, therefore, was this behaviour sensible in the context of liquid investment markets, as Keynes argued; it became an institutional necessity.

However, this produced a further important paradox. Even where individual institutional fund managers judged that particular share prices were 'crazy', they would nevertheless feel it essential to purchase them for fear of not meeting the benchmark if they did not. In this way, paradoxically, 'irrational' behaviour (buying shares at what was judged to be grossly overvalued prices) was at the same time 'rational' (acting so as to keep up with the benchmark that determined remuneration and reputation).[32] Those who baulked at the irrational behaviour and refused to jump were duly punished.[33]

---

[32] Several economists have attempted to explore the phenomenon of herd behaviour in areas such as investment and have addressed explicitly the issues raised by Keynes in the previous section. Generally, this work has tried to provide an explanation for such herd behaviour within the framework of rational choice. For example, Scharfstein and Stein (1990), who aim to 'develop a clearer understanding of some of the forces that can lead to herd behavior', find that 'under certain circumstances, managers simply mimic the investment decisions of other managers, ignoring substantive private information'. They conclude that 'Although this behavior is inefficient from a social standpoint, it can be rational from the perspective of managers who are concerned about their reputations in the labor market' (p. 466). Using this framework, they provide a herding explanation of the period just before the 1987 stock market crash when money managers did not sell, even though they believed that the market was overpriced and more likely to fall than rise, because they feared being the only manager out of the market if the market rose further. Similarly, Banerjee (1992) develops a sequential decision model in which 'each decision maker looks at the decisions made by previous decision makers in taking her own decision'. He argues that this 'is rational for her because these other decision makers may have some information that is important for her'. He concludes that under these circumstances 'the decision rules that are chosen by optimising individuals will be characterized by herd behavior; i.e. people will be doing what others are doing rather than using their own information'. However, he also concludes that 'the resulting equilibrium is inefficient' (p. 797). The point being made here, however, is that the institutionalisation of the practice of benchmarking adds a further dimension to the problem by removing from the investor/fund manager the power to decide what, under the circumstances, constitutes 'rational' behaviour. In turn, this raises the question of the determinants of such institutional requirements/constraints.

[33] One famous case in the United Kingdom was that of Tony Dye, referred to in the media as Mr Doom. Dye was chief investment officer for a leading asset manager,

Inventing the Price of Shares

In theory, the price of a company's shares is determined by the discounted value of the company's future earnings. This implies that the would-be valuer of a company's shares must decide on what discount rate to use and on how to determine the company's future earnings. Ignoring the decision regarding the appropriate discount rate (which itself can present serious difficulties[34]), attention will be focused here on the calculation of future earnings.

Phillips and Drew. However, at the height of the so-called Dot-Com bubble he refused to hold shares in Internet companies, believing they were grossly overvalued. The consequence was that Phillips and Drew's funds underperformed the benchmark and as a result Dye was dismissed, as it turned out, only weeks before the market finally crashed in March 2000. Interestingly, writing in *The General Theory*, published in 1936, Keynes presciently foresaw both the future advent of benchmarking and the fate of those who, like Drew, refused to abide by the rules of the beauty contest. It is 'the long-term investor, he who most promotes the public interest, who will in practice come in for most criticism, wherever investment funds are managed by committees or boards or banks'. 'The practice', Keynes continues in a footnote, 'by which an investment trust or an insurance office frequently calculates not only the income from its investment portfolio but also its capital valuation in the market, may also tend to direct too much attention to short-term fluctuations in the latter' (p. 157). Regarding the fate of the long-term investor, Keynes had the following to say: it is 'in the essence of his behaviour that he should be eccentric, unconventional and rash in the eyes of average opinion. If he is successful, that will only confirm the general belief in his rashness; and if in the short run he is unsuccessful, which is very likely, he will not receive much mercy. Worldly wisdom teaches that it is better for reputation to fail conventionally than to succeed unconventionally' (p. 158). Zwiebel (1995) provides an explanation for the 'corporate conservatism' that results from this kind of thinking. Within the framework of a rational model based on managerial reputation and career concerns, he concludes that 'within a simple technological and labor market setting, reputational concerns may lead managers to refrain from deviating from the herd' (p. 2). Unlike Scharfstein and Stein (1990), discussed in the last note, in Zwiebel's model managers derive reputation from good relative performance, rather than from undertaking actions similar to those of others. Accordingly, 'managers may have an incentive to outperform one another and clearly have an unwillingness to share private information' (p. 4). Relating this to stock market crashes, Zwiebel concludes that 'While removing funds from the market prior to the crash may have lowered the absolute risk to a fund, it most certainly would have increased risk in its performance relative to other funds' (p. 2).

[34] An example is the following quotation that comes from a report written during the Telecoms Boom on one of Europe's best-performing new entrant telecoms operators by financial analysts in one of the world's best-known financial companies: 'We are using a discount rate of 14% ... At present we have assumed that further finance is

The problem that our would-be valuer immediately encounters in attempting to calculate the future earnings of a company is one of *uncertainty*.[35] And no amount of information is sufficient to entirely solve this calculation problem. The reason is that information, by definition, refers to the past. It is not possible to get information about the future. And there is no necessary correspondence between past information and information that will emerge in the future. This implies that there is necessarily a degree of what I have termed interpretive ambiguity in inferring from current information what will happen in the future. But interpretive ambiguity also implies that different people may arrive at different inferences on the basis of the same set of information. This presents an irreducible dilemma for the would-be valuer.

The attempt to calculate the future earnings of new entrant telecoms operators during the Telecoms Boom was complicated by the fact that because they were new, they had little track record. This meant that the current information set available on these companies provided little guidance on how they might cope with the hurdles with which new firms in this area had to deal. There were also problems in calculating the future earnings of incumbents because telecoms liberalisation and the Internet injected an important degree of novelty into their operating environment, decreasing the usefulness of past information on these companies in the attempt to infer future magnitudes. Accordingly, the analyst faced significant uncertainty in dealing with key determinants of the future earnings of these companies.

provided through debt. It is entirely possible that the company could choose to issue equity, but we have more confidence in our ability to predict future interest rates than to predict at what price future equity could be sold. This does, of course, mean that interest expense could be overstated.'

[35] 'Uncertainty' here is used in the sense of Knight (1921), who argued that 'a *measurable* uncertainty, or "risk" proper ... is so far different from an *unmeasurable* one that it is not in effect an uncertainty at all. We shall accordingly restrict the term "uncertainty" to cases of the non-quantitative type' (p. 20).

Faced with this uncertainty, the financial analyst had little option but to 'invent' the key assumptions and magnitudes that drive the calculation of future cash flow and earnings. This invention process emerges clearly from a reading of the telecoms company reports written by the leading telecoms analysts of the time. There is little attempt in these reports to suggest that the 'inventions' 'fully and correctly reflect all information'. Rather, the language of the analyst usually disarmingly betrayed the discomfort that all decision-makers feel under conditions of uncertainty and interpretive ambiguity. The following quotation from a company report by some of the best-known telecoms analysts working for one of the world's most famous financial companies provides an example (the company concerned being one of Europe's leading new entrant telecoms operators):

> Quite obviously, given [company X's] relative immaturity, it is impossible to value the company using conventional earnings ratios such as price/earnings, price/earnings relative, EPS [earnings per share] growth and even firm value (market capitalization plus net debt)/EBITDA [earnings before interest, tax, depreciation, and amortization] ...
>
> We are using a terminal EBITDA multiple of 10 [in order to calculate the final share price as a multiple of the EBITDA]. Such a multiple suggests substantial growth in EBITDA and EPS even after 2003. We believe (to the best of our ability to predict what will happen in 2004 and beyond) that [company X] will be increasing EBITDA at 12%–15% and EPS at 15%–20% post-2003. We believe that 10x terminal multiple is reasonable relative to growth profiles, the size of [X's] opportunity, its network/technology advantages (fibre, SDH [a new network technology]) and [X's] EPS/EBITDA growth post-2003.
>
> Nonetheless, we realize the inherent volatility and uncertainty in attempting such a valuation.

The invention of the EBITDA multiple is of particular interest as a result of the way in which it was derived (in this and most other reports) and its significant impact on the final calculated share price. Essentially, the multiple was derived from the current experience of 'comparable' telecoms companies. Frequently, in European calculations, the experience of US telecoms companies was used. However, during the Telecoms Boom this had the effect of making the calculation circular. In effect, the overvaluation of the initial companies (due to excessively optimistic expectations) was used to 'value' the other telecoms companies. The circularity produced self-fulfilling prophesies, further fuelling the boom in telecoms share prices.

The processes discussed here have important implications for the 'efficient markets hypothesis'. This hypothesis holds that a capital market is efficient if 'it fully and correctly reflects all relevant information in determining security prices. Formally, the market is said to be efficient with respect to some information set, x, if security prices would be unaffected by revealing that information.' The point, however, is that under conditions of uncertainty and interpretive ambiguity it is not possible for the price of a security to 'fully and correctly reflect all relevant information'. Since under such conditions different people may make different inferences from the same information set – as is implied in the above quotation from the company report – it is not possible to define when prices fully and correctly reflect all relevant information.[36]

---

[36] Further problems arise from the requirement that the security price reflects 'all relevant information'. In practice it is unlikely to be possible to define the set of all relevant information, and from an ex ante perspective, one person's relevant information may for another person be irrelevant. In passing it is also worth noting that it is sometimes claimed that empirical support for the efficient markets hypothesis comes from the apparent fact that individual analysts seem to be unable to consistently beat the market over time in their valuation of shares. However, even if this is true, it does not necessarily support the efficient markets hypothesis. The reason is that the failure of individual analysts to consistently beat the market may be a reflection of their lack of superior capability to deal with uncertainty and interpretive ambiguity, rather than a reflection of the ability of 'the market' to 'fully and correctly reflect all relevant information'. Furthermore, since 'the market' outcome always reflects the balance of the contradictory expectations of buyers and sellers – the seller believes that at the agreed price the share should be sold while the buyer believes the opposite – it is not clear how the market can ever 'fully and correctly' reflect all relevant information.

The Mania Phase of the Telecoms Boom, circa 1998–1999

In this way, rising telecoms share prices, initially justified by the new opportunity for profits opened up by telecoms liberalisation and the Internet, were reflected in the benchmarks, leading, via the beauty-contest process, to further rises in share prices. The surging paper profits that were generated fed the exuberant expectations that soon became associated with this sector and led to reinforcing feedback effects. Simultaneously, this exuberance affected the other financial markets such as those for high-yielding bonds and syndicated bank loans (see Exhibit 8.3). 'Real' markets in the telecoms industry were also affected by the exuberance as owners and managers of telecoms network operating companies, as well as those with a vested interest in supporting them, came to expect significantly above-average returns in the future. They, accordingly, increased their real investment, which, in turn, fed into the market for telecoms equipment and other inputs, sending the shares of companies in these areas into a sympathetic upward spiral (e.g. companies like Lucent, Nortel, Cisco, Alcatel, NEC, Ericsson, and Nokia[37]). In this way, the financial and real markets were closely intertwined.

The processes discussed in this section contributed significantly to the mania phase of the Telecoms Boom that occurred during 1998 and 1999 (see Exhibits 8.7 and 8.8). However, financial markets, taking off under the steam of their own dynamics, soon began to increasingly diverge from the performance of the telecoms companies themselves. In this way financial returns began to diverge significantly from real returns measured in terms of magnitudes such as revenue and earnings of telecoms operators and equipment suppliers. This increasing divergence, as we now know, also created both

---

[37] It is important to note that although closely related, the enthusiasm for the shares of mobile telecoms companies (such as, in the European context, Vodafone, Orange/ France Telecom, and T-Mobile/Deutsche Telekom) was influenced by a number of mobile-specific factors. These factors will not be considered in the present chapter. For a structural analysis of the relationship between telecoms operators and equipment suppliers, see the Layer Model developed in Fransman (2002a).

Exhibit 8.7 *Critical Questions Regarding the Consensual Vision*

Question 1	At what rate will the demand for bandwidth increase?
Question 2	What will happen to the supply of bandwidth and how will demand and supply interact?
Question 3	How many competitors will there be in the market for telecoms services?

Exhibit 8.8 *The Shifting Knowledge Base in the Telecoms Industry: From Operators to Equipment Suppliers*

	R&D as Percentage of Sales
Telecoms operators	
AT&T	0.9
BT	1.8
Deutsche Telekom	2.0
France Telecom	2.2
Telecoms equipment suppliers	
Cisco	13.1
Ericsson	15.4
Lucent	11.8
Nokia	10.2
Nortel	13.1
Sectors	
Telecoms services	**2.6**
Automobiles	4.2
Beverages	2.2
IT hardware	7.9
Media and photography	4.2
Personal care	3.3
Pharmaceuticals	12.8
Software and IT services	12.4

Source: Financial Times R&D Scoreboard, FT Director, 19 September 2000.

incentives and pressures for the management of telecoms companies, often with the connivance of their accountants and auditors, to invent the figures that would help to rationalise the expectations and prices being generated in the financial markets.[38]

PERIOD III: THE TURNING POINT – CIRCA EARLY 2000

Introduction

Kindleberger (2000) has noted that during the mania stage, 'irrationality may exist insofar as economic actors choose the wrong model, fail to take account of a particular and crucial bit of information or go so far as to suppress information that does not conform to the model implicitly adopted'.[39]

Puzzling Failure to Take Account of the Supply Side

A puzzling and significant example of such irrational behaviour during the Telecoms Boom and Bust was the failure to take adequate account of the supply side of the telecoms industry. The Consensual Vision that provided a rationale for the Telecoms Boom was essentially a demand-side story. This is evident particularly from Belief 1 in Exhibit 8.4: the Internet will drive an explosive demand for bandwidth. But what about the supply side? Any introductory economics student knows that price (and therefore revenue and therefore earnings) is determined by demand *and* supply. Yet it is remarkable, reading through the 'explanations' of leading financial analysts of what was happening in the telecoms industry, that virtually no attention was being paid to the supply side. To be sure, the quality financial

---

[38] For example, we now know that innovative practices such as 'capacity swaps' emerged whereby a telecoms operator would increase its revenue by 'selling' capacity to another operator that would also expand its own revenue by 'selling back' identical capacity, thus leaving both companies, in terms of capacity, where they had started but with increased revenue and earnings. Some of the biggest new entrants such as WorldCom and Qwest engaged in activities such as these.

[39] Kindleberger (2000), p. 26.

press did not entirely ignore the supply side. One important example from the *Financial Times*, presented as a contrary note of caution intended to cast some doubt on the prevailing conventional wisdom, was the reporting of the research findings of a small Boston consultancy company that had begun to make estimates of rapidly growing aggregate telecoms capacity and the impact on prices. But this kind of report remained a voice in the wilderness, largely ignored.

The ignoring of the supply side led to a catastrophic failure in investment coordination. Unbelievable as it may in retrospect seem, by September 2001, a year and a half after the beginning of the crash, the *Financial Times* reported that 'only 1 or 2 percent of the fibre optic cable buried under Europe and North America has even been turned on or "lit" ... A similar overcapacity exists in undersea links, where each new Atlantic cable adds as much bandwidth as all the previous infrastructure put together [as a result of improvements in technology and scale].'[40]

Writing now, some three and a half years after the start of the bust, it has become commonplace, even amongst the *cognoscenti*, to recount stories such as this and receive, by way of response, a wistful shake of the head. But surely this kind of phenomenon, with such important implications, begs an explanation. Where were the investment bankers, the financial analysts, the fund managers on the buy side, the journalists, and the academics saying, even on the basis of back-of-the-envelope calculations, 'Hey, this does not add up!' Why did investment bankers, about to pour further billions of dollars into a telecoms company wanting to expand the capacity of its network, apparently not wonder whether other investment bankers, responding to the same incentives and signals, were not doing something similar, logically implying forthcoming overcapacity and plunging prices and profits? At least the benchmarked fund manager had an excuse, being caught up, as Keynes neatly explains, in the spider's web of irrationality and rationality. But clearly this 'benchmarking process',

---

[40] *Financial Times*, 4 September 2001.

undoubtedly one important part of the jumble of interactions that made up the Telecoms Boom, is not by itself sufficient to explain the overall generation of excessive exuberance.

How, then, is this phenomenon to be explained? How adequate are the current explanations given in terms of concepts such as 'greed', 'bouts of optimism', propensity to believe in 'the Emperor's new clothes', etc.? If they are adequate (and this is a tacit implication of the present discussion), then there is far more that unites the economic actors of the modern, ICT-based economy with their ancestors from the economies that produced Tulipomania and the South Sea Bubble than separates them. If true, the implications for economists theorising about how people make economic decisions are as crucial as they are worrying.[41]

---

[41] Rabin and Schrag (1999) tackle implicitly the issue raised by Kindleberger (2000), quoted in this section, where people 'go so far as to suppress information that does not conform to the model implicitly adopted'. Raising the question, 'How do people form beliefs in situations of uncertainty?', Rabin and Schrag note that 'Economists have traditionally assumed that people begin with subjective beliefs over the different possible states of the world and use Bayes' Rule to update those beliefs. This elegant and powerful model of economic agents as Bayesian statisticians is the foundation of modern information economics' (p. 37). However, they go on to note that there is substantial psychological evidence that people suffer from 'confirmatory bias' that departs from Bayesian rationality. (Confirmatory bias exists when a person 'tends to misinterpret ambiguous evidence as confirming [their] current hypotheses about the world' (p. 38).) They conclude on the basis of their model that 'An agent who suffers from confirmatory bias may come to believe in a hypothesis that is *probably wrong*, meaning that a Bayesian observer ... would ... favor a different hypothesis than the agent' (p. 38, emphasis in original). The fundamental assumption made in Rabin and Schrag's story is the existence of uncertainty (i.e. Knightian uncertainty) and therefore the existence of 'ambiguous evidence'. Under these circumstances the agent, by definition, has no way of inferring whether their current hypotheses are more or less correct than other possible alternative hypotheses. Under these circumstances a confirmatory bias may provide a reasonable way of proceeding. However, in this section of the present chapter, the issue under investigation is the failure to take adequate account of the supply side. This failure cannot have been due to uncertainty and corresponding ambiguity. Once pointed out, it would have been clear to virtually all of those involved that changes on the supply side would have a significant impact on the outcome of concern, namely revenues and profits. The question is, why did the otherwise sophisticated players, involved directly and indirectly in the telecoms industry, not take the supply side into consideration? The failure to take adequate account of the supply side remains a puzzle.

The Flaws in the Consensual Vision and the Consequences

The rise in the share price of the telecoms operators (and also the telecoms equipment companies who supplied them) continued until about March 2000. At this time the generalised bull stock market ended and the decline began. Simultaneously, doubts emerged regarding the validity of the beliefs underlying the Consensual Vision that had reigned. These doubts may be summarised in the form of three questions regarding the Consensual Vision. These questions are presented in Exhibit 8.7.[42]

In retrospect, it is clear that the implicit assumptions on which Belief 1 (that the Internet will drive an explosive demand for bandwidth) were based were overly optimistic. Although, as a result of the rapid global diffusion of the Internet, there was an 'explosive demand for bandwidth' – as the new operators and their supporting financial analysts put it in their public pronouncements – it was not explicitly acknowledged that this rate of increase in demand could not continue indefinitely. Telecoms operators – just as their counterparts producing PCs and mobile phones – would soon be forced to live with this fact.

Even more surprising, as already noted, was the under-emphasis in the Consensual Vision of the supply side (Question 2). But crucial changes were taking place on the supply side. In 2000 it was announced, for example, that Lucent Technologies' Bell Labs had pushed 1.6 trillion bits, or terabits, of information through a single optical fibre by using the dense wavelength division multiplexing technique (DWDM).[43] This is enough for 25 million conversations or 200,000 video signals simultaneously and one cable may contain a dozen such fibres. The effects of such technical change were dramatic, contributing to the excess capacity that has already been noted.

---

[42] For a more detailed examination of these three questions, see Fransman (2002a).

[43] DWDM is an optical technology that uses different coloured light waves as communication channels in a single optical fibre, thereby increasing significantly the carrying capacity of that fibre.

However, it was not only technical change per se that was rocking the foundations of the Consensual Vision. The evolving structure and organisation of the entire telecoms industry constituted a fundamental challenge to this vision. The problem was that very few of the participants in this industry understood how the telecoms industry worked and how it was changing.[44]

As had happened in the computer industry earlier, processes of vertical specialisation were radically transforming the telecoms industry. Until the 1980s, the engine of change in the telecoms industry lay in the central research laboratories of the incumbent telecoms operators – famous institutions such as AT&T's Bell Labs, BT's Martlesham Laboratories, France Telecom's CNET laboratories, and NTT's Electrical Communications Laboratories. The research and advanced development that took place in these laboratories created the new generations of technology and equipment that drove the telecoms industry.

The equipment itself, however, was manufactured by a group of specialist telecoms equipment suppliers such as Lucent (then an integrated part of AT&T) and Nortel in North America; Siemens, Alcatel, Ericsson and Nokia in Europe; and NEC, Fujitsu, and Hitachi in Japan. Closed markets and long-term obligational relationships bound the incumbent telecoms operators closely to their equipment suppliers.

By the 1990s, however, this pattern of industrial organisation had changed dramatically. The forces of vertical specialisation that had, at first unnoticed, begun to transform the telecoms industry decades earlier were given legal vent from the mid-1980s when government liberalisation introduced the first elements of competition in telecoms services markets in Japan, the United Kingdom, and the United States. In the United States, MCI and Sprint emerged to challenge AT&T; in the United Kingdom, Mercury took on BT; and in Japan, DDI, Japan Telecom, and Teleway Japan fought with NTT.

---

[44] A detailed analysis of the evolution of the telecoms industry is contained in chapters 1 and 2 of Fransman (2002a).

The entry path of these 'original new entrant operators' was smoothed by the decades of learning and knowledge accumulation undertaken by the specialist equipment suppliers who, in most cases, had cut their teeth through manufacturing equipment for their national incumbent telecoms operator. Rapidly the knowledge of these specialist suppliers had deepened with the result that by the late 1990s they were collectively some four times as R&D-intensive as the incumbent operators who hitherto had powered the engine of technical change in the telecoms industry. By the end of the 1990s, however, the incumbent operators had handed over a large part of their R&D requirements, in addition to their equipment require-ments, to the specialist suppliers. With falling R&D intensities, the incumbent operators became less research and development intensive than the average in industries normally not considered to be 'high-tech', industries such as automobiles, personal care products, and media and photography, and about as R&D-intensive as the beverages industry, as is shown in Exhibit 8.8.[45]

In this way, the R&D engine of the telecoms industry moved decisively from the central research laboratories of the incumbent operators to the specialist equipment suppliers. But this would have crucial consequences for the evolving structure and dynamics of the entire industry.

One of the most important consequences was that techno-logical entry barriers into the network operator layer of the telecoms industry were dramatically lowered.[46] The reason, simply, was that telecoms equipment suppliers such as Nortel and Lucent were willing to supply state-of-the-art equipment to any company that wanted to enter the telecoms operator market, provided they were able to pay. And financial markets, enthused by the Consensual Vision, were willing to provide the funds that enabled the new entrant operators

---

[45] This remarkable fact is documented in more detail in Exhibit 8.2 and is analysed in chapters 2 and 8 of Fransman (2002a).

[46] For a structural analysis of the dynamics of the telecoms industry, see the analysis of the Layer Model developed in Fransman (2002a,b).

to pay. Furthermore, labour markets, oiled by the granting of generous stock options to newly recruited top managers, provided the new operators with the knowledgeable staff they needed, often headhunted from the incumbent operators. Between 1996 and 1999 in the United States alone 144 new telecoms companies went public, raising more than $25 billion.

These events seemed to represent a vibrant market response to the major new business opportunities opened up by telecoms liberalisation and the Internet. They seemed to provide empirical support for the assumptions made in the Consensual Vision (summarised in Exhibit 8.4). Even regulators were delighted, arguing that the market forces that their deregulation measures had unleashed were creating the competitive pressures and incentives that, in marked contrast to the earlier telecoms monopoly era, would stimulate innovation and improve services.

Unfortunately, however, things did not turn out so happily. The problems arose largely from Question 3 in Exhibit 8.7 (How many competitors will there be in the market for telecoms services?). The substantial number of new entrant operators – together with the great increase in investment in new network capacity embodying much improved technology – undermined prices and profitability. This was particularly the case in long-distance and international voice and data services.[47] Only local services and mobile services provided relief from this trend. (In the United States the Telecommunications Act of 1996 had attempted, unsuccessfully, to dislodge the market dominance of the local phone companies such as Verizon and SBC. Particularly in Europe, mobile services remained profitable into 2002, but in the United States strong competition between the mobile operators soon put an end to above-average rates of profitability.)

---

[47] This was the general picture although some sub-areas were profitable, such as private lines (data networks for businesses) and frame relay services (switched data access). However, Internet transmission provided little profit. (I am grateful to Arno Penzias for pointing this out to me.)

The collapse in prices meant that both the revenue and the earnings of incumbents and new operators alike were significantly below what investors had expected. The problem in this high fixed-cost industry was that large sums of money had to be spent on rolling out networks well in advance of the compensating revenues that would eventually pay for these investments. During the Telecoms Boom the exuberant expectations of investors (shaped by the Consensual Vision) plugged the gap between investment costs and the anticipated revenue streams that would cover them. The collapse in prices, however, meant that these future revenue streams were unlikely to be forthcoming. Financial markets that were exuberant quickly became disenchanted.

The collision between Consensual Vision–shaped expectations and the reality of falling prices and profitability put enormous pressure on telecoms operators. It was this pressure that explains the transgressions of WorldCom – accused of fraudulently reporting an excess of up to $9 billion in earnings – and the similar misdemeanours by companies such as Qwest and Global Crossing. Caught in the web of false expectations that they themselves had helped create, these companies did everything they could to avoid disappointing the markets that fed them and kept them alive. In short, the bonanza foreseen by the Consensual Vision proved illusory.

PERIOD IV: THE BUST – CIRCA EARLY 2000 TO 2003

Period IV, the final period in the cycle of the Telecoms Boom and Bust, was characterised by several events. The first, which followed from the growing contradiction that had emerged in Period III between the value of telecoms financial assets, on the one hand, and the real performance of telecoms companies (both operators and equipment suppliers), on the other, was the dramatic devaluation of these financial assets (not only equities but also bonds and bank loans). The drastic fall in the share prices of incumbent telecoms operators and several of their new entrant rivals from early 2000 in the United States and United Kingdom is shown above in Exhibits 8.5 and 8.6.

However, the fall in share price also indicated a radical shift in underlying 'market sentiment' toward the telecoms industry. With a more pessimistic outlook for the telecoms industry, the external supply of capital to its companies (both operators and equipment suppliers) largely dried up. This put severe pressure on these companies as the effective rate of interest that they had to pay on outstanding borrowing increased significantly (often as a direct result of downgrading by the credit rating agencies). Some of the operators were still not generating sufficient revenue with which to pay back the sums they had borrowed to expand their networks and supporting assets. Some of the companies (operators and equipment suppliers), in their enthusiasm during Period II, had borrowed large sums to fund mergers and acquisitions and now faced growing debt service costs.

To make matters worse, the market for telecoms services slowed as domestic and global recession set in. The market for telecoms equipment fell even more dramatically as the telecoms operators, suffering under substantial excess capacity and under severe financial pressure, slashed their orders for equipment. Major equipment suppliers – such as Lucent, Nortel, Cisco, Siemens, Alcatel, NEC, and Fujitsu – and smaller suppliers were hit hard, contributing to even further falls in the share prices of telecoms companies.

The result was a widespread financial crisis amongst the firms in the telecoms industry. All of them tried desperately to restructure in an attempt to cut costs. However, some – including several that had led the pack during the Telecoms Boom, such as WorldCom, Global Crossing, and Wintel – eventually filed for protection and went bankrupt.[48]

---

[48] However, filing for protection and going bankrupt did not mean that they exited from the industry. Indeed, by eliminating their obligations to several categories of creditors, some of them emerged fitter, though leaner, and soon reentered the market. These included WorldCom (which reemerged under the guise of MCI, the company that WorldCom had acquired) and Global Crossing, which was acquired by a Singapore state-owned company.

In the throes of the financial crisis one of the central beliefs that had underpinned the Telecoms Boom was turned upside-down. This was the belief that the new entrant telecoms operators will outcompete the incumbents in providing the bandwidth demanded by the Internet (i.e. Belief 2, Exhibit 8.4 shown above). However, as the financial crisis soon demonstrated, the incumbents had a key resource that the new entrants lacked: a reasonably reliable cash flow from their traditional core businesses. True, one of these core businesses – namely, fixed-line (land-line) telephony services – was already beginning to be attacked.[49] Nevertheless, over the next few years many incumbents demonstrated that with aggressive cost-cutting they could turn their traditional core revenues into reasonable net cash flows that could be used to reduce their level of indebtedness.

In addition, many incumbents still dominated important markets in the telecoms industry, such as local access markets (responsible for connecting homes and businesses to the broader telecoms networks), that in turn gave them the ability to dominate other markets, such as the market for broadband services. Furthermore, many of the incumbents had also diversified into mobile communications, a sector that continued to improve its performance in the first few years of the new millennium. By the beginning of 2004 it seemed that many of the incumbents had consolidated their positions, achieved financial stability, and begun looking forward to the new challenges facing them. Accordingly, far from being the dinosaurs that many had predicted during the Telecoms Boom, by the early 2000s the incumbents looked more like the great survivors. The Telecoms Boom and Bust, 1996–2003, had run its course, ending in financial crisis, shake-out, consolidation, and a relative strengthening of the incumbents and some of the new entrants.[50]

---

[49] By a combination of competition, regulatory change, pressure from mobile-fixed substitution, and technical change (e.g. the adoption of competing voice-over-the-Internet services).

[50] For a detailed analysis of the responses of BT, Deutsche Telekom, and France Telecom to the Telecoms Bust, see M. Fransman, 'Surviving the Telecoms Bust: BT, Deutsche Telecom, and France Telecom', mimeo.

DISCUSSION AND IMPLICATIONS

Introduction

In this section the following will be discussed:

1. Beliefs and theories of the business cycle
2. A puzzle: Why was the consensual vision believed?
3. Rationality, bounded rationality, and Gurus.

Beliefs and Theories of the Business Cycle

Some attempts have been made to understand the Telecoms Boom and Bust, 1996–2003, through the prism of business cycle theory. However, although such attempts may provide partial illumination, they are not sufficient as explanations of this boom and bust. This is so for at least two reasons.

The first is that as Kindleberger (2000) reminds us,[51] it is necessary to distinguish between business cycles and financial cycles. Although the two may interact in various ways (most notably through the mechanism of changes in the interest rate and credit), they have their own specific dynamics. It would certainly not be correct to attempt to reduce financial cycles to business cycles. Enough has presumably been said in the present chapter to make a convincing case that some important aspects of the Telecoms Boom and Bust, 1996–2003, though not all, had to do with the specific processes of financial cycles.

The second reason why (in general) business cycle theory per se is not sufficient is that, as noted earlier, although it does deal with the cost side of the calculation that investors in real and financial assets have to make, it does not deal adequately with the benefit side. More specifically, the alleged benefits arising from the 'opportunities for

---

[51] 'Financial crises are associated with the peaks of business cycles. We are not interested in the business cycle as such, the rhythm of economic expansion and contraction, but only in the financial crisis that is the culmination of a period of expansion and leads to downturn. If there be business cycles without financial crises, they lie outside our interest' (Kindleberger 2000, p. 1).

above-average returns' that supposedly were available in the telecoms industry were an important part of the processes that drove the Telecoms Boom and Bust. However, these benefits, and the beliefs that underlay them, remain unanalysed and unexplained in most business cycle theory. This is evident in the following (highly compact) summary of the Keynesian and Austrian business cycle theories.

To grossly simplify, the main driver in the Keynesian theory is the volatility of investment demand. Investment, in Keynes's memorable phrase, is subject to the 'animal spirits' of investors. A sufficient increase in investment, caused by optimistic spirits, may increase household incomes and expenditure that will have further effects leading to an economic upturn. However, later a downturn may occur as optimism turns to pessimism.

According to Hayek's version of the Austrian theory, if short-term interest rates fall below their 'natural' equilibrium level (which equates the savings of households with the investment of firms), credit and investment will increase too rapidly relative to savings. This will lead to a mismatch between future output (driven by the increase in investment) and future spending (which will be reduced by the fall in short-term savings). Accordingly, there will be overinvestment (leading to excess capacity) as well as unsustainable investment in inappropriate areas.

Both these theories depend on investors' expectations of opportunities for future profit.[52] These expectations are also at the heart of *The Economist*'s own Austrian-like explanation of the generalised boom and bust that occurred in the late 1990s and early 2000s:

> Firms overborrowed and overinvested *on unrealistic expectations about future profits* and the *belief* that the business cycle was dead. Consumers ran up huge debts and saved too little, *believing* that an ever rising stock market would boost their wealth. The boom

[52] Beliefs and expectations are more tacit in this too brief account of Hayek's theory, although Hayek himself and many Austrian economists have been very much concerned with expectations, how they are formed, and their implications.

became self-reinforcing as *rising profit expectations* pushed up share prices, which increased investment and consumer spending. Higher investment and a strong dollar helped to hold down inflation and hence interest rates, fuelling faster growth and higher share prices. That virtuous circle has now turned vicious.[53]

The question is why were these 'unrealistic expectations', which play a key role in the causal explanation offered in all three accounts, formed in the first place? The answer must necessarily depend on an understanding of how the interpretive frameworks of the investors were constructed. Unfortunately, a discussion of this important, but complex, issue lies beyond the bounds of the present chapter.[54] Nevertheless, it is clear that any complete explanation of the Telecoms Boom and Bust, 1996–2003, or of booms and busts more generally, must delve into the question of how unrealistic expectations come to be formed in the first place and are later abandoned, often becoming overly negative and therefore still unrealistic.

A Puzzle: Why Was the Consensual Vision Believed?

In this chapter it is argued that the Consensual Vision, constructed by financial analysts such as Jack Grubman in tacit collusion with many others with a vested interest in a telecoms boom,[55] played an important role in providing a rationale for, and justifying, what began as enthusiasm for this sector and ended in mania and panic. However, to the extent that this account is accurate, an important puzzle is raised: Why was the Consensual Vision believed?

This is a puzzle because, as the earlier discussion of the flaws in the Consensual Vision showed, some elementary analytical mistakes were made in its construction (notably, the neglect of the supply side).

---

[53] *The Economist* (2002), p. 4, emphasis added.

[54] For recent writing on interpretive frameworks in economics, see Loasby (2001, 2003).

[55] Such as telecoms shareholders, other investors in telecoms, and telecoms company managers.

With hindsight it seems clear that these mistakes could have and should have been foreseen.

Why, then, was the Consensual Vision believed? Part of the answer was that the Consensual Vision itself was not a static, stand-alone analysis of what was happening to the telecoms industry, inviting discussion, debate, and criticism. Rather, the Consensual Vision evolved. And it evolved in the earlier part of Period 1 (see Exhibit 8.1) in a context where (as the earlier discussion of WorldCom showed) new entrant telecoms were already performing extremely well. The burgeoning Internet and the enthusiasm it generated was used as additional 'evidence' to support a story about the above-average returns that were to be made in the telecoms industry.

In asking why the Consensual Vision was believed it is crucial to remember that this 'vision' was self-serving, intended by investors in the telecoms industry to justify the investments that they themselves had made as well as to persuade others. In this sense the Consensual Vision was ideology rather than scientific analysis. Seen from this perspective, people believed what they wanted to believe. They were willing to be seduced by a set of arguments that gave them comfort. Mechanisms such as benchmarking the performance of fund managers and beauty contests (analysed earlier in this chapter) served to reinforce the virtuous circle (that would, alas, soon turn vicious). With narrow self-interest as the overriding force, investors in the telecoms industry were willing, in Kindleberger's (2000) words, to 'go so far as to suppress [consciously or unconsciously] information that [did] not conform to the model implicitly adopted'.[56]

Organisational Routines and Biased Incentives

There were further mechanisms that reproduced and enhanced the virtuous circle. Two organisational routines in particular were singled out in the public debate that followed the Bust.

---

[56] Kindleberger's (2000), p. 26. The discussion of 'confirmatory bias' in note 43 above is, clearly, relevant here too.

The first was the conflict of interest that existed in investment banks whose biased incentives led them to produce biased 'information'. One version of this biased incentive hypothesis is provided in the following quotation:

> Wall Street has always struggled with conflicts of interest. Indeed, an investment bank is a business built on them. The same institution serves two masters: the companies for which it sells stock, issues bonds, or executes mergers; and the investors whom it advises. While companies want high prices for their newly issued stocks and low interest rates on their bonds, investors want low prices and high rates. In between, the bank gets fees from both and trades stocks and bonds on its own behalf as well, potentially putting its own interests at odds with those of all its customers. But in recent years, those inherent conflicts have grown worse.[57]

More generally, the argument is that the analysts working for an investment bank might bias the recommendations they make in order to suit the interests of the corporate clients of the bank. It is this biased incentive hypothesis that supposedly explains the remarkable fact discovered by New York Attorney General Eliot Spitzer, in an investigation into the stock market boom and bust. In *Business Week*'s words, 'In some of the e-mail turned up by Spitzer, analysts disparage stocks as "crap" and "junk" that they were pushing at the time.'[58]

Another variant of the biased incentive hypothesis applies the argument to the incentive regime governing the behaviour of managers, particular attention being paid to the practice of giving managers stock options. This practice was influenced (or perhaps justified) by academic discussions about principal-agent problems.[59] By giving the agents (managers) stock options, the argument went, their

---

[57] *Business Week* (2002), p. 36.   [58] Ibid., p. 37.

[59] These problems stem from the potential for conflict between the interests of principals and their agents, in this case owner-shareholders and their managers.

incentives and interests would be more closely 'aligned' with those of the principals (owner-shareholders). In practice, however, not only were the managers in this way incentivised, they were over-incentivised to produce the 'right kind' of company performance that would please the markets, raise the price of their share options (or prevent them falling), and maximise their own rewards. In the words of Robert J. Shiller, author of *Irrational Exuberance*, 'It's finally dawning on people that this incentive system we've given managers based on the value of stock options has encouraged management to puff up their companies a lot.'[60]

These organisational routines and the biased incentives they produced certainly contributed to the cumulative causation that fuelled the Telecoms Boom. In particular, they contaminated the 'information' on which calculations were based and distorted the 'knowledge' about the telecoms industry that people were trying to derive from this information. In short, they helped to make more believable during the boom period a Consensual Vision based on fundamental flaws.

Rationality, Bounded Rationality, and Gurus

It is not so long ago that many economists made the assumption (explicitly or implicitly) that actors had perfect information and knowledge and made optimal decisions on this basis. However, objecting to the lack of realism in this assumption and taking a behavioural perspective, Herbert Simon proposed the alternative of 'bounded rationality'.[61] Seeing human beings as essentially

---

[60] *Business Week* (2002), p. 39. One of the authors of the paper credited with launching the debate on agency problems, Michael Jensen, professor emeritus at Harvard Business School and initial supporter of stock options as a way of aligning the incentives of owner-shareholders and their managers, now argues that stock options need to be redesigned. Specifically, they need to be exercised only after the passage of a long period. This will give managers a long-term interest in their companies. What will happen to managers' behaviour over the short period that exists before the expiry of the contractually defined 'long period' remains unclear.

[61] See, for example, Simon (1959).

'information processors' who are constrained by their 'scarcity of attention',[62] Simon put forward the proposition that people do not make optimal decisions based on a complete information set but rather decide on the basis of the information they have selected,[63] within the constraint of their scarce attention. Their decisions would be rational and optimal, not absolutely, but relative to their selected information set (i.e. they would be boundedly rational).

How would the Simonian decision-maker have decided, in the context of the Telecoms Boom, whether or not to invest in the telecoms industry? Or, to put the question more starkly, is there a place in Simon's analysis for the decision-maker who had become caught up in the processes of the Telecoms Boom outlined in this chapter?

The impression one gets in reading Simon's writings is that, in common with most writers in mainstream economics, he views decision-makers as 'sensible' people who will make reasonable attempts (taking account of information costs and scarce attention) to collect objective information that will be relevant to the decision in question. Furthermore, Simon was sophisticated enough to insist that this is not purely an individual matter, but that people are embedded in organisations and institutions and subjected to psychological influences that have a bearing on the information they collect and the processes they use (procedural rationality) and therefore on the ultimate decisions they make.[64] But his insistence on the 'rational' part of

---

[62] Until his death in February 2001, Herbert Simon held the view of human beings 'as information processors'. Furthermore, he believed that 'human beings are serial information processors: we can attend to at most one thing at a time' and that this was a 'fundamental axiom underlying the principle of scarcity of attention' (Simon, 2002). Simon argued that 'bounded rationality' was one of the major consequences of the scarcity of attention.

[63] For a more detailed analysis of Simon's views on the selection of information, see Fransman (1994c), pp. 725–32.

[64] 'Administrative man is limited also by constraints that are part of his own psychological make-up – limited by the number of persons with whom he can communicate, the amount of information he can acquire and retain, and so forth. The fact that these limits are not physiological and fixed, but are instead largely determined by social and even organizational forces, created problems of theory construction of great subtlety; and the fact that the possibilities of modifying and

bounded rationality reveals that he saw the whole process of decision-making as a rational one, even though he wanted to qualify the extent to which it is rational. However, problems confronting Simon's perspective begin to emerge when (within the context of this chapter) the fundamental question is posed: What information set does the Simonian decision-maker use (circa 1998/1999) on the basis of which to decide whether or not to invest in the telecoms industry? Simon's own answer to this question (implicit in his writings) is that it will depend on the information that the decision-maker has *selected*. Simon argues that attention plays a dual role. Not only does its scarcity limit the amount of information that can be selected. Attention also serves as a selection mechanism, allowing the decision-maker to focus on particular subsets of the total set of available information. In this way, attention economises on its own scarcity by allowing the decision-maker to process only a limited amount of the total information available.

But this raises further problems by moving the questions one stage back. What determines the subsets of information that the decision-maker's attention will select? Concretely, for instance, what determines whether the information that the decision-maker selects is a report by Jack Grubman or a book on past booms and busts in the railways, electricity, and automobile industries?[65] The fact that the decision-maker in question is a fund manager who regularly receives company reports from Salomon Brothers, including Grubman's, does not deterministically imply that the decision-maker will not feel the need to pursue a 'deeper' understanding of industrial and financial dynamics in an attempt to learn from past experience.

Pursuing these kinds of questions leads quickly to an abandonment of the insistence that the process is 'rational', even boundedly so, for the simple reason that it becomes impossible to define

relaxing these limits may themselves become objections of rational calculation compounds the difficulties' (Fransman 1994c, p. 199).

[65] For one such book, see Nairn (2002).

boundary conditions separating a rational selection of information from one that is not. That people select information, that numerous factors determine which subsets of information are selected, and that for practical purposes the process of selection is nondeterministic seems to be a fact of life that leaves little room for notions of rationality. Furthermore, this fact of life helps us to make sense of the beliefs and expectations that shaped the Telecoms Boom and Bust, 1996–2003.

Gurus

At this point it is worth adding some comments on the role of Gurus in the Telecoms Boom and Bust, 1996–2003. It is clear that Gurus played an important role in the boom and bust. Jack Grubman could move markets (as could his counterparts such as Mary Meeker, Henry Blodget, and Abby Cohen in the so-called dot-com arena[66]).

But what does this imply about the decision-making process? Why is it that so many apparently confident, intelligent, and institutionally well-placed individuals selected Gurus for their prime information?[67]

To be sure, there are several good reasons for turning to gurus. To begin with, the Guru's perceived attributes of foresight, wisdom, and well-connectedness give comfort to those making decisions that are inevitably permeated by Knightian uncertainty.[68] At the same time, the Guru allows the decision-maker to economise on the scarcity of their attention by effectively 'outsourcing' the job of information selection and information processing to the guru. How comforting to know that one does not have to go through the cumbersome and costly task of deciding what information is needed, and interpreting it, in order to make the decision. It has already been done – by the Guru.

---

[66] See, for example, Cassidy (2002).
[67] One example is Walter Scott, quoted in note 12.
[68] More research is needed to understand better how these perceptions are formed that determine who becomes a Guru and who does not.

However, serious problems may result from the use of a Guru. We have seen that Gurus obviate the need to process information while they provide a way (though not a rational way) of coping with uncertainty. But Gurus do not provide their followers with a way of deciding whether the 'information and knowledge' they are offering is biased or not. Indeed, precisely because their role eliminates or reduces the need of their followers to process their own information in order to arrive at their own conclusions, Gurus may be offered a screen behind which they can hide their biases. This danger may be referred to as Guru Hazard. There seems to be strong grounds for concluding that both the use of Gurus and Guru Hazard played an important role in both the Telecoms and the Dot-Com booms and busts.

Finally, a necessary implication of the use of Gurus is that they may be wrong. Unfortunately, however, their followers may have no way of knowing they are wrong until it is too late. For example, there is scant comfort for telecoms investors to read in *Business Week* that 'Grubman argues that he truly believed in the stocks he recommended, even if he was wrong.'[69]

CONCLUSIONS

Starting with a periodisation of the Telecoms Boom and Bust, 1996–2003, the main concern of this chapter has been to understand some of the causal processes and mechanisms that have been involved and to discuss some of the questions and implications that emerge. In this concluding section attention will be turned to the question of whether there are lessons that may be learned.

Are there lessons that may be learned from the Telecoms Boom and Bust that may reduce the chance or the severity of what Charles Kindleberger (2000) has called 'manias, panics and crashes'? Or are we fundamentally and unavoidably 'in the same boat' as those who produced phenomena such as Tulipomania and the South Sea Bubble,

---

[69] *Business Week* (2002), p. 42.

despite what we like to think of as our far more sophisticated economy based on complex information and communication technologies,
theories, and models?

To remain at the pragmatic level, three questions will be briefly
examined:

1. Is it possible to encourage more 'independent research' in the system that
   will make the system less susceptible to the bouts of excessive optimism
   and pessimism associated with booms and busts?
2. Is it possible to give greater weight to calculations of long-term prospective
   yields to achieve the same purpose as in Question 1?
3. Are there institutional reforms and innovations that can be made so as to
   produce a systemic way of 'stripping the Emperor', that is, challenging the
   conventional wisdoms that are an endogenous part not only of booms and
   busts but of everyday life?

Of the three questions, the first has been addressed most directly in the reforms that have been proposed by financial regulators in
the wake of the bust. Specifically, it has been proposed, inter alia, that
research functions in financial institutions such as investment banks
should be separated organisationally and in terms of incentives from
the institution's other activities, that research should be separately
costed and marketed so that the purchasers of research will be able
through their purchase decisions to exercise control over the quality
of the research, and that mechanisms be found to ensure that a
minimal amount of research is produced by 'independent' researchers.
How effective are proposals such as these likely to be?

In answering this question, a further question needs to be posed:
When can research be said to be 'independent' – independent of what?
The present chapter has suggested that the Consensual Vision that
dominated thinking during the Telecoms Boom, which was constructed and reproduced through a wide variety of mechanisms,
strongly influenced many of the assumptions that formed the starting
point (and interpretive framework) for much of the research that was
done. This suggests that it is necessary to distinguish between organisational independence (i.e. independence from specific organisations)

and what may be called ideological independence (i.e. independence from conventional wisdoms such as the Consensual Vision). However, as is immediately apparent, any attempt to produce an effective degree of ideological independence in the system will be extremely difficult to achieve. Certainly, there seems little reason to believe that creating organisational independence (e.g. by separating research organisations from others) will lead to the creation of ideological independence. The idea of organisational independence does not pay sufficient attention to the broader question of how ideas and beliefs are constructed and modified in a socioeconomic system.

There are also reasons to doubt the effectiveness of attempts to give greater weight in the system to calculations of long-term prospective yields. Keynes provided one of the reasons when he discussed the assumption that 'the existing market valuation [of financial assets] ... is uniquely *correct* in relation to our existing knowledge of the facts which will influence the yield of the investment, and that it will only change in proportion to changes in this knowledge'.[70] This assumption is very much in the mould of the efficient markets hypothesis.[71]

However, Keynes points out that 'philosophically speaking, it cannot be uniquely correct, since our existing knowledge does not provide a sufficient basis for a calculated mathematical expectation. In point of fact, all sorts of considerations enter into the market valuation which are in no way relevant to the prospective yield.'[72] In similar vein, Keynes points out elsewhere that 'The outstanding fact is the extreme precariousness of the basis of knowledge on which our estimates of prospective yield have to be made. Our knowledge of the factors which will govern the yield of an investment some years hence is usually very slight and often negligible.'[73] Furthermore, as noted earlier in this chapter, Keynes produced a number of other

---

[70] Keynes (1961, p. 152), emphasis in the original.
[71] 'The efficient markets theory asserts that all financial prices accurately reflect all public information at all times' (Shiller 2000, p. 171).
[72] Keynes (1961), p. 152.   [73] Ibid., p. 149.

reasons for suggesting that stock markets are inherently short-term oriented and inevitably pay little attention to calculations of long-term prospective yield.

Nonetheless, these arguments have not prevented the establishment of a number of investment funds, in the wake of the bust, purporting to take a long-term view of returns and eschewing short-term benchmarking. However, while Keynes acknowledged the existence of such individuals in the financial markets, and recognised the potentially important impact of these individuals, he came to the ultimate conclusion that 'Investment based on genuine long-term expectation is so difficult today as to be scarcely practicable.'[74] To the extent that Keynes's arguments are accepted, therefore, we have reason to doubt the effectiveness of the proposal contained in Question 2.

This leaves Question 3, attempting to create systemic ways of challenging conventional wisdoms. In dealing with this question it is first necessary to understand how the existing system sometimes creates conventional wisdoms, in this case a Consensual Vision of what was believed to be happening in the telecoms industry where above-average returns were thought to be available.

The processes that generated the Consensual Vision are far too complex to describe adequately here (and further research would be required to do so). Nevertheless, it is possible to detect the broad outlines of these processes. The starting point, as noted earlier, seems to have been the new opportunities for profit generated by telecoms liberalisation in the era of voice communications. These opportunities resulted in the emergence, first and notably in the United States, of a number of new entrants that challenged the incumbents and quickly became highly profitable.[75] In response, telecoms equipment and other telecoms input suppliers grew and raised their profile. With the IPOs of these companies and the rapid rise in the price of their

---

[74] Ibid., pp. 156-7.

[75] WorldCom in a case in point in the US and Mobilcom in Germany followed a very similar evolutionary path.

shares, the attention of other players was quickly attracted. These included investment bankers and their equity researchers, stock brokers, institutional and private investors, and fund managers.

The Internet and the data era added fuel to the fire. Gurus such as Grubman soon emerged in order to articulate and provide a rationale for the hopes and aspirations of these players, all of whom had developed a vested interest in exuberant aspirations for the telecoms industry. The media soon came to play an important role. For example, newspaper features and even TV programmes reflected, reproduced, and further embellished the growing perceptions of a new bonanza. To be sure, the press also articulated doubts and misgivings about the growing conventional wisdom, harking back to earlier episodes such as the railway and electricity busts and on occasion even pointing to some of the flaws in the Consensual Vision. But these voices tended to be drowned out.

Evolutionary thinking teaches that variety is one of the key ingredients of the health of a socioeconomic system. Not only does it provide, with selection processes, the grist for the evolutionary mill. It also provides a systemic way of coping with uncertainty. In an uncertain world, by definition, there is no way of knowing, ex ante, what is the right way forward. In such a world, variety in thinking provides a number of alternative ways forward. The Consensual Vision in the telecoms industry produced a dangerous situation, precisely because it destroyed variety in thinking.

The question is whether it is possible, through institutional innovation, to produce a greater variety in thinking, particularly at those times and in those areas where variety is lacking. We do know that the pressures against variety in thinking can be extremely strong[76] and, therefore, that the task is not an easy one. But given the importance of the

---

[76] Relevant here is the work of Thomas Kuhn (1966) on the dominance of paradigms in scholarly thinking and the role played by 'invisible colleges' consisting of groups of people united by background and interest. Paradigmatic thinking, however, discourages variety of thought.

issue and the potential benefits that could be produced it is suggested that this question merits further close attention.[77]

At a more general level it may be concluded from the analysis in this chapter of some of the processes and mechanisms involved in the Telecoms Boom and Bust, 1996–2003, that the failures that have been identified are quintessentially human failures. This much is apparent in some of the terminology that it has been felt essential to use in analysing financial cycles –words such as 'mass psychology', 'fetish of liquidity', 'rationalisation', 'greed', 'mania', and 'panic'. It is this human dimension that ties us closely to those who produced Tulipomania and the South Sea Bubble, despite the more sophisticated technology and knowledge that separates us.

---

[77] One of the notable characteristics of the Telecoms Boom and Bust, 1996–2003, was the relative absence of 'corrective' research produced by universities. Why universities failed to muster a more vigorous challenge to the flawed thinking in the Telecoms Industry (and the dot-com arena) is not immediately apparent. But this institutional failure should form a part of any discussion intended to contribute to a greater degree of systemic variety in thinking.

9   Innovation Ecosystems, New Waves of Industrialisation, and the Implications for China[*]

How might innovation ecosystems fit into a government's innovation policy? In this chapter the case of China is examined based on a policy report prepared by the author of the present book for the then-incoming Chinese government of Xi Jinping. The differing roles of national, sectoral, regional, company, and societal challenge innovation ecosystems are distinguished.

BACKGROUND

In 2012 the Chinese government, in preparation for the new leadership of Xi Jinping, decided to invite a number of Fortune 500 companies to prepare several reports for the new government suggesting what the companies thought the government should do. Four areas were selected. The first of these was on innovation. The six companies invited to address this area were Caterpillar, Dow Chemical, Hitachi, Mastercard, Michelin, and Renault.

I, the author of the present book, was invited by the China Development and Research Foundation (CDRF) of the Chinese State Council, the institution entrusted with organising the project, to join this innovation team. The topic that the team was invited to address was 'Innovation and New Wave Industrialisation'. For the companies a condition of their participation was that their CEO would sign off on the team's final report. As an appointee of CDRF I was specifically asked to act as a 'sparring partner' to the multinational companies with the aim of sharpening the analysis provided in the final report.

[*] See also Fransman, M., 2018. 'Inventing and designing a Mobility Innovation Ecosystem for Chinese cities to combat congestion, pollution and global warming: putting it all together and making it happen', in Jin Zhang and Zhang Laiming (eds.), *China and the World Economy: Transition and Challenges*. London: Routledge.

After the team's final report was submitted I was requested by CDRF to prepare my own report to be titled: 'Innovation, New Waves of Industrialisation, and the Implications for China'. The present chapter is largely a reproduction of my original report with only a few omissions and some minor additions.

The CDRF asked the following six questions of the multinational companies, the fifth of which dealt specifically with innovation ecosystems:

1. What exactly are the trends of the third technology revolution?
2. What are the trends of innovation models at the global level and the trends of innovation policy?
3. What are the mechanisms of the collaborative innovation?
4. What could be the relationships between the government and the market?
5. How to create a sustainable and effective innovation ecosystem?
6. How to secure that the Report addresses the government's interests and [in] the appendix the company interests?

INTRODUCTION

China has embarked on a remarkable transition – from a country whose economic dynamic has been largely based on low cost (though often high quality) manufacturing, using technologies and practices that have come mainly from outside, to a country increasingly capable of internally generating novelty.

However, this transition, of the greatest importance not only for the Chinese people but also for the functioning of the global economy, is inherently problematical.

Let us begin with novelty itself. It is novelty that is the main driver of the capitalist economy, making it, as Joseph Schumpeter observed, a restless system, incessantly in a process of change. Novelty is the essence of innovation, which Schumpeter defined as including not only new products and services, and new technologies and processes, but also new forms of organisation and new markets, ways of marketing, and business models. To this we should also add new ways of thinking.

However, Schumpeter, drawing explicitly and heavily on Karl Marx, also pointed to the two-edged sword that is innovation. Novelty generates new possibilities. But it also destroys the old, often with difficult consequences. Furthermore, as we are now only too aware, if we extend the discussion of innovation as Schumpeter did to the dynamic interplay between innovation and the financing of, and investment in, innovation, we have to come to grips with other drivers of the restless capitalist system such as irrational exuberance, greed, panic, and contagion in financial markets. Apparently, the generation of novelty is not an unmixed blessing.

But the problem goes even deeper. The reason is that novelty can never be an end in itself. It can only be a means. Something new is not necessarily in all respects better than something old. Furthermore, the new, even when it is obviously significantly more advanced than the old, is not always demanded. Concorde, the superior supersonic airplane, failed to pass the market-selection fitness test and soon became commercially obsolete.

The main implication is that the spotlight necessarily then moves to focus our attention on the *ends*. But this only deepens our problems. What are our ultimate goals for our societies and, indeed, for person-kind generally? This is a crucial but troubling question. It is also paradoxical. Because although almost all of us have, at one time or another, had the good fortune to experience that state of mind to which we might attach words such as 'fulfilment' or 'happiness', we find it extremely difficult to turn this sought-after frame of mind into practical goals that may serve to orient society's actions and inter-actions. We also find it a hard task to define the conditions that are necessary and sufficient to produce this state of mind in a large proportion of the population.

But, of course, these difficulties do not imply that we should desist from posing the crucial question of what we should be aiming to achieve. For even if this will not produce a consensual answer, the mere posing of the question is likely to stimulate discussion and debate that will encourage the self-examination and critical awareness that surely is an essential part of any healthy society.[1]

LONG AND SHORT WAVES OF ECONOMIC ACTIVITY

As Schumpeterian economists have observed, the history of capitalist development has been punctuated by periods when clusters of radically new technologies have emerged. Five such periods have been identified since the first industrial revolution began in the 1770s in Great Britain. These are shown in Exhibit 9.1.

The emergent new technologies have had two immediate principal effects. First, they have created new possibilities and new opportunities. Second, they have resulted in dramatic falls in relative prices of at least an order of magnitude (e.g. a huge drop in the *cost of power* from the water-powered loom, to steam-engine driven machinery, to electrical machinery; significant falls in the *cost of transport* with the emergence of the steam engine and the later development of the internal combustion engine; and the substantial decrease in the *cost of processing, storing, and communicating information* with the advent of information and communications technologies.)

These new possibilities and opportunities, together with the high-powered incentives created by the radical fall in relative prices, created new channels for lucrative investment. As investment is made in the newly opening areas so total factor productivity increases and with it so does GDP and employment. Although, as we have noted, the opposite side of the same coin is the destruction of some older industries, products, technologies, and markets (however, usually not total destruction), on balance the new industries driven by the new technologies have provided sufficient impetus to increase significantly aggregate output and employment.

---

[1] Stiglitz, J., Sen, A., and Fitoussi, J.-P., 2009. *Report by the Commission in the Measurement of Economic Performance and Social Progress*. www.stiglitz-sen-fitoussi.fr.

Exhibit 9.1 *Long Waves of Economic Activity*

Technical Change and Economic Growth: Five Periods

Date	Age	Events	Industries
From 1771	'Industrial Revolution'	Arkwright's water-frame mill opens in Cromford; Watt's steam engine; Crompton's spinning mule	Mechanised textile industry; machinery
From 1829	Steam and railways	Stephenson's 'Rocket' steam locomotive wins contest for Liverpool-Manchester railway; steam power applied to many industries (including textiles)	Railways; steam engines; iron and coal-mining; telegraph
From 1875	Steel, electricity, heavy engineering	Carnegie's Bessemer steel plant opens in Pittsburgh; steam engines for steel ships; electrical equipment; copper cables	Steel, steam-driven steel ships; electricity; telephone
From 1908	Oil, cars, mass production	First Model-T produced by Ford in Detroit; internal combustion engine; oil and oil fuels; rubber; home electrical appliances	Mass-produced cars; oil; petrochemicals; rubber; home electrical products
From 1948	Information and telecommunications	Shockley's transistor; computers; telecoms equipment; Intel's microprocessor; networked computing	Telecoms equipment and networks; computers; semiconductors and devices; software; consumer electronics; Internet

Source: Adapted from Perez (2002) and Fransman (2007).

But the ball does not stop here. And this is where financial markets enter the picture. Some investors soon discover that there are relatively attractive returns to be earned in the new areas. As Charles Kindleberger,[2] the great scholar of booms and busts, observed, there is nothing that gets colleagues, friends, and neighbours excited as much as the knowledge that a great deal of money is being made. Expectations about these areas, accordingly, become exuberant. And financial markets seem, under these conditions, inevitably to over-shoot, despite all the lessons from the past that council caution – from Tulipomania to the South Sea Bubble and on. Eventually, financial asset prices, and the prices of some real assets, become unsustainable and the inevitable then happens – panic and rapid asset depreciation occur.

In the real economy, at the level of companies, the first success-ful movers into the new areas, being the first to acquire the distinctive new competences required, and therefore with limited entry by com-petitors, enjoy a temporary monopoly power and earn relatively high profits. This fuels the financial bonanza. But soon, as Schumpeter observed, competitors jump on the bandwagon and profit margins unavoidably become eroded, contributing to the downturn. Eventu-ally, average profits fall and productivity slows down, leading to a moderation of economic growth and even, depending on the severity of the disruption in financial markets, to a decline in growth.

Radically new technological revolutions usually require new institutions and new facilitating conditions if they are to have a significant impact. These may include new supporting and comple-mentary technologies; new skills and new approaches provided by schools, training institutions, and universities; new infrastructure; and perhaps new forms of funding, state intervention, and regulation. These requirements and the costs and difficulties of providing them often make it difficult for the countries that have dominated

---

[2] Kindleberger, C. P., and Aliber, R. Z., 2005. *Manias, Panics and Crashes: A History of Financial Crises*. Hampshire: Palgrave Macmillan.

preceding waves to make the adaptations needed to maintain their position in the new wave. Great Britain provides a good example having initiated the first wave (in textile machinery) and performed successfully in the second (steam and railways). Remarkably, for example, at the beginning of the First World War the Clyde River alone in Glasgow, Scotland, built one-third of British shipping tonnage and almost one-fifth of world tonnage, a total greater than all German shipyards combined. But in the third, fourth, and fifth waves Britain fell rapidly behind as, notably, the United States and Germany soared ahead.[3]

The new revolutions create new opportunities for some emerging countries that are able to leapfrog over the previous waves and create the conditions needed for the new wave. A good example is the catch-up, first of Japan and then Korea and Taiwan, in the area of information and communications technologies, technologies that were not invented in East Asia.[4] This new entry and the global competition it has provided has given a significant boost not only to the new entrant countries and their companies but also to the global economy.

However, these great leaps forward are few and far between. In the more normal times technical change is incremental rather than radical, causing ripples of new economic activity rather than huge waves. Although Schumpeter focused on radical technical change, the cumulative effect of incremental technical change should not be underestimated. The example of smartphones is a case in point.

Some have suggested that at the present time we are witnessing the emergence of the beginnings of a new long wave of economic activity. They point to the technological advances that have taken place in areas such as information and communications technologies, biotechnology, stem cells and regenerative medicine, nanotechnology

---

[3] Fransman, M., 2007. *Edinburgh, City of Funds*. Edinburgh: Kokoro.
[4] Fransman, M., 2010. *The New ICT Ecosystem: Implications for Policy and Regulation*. Cambridge: Cambridge University Press.

and new materials, renewable energy, 3-D printing, etc. Others, however, are more cautious, not denying the breakthroughs in areas such as these, but more sceptical that collectively they are sufficient to generate the kind of aggregate growth-raising impetus created by the five earlier long waves.[5] To the extent that an order-of-magnitude fall in the real price of key products, services, and technologies is a necessary precondition for long wave impacts, there are reasons for caution on this issue. Time will be the ultimate arbiter.

THE IMPORTANCE OF GROWING GLOBALLY COMPETITIVE INDIGENOUS COMPANIES AND THE IMPLICATIONS FOR CHINA

Introduction

It is clear from economic history that it is *enterprises* (aided by institutional innovations such as the advent of the joint stock company) that play the leading role in seizing the opportunities provided by the new technologies and turning them into profits and national growth in output and employment. This is evident from Britain's transformation in the first industrial revolution and from the performance of catch-up countries thereafter. Indeed, growing globally competitive indigenous companies is a necessary condition for successful performance both in the new wave of radical technological change and in the ripples of incremental change that occur thereafter. But the growth of both companies and their global competitiveness does not happen automatically. It is something that must be made to happen. For China this is one of the most important challenges, the success of

---

[5] A particularly important contribution in this connection is the quantitative work of Robert Gordon, who argues that the absence of radical innovation is leading to a significant slowing of economic growth. Gordon, R., 2016. *The Rise and Fall of American Growth: The U.S. Standard of Living since the Civil War.* Princeton, NJ: Princeton University Press. Also see Gordon, R., 2012. 'Is US Economic Growth Over? Faltering Innovation Confronts the Six Headwinds', NBER Working Paper 18315, August.

http://faculty-web.at.northwestern.edu/economics/gordon/is%20us%20economic%20growth%20over.pdf.

which will heavily influence the achievement of many of the country's other goals.

What Needs to Be Done to Grow Globally Competitive Indigenous Companies in China? Trade, Investment, and Market Failure

Any catch-up country starts with a great dilemma. Both its companies and its institutions (what Nobel Laureate Douglass North calls 'rule of the game') as well as supporting organisations – such as banks and other financing bodies, universities, other research organisations, and legal systems – are weak relative to those in the leading countries. It therefore faces an uphill struggle.

But this does not mean that the catch-up country has no weapons in its armoury. Amongst its weapons are lower factor costs (particularly skilled labour), perhaps a favourable exchange rate, and the fact that the very weakness of its institutions and supporting organisations may make them more flexible and adaptable to the new conditions required by the new technologies (vested interests in these bodies may be relatively weak precisely because of their overall ineffectiveness). With good policy and strong state leadership it is possible that over time these weapons can be mobilised and turned to the purpose of building globally competitive indigenous companies together with the facilitating institutions and organisations that they require.

It is here that the question of the respective roles of the state and the market, one of the key questions posed by the CDRF to the six multinational companies, becomes important. To what extent can the task at hand – growing globally competitive indigenous companies together with supporting institutions and organisations – be left to the market (i.e. to the collective decisions of private firms, consumers, and non-government-controlled entities)? To what extent is it necessary for the state to intervene and in what ways?

These questions soon become pressing at the country's borders. To what extent should the inflow of foreign goods and services and foreign direct investment be left to global markets and the domestic market to decide? In answer to this important question some like to tell an optimistic story of the benefits that will flow to all in the global system as largely unrestrained markets allocate resources globally according to the endowments of each country (i.e. endowments of labour, capital, and natural resources) thus optimising not only global social welfare but also the social welfare of each country. This is the conventional economic theory of comparative advantage.

Historically, however, this optimistic story has soon run into difficulties. The first problem is that left to themselves global markets and the flows of trade and investment that they drive are likely to leave little room for the growth of globally competitive companies in follower countries. While relatively low factor costs (i.e. costs of labour or capital) and/or raw material costs may provide some opportunities in these countries under free trade conditions for some viable corporate growth, the historical experience on the whole has been that these opportunities have been deemed insufficient by the political decision-makers in the follower countries. Accordingly, the general rule – from the first catch-up countries, the United States and Germany, to later catch-up countries such as Japan, Korea, and Taiwan – has been for the state to interfere with free global markets through the use of indigenous enterprise–encouraging tools such as import quotas, tariffs, subsidies, and restrictions on inward investment. The ultimate success of these countries despite their interference with market forces stands in strong contrast to the optimistic story of free trade referred to earlier. However, once indigenous companies and their competences become more competitive globally, so more and more room is created for market forces to play a greater role.

The second problem with the free market story is that sometimes markets simply do not work efficiently. One of the most important findings in economic research over the last few decades is the rigorous demonstration of this fact. A few examples will make this clearer.

To begin with, markets produce their best results when all the players in the system have the same perfect information. In reality, however, players usually have asymmetric information (some have information that others do not) and their information is incomplete (they do not know what they must know in order to make optimal decisions). Significant further problems are presented by irreducible uncertainty (which exists when probability distributions cannot be defined and therefore probabilistic decisions cannot be made and optimal decisions, accordingly, cannot be determined).

This is particularly important in the area of innovation where, by definition, uncertainty rules. (If we know the outcomes of ex ante investments in innovation, even probabilistically, we would not have to undertake the search that is the essence of research.) Under conditions of uncertainty, by definition, we do not *know* the outcomes and can only *imagine* them. Under such conditions it is not possible to define optimal outcomes.

It can be demonstrated that key markets in the capitalist economy are subject to significant market failure, for example, credit, labour and knowledge markets.[6]

In the case of credit markets, for instance, think of an entrepreneur who supposes she has a great new innovation to commercialise. But in order to do so she needs money. How does she persuade the provider of money (e.g. venture capitalist or bank) to lend it to her? How is the lender to evaluate the information she gives? Is she being too optimistic and 'spinning' the opportunity? Even if the lender believes she is being honest, how does the lender deal with the possibility that the would-be borrower is being overly optimistic? Of course, there is also a chance that the borrower is being downright opportunistic, lying about the prospects. If the lender turns to a third party for advice how do they decide whether the judgement of the third party is any more reliable, and besides, what are the costs of this advice? It is because of problems such as these that early-stage

---

[6] A recent demonstration is contained in the paper on industrial policy by Harvard economist Dani Rodrick. See Rodrik, D., 2008. *Normalising Industrial Policy*. Harvard University.

    www.hks.harvard.edu/fs/drodrik/Research%20papers/Industrial%20Policy%20_Growth%20Commission_.pdf.

innovation (particularly when there are no prototypes that may aid decision-making) is often underfunded by the market, leaving the state to fill the gap in order to fuel innovation.

In the case of labour markets there is often a problem with market failure relating to in-firm training. The problem is that having invested in the training of an employee the employer may fail to appropriate an adequate reward from the investment if the employee is headhunted by another employer. This may result in underinvestment in crucial in-firm training if left entirely to the labour market. There are, however, institutional innovations designed to deal with this problem. The Japanese, for example, developed lifetime employment as a solution. However, while this practice has many benefits (including, apart from a stronger incentive to invest in training, loyalty and sometimes good intrafirm flows of information), it also has its costs. These include limited inter-firm flows of knowledge and difficulties for companies unable to reduce labour costs through dismissal in times of economic downturn.

In the knowledge market, another crucial capitalist market, major market failures arise from uncertainty (already discussed). Uncertainty considerably reduces the market incentive to invest in knowledge creation because the investor does not know what returns are likely. This is a key justification in all countries, not only catch-up ones, for state investment in schools, universities, and government-funded research programmes or institutes.

These and other market failures carve out a sizable domain where not only is it legitimate (logically) for states to intervene but where state intervention provides the only way forward. This is as true for the Chinese state as for any other.

THE ROLE OF GLOBAL INNOVATION ECOSYSTEMS (GIES)

The Conceptualisation and Role of GIEs

Like motherhood and apple pie, 'innovation ecosystems' have come to be seen as one of the 'great goods'. Construct your innovation ecosystem, like Apple for example, and the world will be yours. Unfortunately, however, the concept of 'innovation ecosystem' has not been well defined, is used in inconsistent ways by different writers and in different settings, and has obscured significant complexity.

At the heart of the concept is the assumption that those who jointly create value through innovation interact with one another and are interdependent with the result that they may, collectively, reasonably be seen as part of a *single system*.

But this raises the first conceptual problem: Where are the *boundaries of any particular innovation ecosystem* that include some but omit others? This is a problem because in a modern economy there are many links of various kinds that connect large numbers of the economy's agents. In dealing with this problem a subjective judgment needs to be made regarding who is mainly responsible for creating and implementing the many processes that lead to innovation in a given area. Inevitably, this subjectivity means that different analysts may come up with different innovation ecosystems.

Solving the boundary problem also entails selecting the components of the system, i.e. the *'players'* in the system as well as those who determine the *rules of the game (institutions)* according to which the players play and the *facilitating and frustrating factors* that also shape the innovation process.

Significantly, this discussion implies that *'innovation ecosystems' are not real objects* that exist in the world the way, say, atoms, elephants, and machines do. Rather, they are *conceptual constructs* that can be constructed in different ways with different contents.

The Players in the Innovation Ecosystem

But who are the players who jointly create value through innovation that are the object of attention? To answer this question, we need to define what we mean by 'innovation'.

In doing so we will follow Schumpeter, whose definition informs the currently internationally accepted definitions of innovation adopted by organisations such as the OECD. According to

Schumpeter, innovation includes new products and services; new processes and technologies; new forms of organisation; new markets, business models, and ways of marketing; and, we should add, new ways of thinking. Other definitions are, of course, also possible.

Business Enterprises

From Schumpeter's definition it follows that *business enterprises*, and in particular those within them who 'carry out' the processes in these enterprises that lead to innovation, constitute the *engine of the innovation ecosystem*. The reason is that in general it is enterprises that create new products and services, new processes and technologies, etc., rather than other players in the ecosystem such as funders, universities, regulators, etc.

But this first approximation in defining the players in the ecosystem creates further problems since 'enterprises' and 'universities' etc. are also conceptual constructs that have to be deconstructed and disaggregated if we are to understand innovation.[7]

Indeed, these players in an innovation ecosystem are themselves complex subsystems of the innovation ecosystem. Take as an example large companies. As we will see later, we may think of a large company as consisting of a number of functionally differentiated players who jointly possess the knowledge embodied in the competences and routines that allow the company to do what it needs to in order to survive and hopefully thrive. As far as the company's innovation is concerned, it may make sense to distinguish the following internal players: those in corporate strategy; research, usually located

---

[7] The Cambridge University economist Edith Penrose put this insightfully when she said that 'A "firm" is by no means an unambiguous clear-cut entity; it is not an observable object physically separable from other objects, and it is difficult to define except with reference to what it does or what is done within it. Hence each analyst is free to choose any characteristics of firms that he is interested in, to define firms in terms of those characteristics, and to proceed thereafter to call the construction so defined a 'firm'. Herein lies a potential source of confusion' (Penrose, E., 1959. *The Theory of the Growth of the Firm*. Oxford: Oxford University Press, p. 10). As with a 'firm' so with an 'innovation ecosystem'.

in specialised research laboratories; development, located in the firm's business units; and marketing and sales, also in the business units. But even these 'players' need to be disaggregated since not all of their members are involved in the generation of novelty (i.e. innovation).

As this brief discussion makes clear, defining the 'players' involved in the innovation processes of an innovation ecosystem is no simple matter.

Customer-Users

This brings us to a key issue. The overall goal of innovation ecosystems, paradoxically, is *not* innovation per se (e.g. creating a new product or process). Rather, it is to *generate added value* for the customer-users of the innovation. The *incentives of the ecosystem* are geared towards added value, not innovation itself. A new product or process may or may not add value. The ultimate test is whether the innovation is *adopted* in the market by customer-users. More generally, for an innovation to be *economically significant* it must be *diffused* (a requirement on which Schumpeter insisted).

It is crucial, therefore, that our conceptualisation of innovation ecosystems includes *customer-users* as a crucial set of players in the system. This requires a focus on the process of value-creation, a process that may be facilitated by innovation.

But we also need to explore further the *symbiotic relationship* (symbiosis = living together) between customer-users and the companies that create value for them. This relationship is complex and can take many different forms with different degrees of customer involvement.

However, in all company–customer relationships there is one essential characteristic: companies specialise in *producing* the goods and services concerned, while customer-users specialise in *consuming* them. Production and consumption generate two overlapping, but nonidentical, sets of knowledge. In order to innovate, companies need feedback from the customer-users of their products and services (although they will often have to go beyond this feedback in making imaginative conjectures regarding how they might create additional value for their customer-users). Furthermore, in some circumstances it may be possible to construct processes that will allow customers to become more directly involved in the innovation process so that they become co-innovators, by generating customer-created innovations. In this way the sharp distinction between the *producers* of innovations and the *consumers* of these innovations may become blurred with both producers and customers playing a part in the innovation process.

Universities

A key player in most innovation ecosystems is universities that train skilled person-power, do research, and, increasingly, commercialise that research. As largely publicly funded organisations they are designed in part to overcome the knowledge-creation market failure referred to earlier.

But universities are also complex sub-ecosystems, acting as players in broader innovation ecosystems. Their goals and the aims of their members, particularly in the area of research/knowledge creation, are fundamentally different from those of companies.

The goal of companies is to generate value in the form of revenue that is sufficient to at least cover costs and earn a profit that will make it worthwhile staying in business. Failure to do so means either bankruptcy or getting subsidies from the state or financial institutions. (The ability of Chinese state-owned enterprises sometimes to get such subsidies is a crucial factor influencing their innovation behaviour since it gives them a 'soft budget constraint' that allows them to carry on doing things that would have been ruled out under a 'hard' budget constraint.)

In pursuit of this goal, innovative companies try to create new knowledge. Generally, however, they do so in a top-down way. Typically, R&D budgets are created (usually according to a rule of thumb based on an assumed desirable R&D to sales ratio). This budget is managed by R&D managers who have agreed on specific R&D value-related objectives. R&D projects are then selected with researchers and developers encouraged to contribute to the objectives.

In universities, however, the knowledge-creation process is typically bottom-up. Usually university researchers are employed according to their expertise in specialised areas but are given a wide degree of freedom to choose areas in which to research. Their main constraint is not whether or not they create commercial value, as in the case of company researchers, but whether they contribute to knowledge. The latter is usually judged according to publication in peer-reviewed journals and acknowledgement by learned societies, although increasingly patents have been added as a supplementary measure of performance. Frequently, university researchers are motivated just as much by the status bestowed by promotion and the prestige provided by being regarded as a high-flying academic as they are by money.

But researchers are not the only player in universities who matter in terms of innovation. There are also the university's leaders and top management who have additional goals such as fund-raising, attracting students, and acquiring better reputations; commercialisation managers who try to generate value, including spin-offs and start-ups, from research; students themselves, who are generally motivated by many other considerations; and those who fund universities in one way or another. All these interacting 'players' make universities what they are and influence the role they play in the broader innovation process in innovation ecosystems.

Given the very different motivations and knowledge-generation processes in companies and universities, it is no surprise that their symbiotic interface is difficult to design and manage and that the benefits to each vary widely. Exhortation by government policy-makers to 'link universities and companies more closely' often fails to come to grips with the complexities involved. A deeper analysis of the problems and a more careful consideration of the optional ways of designing this interface would often bear fruit.

Other Players, Institutions, and Facilitators and Frustrators

There are many *other key players* in innovation ecosystems including the providers of capital (e.g. banks, venture capitalists and angels, and capital market players), intermediaries who may assist both the creation and diffusion of innovations, knowledge-intensive professionals (such as consultants, lawyers, accountants), regulators, and policymakers. There is no room here, however, for a more detailed analysis of their role.

In addition, there are the *institutions* (defined by Nobel Laureate Douglass North as 'the rules – both formal and informal – of the game') in which the players are embedded, which shape and constrain their behaviour, and which define both incentives and disincentives. These institutions can facilitate and, in some cases, frustrate the innovation process. They include *legal institutions* (e.g. law of property, law of contract, IP law, the rule of law, competition law, etc.), *standardisation* (which may facilitate modularisation, coordination, and interoperability but may also constrain these processes), and *de facto practices* (an interesting recent example of which is the de facto – rather than de jure – redefinition of the acceptability boundary between tax evasion and tax avoidance in the wake of the global financial and fiscal crisis).

These must be added in order to understand the innovation process, making an innovation ecosystem a complex system consisting of complex subsystems.

The Performance of Innovation Ecosystems

Given the complexity of GIEs it should come as no surprise that there is no reason for believing that they are, or will over time become, 'efficient' or 'optimal'. Indeed, for the same complexity reason, it is impossible to define analytically what should be meant by 'efficient' or 'optimal' in this context. The inherent uncertainty that is a key characteristic of GIEs is a major contributor to the problem.

This does not mean, however, that no attempt can be made to measure (and therefore monitor) the *performance* of the GIE (although attributing causality to the different factors that drive performance is a difficult, perhaps even impossible, matter to solve).

So how should the performance of GIEs be measured?

The first point to make is that measuring innovation itself is problematical. The three main indicators – R&D, patents, and citations – are riddled with imperfections. For example, R&D is an input measure, but it is output that we want. More R&D expenditure does not necessarily mean more innovation and value-creation.[8] The total number of granted patents, a measure that is often used, tells us little about the values that result, and weighting patents by revenue generated is a difficult task. The same problem arises in the case of citations. It is as a result of these defects that organisations such as the OECD have tried to extend the measurement of innovation to include data on other outcomes such as proportion of a company's revenue that comes from new products, processes, and forms of organisation. While these measures do help, their usefulness is limited by asymmetric information constraints that result from making firms themselves the measurers of their own performance.

More important is the fact that, as mentioned earlier, it is not innovation itself that we are interested in but its use as a means to achieve other final objectives. In the case of companies these include increases in competitiveness, productivity, profits, and growth, while in the case of countries they include total factor productivity, GDP, and employment growth as well as social objectives such as improved health, education, and environmental conditions. Furthermore, we would like to know how *globally competitive* the players in the GIE

---

[8] Significantly, Apple, as measured by R&D intensity (i.e. R&D as a percentage of sales) is a *low-tech* company, but one that is high-innovation! For example, in 2011 Apple's R&D intensity was 2.2 per cent. This compared with Google's 14 per cent, Microsoft's 13 per cent, Samsung's 9 per cent, and IBM's 6 per cent. Two key reasons for Apple's good innovation performance is that the company's success is largely due to design, the expenditure on which is usually excluded from R&D data, and its highly effective innovation ecosystem, which mobilises important value contributions by complementors such as application developers. The Apple example councils caution regarding an uncritical use of R&D as a measure of innovation performance.

are, not only the companies but also the other players such as universities, other research organisations, hospitals, and schools. For if the players are behind the global frontier it is possible for their performance to be improved. Innovation, we know, makes the most important contribution to the achievement of these final objectives, but the precise causal link is often difficult to establish.

One of the measures of GIE performance should be global performance. Here two indicators are potentially helpful. The first is exports, both at company level (e.g. the proportion of sales exported out of China) and at country level (e.g. exports from China as a proportion of world exports by product category).[9] These measures allow us to distinguish *company competitiveness* from *country competitiveness*. These two do not necessarily go together. In many areas China enjoys country competitiveness while its own companies are not globally competitive in the area. The second measure, relevant at company level, is data on market share by product category. Japan has put these measures to good effect in a critical evaluation of Japanese performance in the ICT sector.[10]

Many measures of GIE performance can and should be made so as to get a reasonable idea of how the ecosystem is performing since, as noted, there is no inherent reason to assume it is performing well or that its performance is improving over time. But it is as well to be aware that the overall judgement of performance is likely to be a tricky affair.

Globalisation and Global Competitiveness

Innovation ecosystems have simultaneously both a *local* and a *global* existence. In any country the players in the innovation ecosystem are embedded in local interactions with other players under the influence of local institutions, facilitators, and frustrators. But at the same time,

[9] This measure is relevant in the case of the tradeable goods and services sector.
[10] Fransman, M., 2014. 'Models of Innovation in Global ICT Firms: The Emerging Global Innovation Ecosystems'. JRC Scientific and Policy Reports – EUR 26774 EN. Seville: JRC-IPTS.

they are also part of a global innovation ecosystem. This is most obviously the case for those players that have a direct global involvement through activities such as exports, imports, outward and inward investment, participation in international trade fairs and conferences, etc. But even those players producing only for the local market will be aware through multiple channels of relevant things happening abroad.

As we have already noted, an important issue regarding the performance of innovation ecosystems relates to the global competitiveness of key players. The more globally competitive they are, the more opportunities they will have to engage in various ways outside China and hence learn from and access global knowledge pools. The increasing importance of knowledge located in other countries is one of the most important trends to emerge in the last decade, a trend that is fundamentally reshaping the global economic system and the way it works. The reason is that R&D, and innovation more general, goes together with GDP. And global GDP is being rapidly redistributed globally away from the traditional 'developed countries', such as the United States, European countries, and Japan.

This has two important implications for innovation ecosystems. First, more knowledge will be generated outside the so-called developed countries, making it increasingly important to connect to knowledge in the 'growth countries'. Second, no country – even China and India, which are expected to be the largest economies in 2050 – will be able to generate all or even most of the knowledge it will require. Increasingly, therefore, *innovation ecosystems must go global, plugging into the knowledge that is generated outside the home country* while at the same time fostering the symbiotic relationships between players domestically that will drive innovation within the country.

Lessons from Japan, Korea, and Taiwan
It is here that Japan, Korea, and Taiwan offer important lessons for China.

In my view the most important lesson from Korea and Taiwan (and Japan in its early catch-up phase) is how to grow globally competitive indigenous companies that power domestic GIEs while driving the growth of GDP, employment, and social development. Summarising complex processes, it may reasonably be concluded that in these countries the state played a key role in facilitating the emergence of indigenous companies and enabling them to rapidly learn from abroad by fostering, and for a long while protecting, the learning process. In all these countries key sectors were selected, sectors that would not have survived in the short run under free trade, and high-powered incentives were used to encourage firm learning in a way that produced increasing global competitiveness.

From the mid-1960s Korea and Taiwan in particular required that their companies in the selected sectors (that did not immediately enjoy a global competitive advantage) *first* prove themselves in export markets in order to qualify *later* for the 'carrots' that were provided as rewards (such as subsidised-interest loans from state financial institutions, tax breaks of various kinds, favourable exchange rates for exporters, other forms of state assistance in export markets, etc.). This requirement ensured that emerging companies in Korea and Taiwan plugged rapidly into *global markets*, learning from *global customers and competitors* (unlike other emerging countries at the time in Latin America and places like India and Pakistan where companies and industries were protected under import-substituting policies and incentivised to produce for protected local markets).

Furthermore, unlike in Europe where single national champions were frequently chosen,[11] the authorities in Japan, Korea, and Taiwan ensured that there was *strong competition* between *multiple* rivals in domestic markets (e.g. cars, semiconductors, computers, consumer electronics, etc.).

---

[11] See, for example, Owen, G., 2010. 'Industrial policy in Europe since the Second World War: what has been learnt', ECIPE Occasional Paper No. 1/2012, Department of Management, London School of Economics.

At the same time as encouraging these high-growth, innovation-intensive sectors where they did *not* immediately enjoy a competitive advantage, the policymakers of these countries took advantage of sectors where they *did* have a competitive advantage (such as textiles, clothing, plywood, trainers, toys, etc.). This policy of 'walking on two legs' took full advantage of global markets and knowledge and eventually, after several decades, resulted in the achievement of global competitiveness that was first elusive in the chosen protected and nurtured markets.

The case of Japan, however, is more complicated.

The Japanese Paradox

The more recent experience of Japan presents an important paradox. Japan leads the world in areas of innovation such as gross expenditure on R&D as a proportion of GDP, business expenditure on R&D as a proportion of GDP, patents, and broadband speed. These are the targets that many policymakers such as the European Commission have prioritised. However, Japan has not performed particularly well in terms of indicators like growth in real GDP and global market share of Japanese companies in important sectors such as ICT (although in other sectors like motor cars, cameras, and optical devices Japanese companies have done much better). Why this discrepancy?

There are multiple factors that enter into an explanation of the Japanese Paradox. These include the bursting of the Japanese financial bubble in 1989 and the subsequent 'lost decade', which negatively impacted on Japanese companies, dependent to a significant extent on the local market; the relatively high yen exchange rate; and relatively high Japanese labour costs. But together with these causes there has been another crucial determinant: the inward-looking nature of many Japanese companies, measured by their relatively low ratio of sales outside Japan to total sales, compared with their main global competitors.

Japanese policymakers sometimes refer to this cause as the Galapagos Effect, alluding to Darwin's explanation of the evolution of unique species on the individual, separated islands of Galapagos. They suggest that in many cases the goods and services of Japanese companies, while well adapted to the high-income, sophisticated markets of Japan, have not necessarily been as well suited to the tastes and preferences of other global markets. In strong contrast, for example in the ICT sector, companies from Korea and Taiwan – such as Samsung, LG, TSMC, HTC, and Acer – with relatively small domestic markets and with strong export encouragement from their governments from the mid-1960s, have focused far more on the most important global markets. The result has at times been startling. For example, 'Samsung Electronics posted four times as much net profit in the third quarter [of 2011] as Japan's 19 main listed technology *and* consumer electronics companies combined.'[12]

The Seductiveness of the Chinese Market: A Chinese Danger

The Japanese Paradox has important implications for the growth of globally competitive Chinese companies, whether state-owned enterprises (SOEs), privately owned enterprises (POEs), small- and medium-sized enterprises (SMEs), or emerging Chinese multinational corporations (MNCs).

The problem is the lure of the domestic Chinese market, which, like the Japanese market from the 1950s to the 1970s, is growing rapidly and which in many cases offers handsome rewards in terms of profitability and growth. However, it would be a big policy mistake to allow this inward-looking focus to go unchallenged. The reason is that an inward focus will mean that Chinese companies, both large and small, will forgo the opportunities for learning and knowledge acquisition that could result from global innovation involvements. An important challenge for Chinese policymakers, therefore, is to incentivise greater global involvement by all categories of Chinese companies. This is equally important for Chinese SMEs (as illustrated, for example, by the 'born global' Indian software SMEs that

---

[12] *Financial Times* (2012).

have made such an important contribution to India's burgeoning software sector, which has contributed significantly to the transformation of the Indian economy).

The Importance of Encouraging Variety in Innovation Ecosystems

In this chapter both the complex nature of innovation ecosystems and the ubiquitous importance of uncertainty have been highlighted. In short, we simply do not know, and cannot know, what will happen to technologies, products and services, and markets in the longer-term future. How should policymakers deal with the predicament that this creates?

One key answer is that they should try and ensure that their innovation ecosystems generate *variety*. As Schumpeterian-evolutionary economics has demonstrated, *variety* plus *selection* are the main drivers of the evolutionary processes that transform economic systems.[13] It is innovation that generates variety. The market provides one of the most important mechanisms for selecting from this variety (although there are also many other mechanisms that coexist with the market in selecting, such as in-firm ways of selecting or rejecting R&D projects and the research selection procedures of government and other research-funding bodies). Under conditions of complexity and uncertainty, although we cannot know which technologies, products and services, and markets will ultimately be selected, we can try to ensure that global innovation ecosystems generate a variety of alternatives so that there is a wider range of opportunities from which to select. For this reason, it is suggested that a healthy global innovation ecosystem is one that succeeds in generating significant variety.

---

[13] For an elaboration, see Fransman, M., 2010. *The New ICT Ecosystem – Implications for Policy and Regulation*. Cambridge: Cambridge University Press.

There Is No Magical Model for GIE Design and Management

Just as with marriage and parenting, there is no magical model for GIE design and management. Its effectiveness depends on many things: the players concerned and their strengths and weaknesses, the quality of its institutions, the political priorities and constraints that exist, and the presence of facilitating and frustrating institutional forces.

Having said this, however, and again just as with marriage and parenting, a good deal of progress may be made through careful analysis, thoughtful and sensitive policy design, and a healthy dose of common sense. Nevertheless, as in the other two areas, this does not mean that we should succumb to the error of thinking that we are, or ever can be, in full control. For we are dealing with a complex system of complex systems that have their own dynamics that we may be able to influence but will never fully control.

HOW SHOULD CHINA USE THE IDEA OF GLOBAL INNOVATION ECOSYSTEMS?

Chinese policymakers should use the idea of GIEs as an important conceptual policy tool at five interconnected levels:

1. The *national* level
2. The *sector* level
3. The *regional* level
4. The *company* level
5. The societal challenge level.

The National-Level Global Innovation Ecosystem

It is at the national level that the official Chinese document aimed at 'speeding up the building of a National Innovation System' focuses as part of implementing The National Guideline for Medium- and Long-Term Plans for Science and Technology Development, 2006–2020.[14]

---

[14] China Government, 2009. 'Opinions on Deepening the Reform of the Scientific and Technological System and Speeding up the Building of a National Innovation System', 20 December 2009 (no author or publisher mentioned).

This guideline sets out the goal for China to become an innovative country by 2020 and a scientific and technological leader by 2050. Achieving this goal will require significant changes in the structure and dynamics of the country's innovation ecosystems and in particular in its enterprises – SOEs, POEs, SMEs, and emerging Chinese MNCs – and innovation-related institutions.

At the national level the concept of GIEs is useful for Chinese policymakers as a way of mapping, first, the kinds of enterprises (SOEs, POEs, SMEs, and emerging Chinese MNCs) that are the engines of the ecosystem and, second, the main institutions and facilitators that can support them.

State-Owned Enterprises

Here the vexed and ongoing debate about the role, strengths, and weaknesses of the SOEs is of great importance because of the size, number, and positioning of these enterprises in the Chinese economy. This is not the place to delve into the important considerations and debates involved. However, from an innovation and innovation ecosystems perspective, a key set of questions deals with the ways in which innovation currently happens, and in some cases fails to happen, in SOEs in different parts of the economy.

My own view, in brief, is that it is not state ownership per se that constrains innovation in China's SOEs. There are too many examples of large companies that have grown to become globally competitive under state ownership – including the cases of Pohang Steel in Korea, Embraer aircraft in Brazil, and national rail companies in countries like Japan, France, and Germany – for state-ownership in itself to pose a problem. Of far greater importance is a combination of the *external environment* of SOEs – in particular the extent to which they face fiercely competitive rivals and their symbiotic positioning in dynamic GIEs – and their *internal organisation*, especially their incentive structures and the ways in which they design and manage their innovation processes. The successful performance of some of the spin-out companies from Chinese research institutes (such as the

Institute of Computer Technology of the Chinese Academy of Science) that were in effect state owned but, crucially, not state managed but independently managed by incentivised managers, suggests that under the right conditions such enterprises can rapidly become globally competitive. Legend Computer, now Lenovo, which emerged from the Institute of Computer Technology, is a shining example.

However, a key issue, in addition to a strongly competitive environment, is SOEs' *soft budget constraint* provided by state-led financial support for enterprises that run into trouble and are deemed by policymakers to be too important to fail. (The bailout of Western banks in the wake of the global financial crisis, however, has taught us that this problem is not confined to China.) There is little that concentrates the innovative mind in enterprises so much as a threatening external environment coupled with a hard budget constraint.

These kinds of issues need to be examined, with detailed empirical evidence, in order to decide what needs to be done to make SOEs more innovative and globally competitive. This requires a large study programme.

Privately Owned Enterprises
Huge strides have been made by China's POEs with a few truly outstanding innovative and globally competitive companies such as Huawei, Lenovo, and Haier leading the pack. The lessons that are to be learned by other Chinese companies from the experiences, learning, and innovation processes of these leaders are extremely important. But these leading companies are still only the tip of the iceberg and their total number is not great.

A key issue, as discussed earlier in this chapter, is how more Chinese POEs can become *globally* competitive. This involves making sure that they do not become totally seduced by the attractions of the Chinese market but that they simultaneously use this market as a springboard for a range of innovation-related involvements outside China, especially in key global markets. One way of doing this, à la Korea and Taiwan, is by incentivising not exports per se but the broader innovation process of *learning by exporting*, which is very different from simply selling goods and services abroad, involving as it does innovation employees in the company and not only sales and marketing people. Another key way is by encouraging the development of *company-level global innovation ecosystems* (discussed in more detail below). China needs to avoid the pitfalls of the Japanese Paradox discussed earlier.

Research Institutes

Key questions with which Chinese policymakers have long been grappling relate to the transformation of research institutes (such as universities, Chinese Academy of Sciences institutes, and ministry and other government-funded research institutes). Again, there is insufficient space here to delve into the major issues and so I will confine myself to only a few points.

The main point is the importance, referred to earlier, of generating *variety* of research in Chinese GIEs. The policy implication of this requirement is that as far as feasible there should be *multiple sources* available for the funding of research. This will encourage different approaches, priorities, and objectives of research. Often it will be sensible to separate policy-making and implementation from research. One way of achieving this is to have research funds allocated by peer-researchers to competing funding applicants. This is particularly useful in the funding of basic research, which tends to be underrepresented in company research. Attention also needs to be given to the research selection procedure to ensure that both quality and variety are objectives. Opening Chinese research programmes to global participation is one important way of giving GIEs the international exposure that they need, and another is the engagement of Chinese researchers in overseas research programmes.

The desirable connections that should be created between nonenterprise research organisations and Chinese and foreign enterprises is another important issue. This has been briefly touched on earlier in the discussion of universities, but far more needs to be said, which, unfortunately, cannot be discussed here.

Sector-Level Global Innovation Ecosystems

A good deal of the attention of Chinese policymakers concerned with innovation should be paid to identifying and analysing *sector* GIEs. However, as far as I am aware, official Chinese documents make little or no reference to sector GIEs.

The reason why the sector is a crucial unit of analysis is that the dynamics of innovation and the role of institutions as facilitators and frustrators of innovation differ fundamentally by sector. Furthermore, countries are globally competitive in only some sectors; none is or can be competitive in all.

For example, the ICT, bio-medical, financial services, automobile, and alternative energy sectors, conceived of in terms of GIEs, are fundamentally different and work in different ways. The players in each sector are different, as are the institutions, facilitators and frustrators, and science and technology bases supporting them. Accordingly, policies that make sense in one sector may not work in another. It is therefore essential to differentiate science, technology, and innovation policy by sector. Taking these points on board it is significant that at the end of 2012 the British government (specifically the Department of Business, Innovation and Skills) declared that it would be focusing more attention on sectors in its policies.[15]

The first thing that Chinese policymakers should do is make the strategic choice regarding which sectors should be prioritised. The selection of sectors, in addition to obvious political and security considerations, should also take into account that China should not, and indeed cannot, try to become globally competitive in all sectors.

---

[15] See Department for Business, Innovation and Skills, 2012. 'Industrial Strategy: UK Sector Analysis', BIS Economics Paper No. 18, September. An example of a good official study of a sector innovation ecosystem is the BIS study of the life sciences sector in the United Kingdom done in 2010. See http://bis.gov.uk/assets/biscore/economics-and-statistics/docs/i/12-1140-industrial-strategy-uk-sector-analysis.

Accordingly, account must be taken of the international division of labour, and the sectors in which China already is, or may become, globally competitive, in sector selection.

A detailed analysis of the GIE in each sector then needs to be developed in order to understand the components of the sector ecosystem, how it works, and its strengths and weaknesses. This requires the creation of an *evidence database for each sector* that will provide the information to aid the analysis of each sector GIE in order to deal with the questions and issues raised in this chapter. The database also must provide the information that will be used to judge the *performance* of the GIE and its major players.

The final step is the policy-making process. Here, in view of the complexity of GIEs and the omnipresence of uncertainty already discussed, it is suggested that *policy be conceived of as a process*, rather than as a static instrument such as a plan. The process might involve the preparation of an initial report on the sector GIE, identifying the main players (and in particular the main enterprises involved by name), the key institutions, facilitators and frustrators, and various performance indicators. The strengths and weaknesses of the GIE should be clearly identified. Finally, possible policy measures should be suggested.

This report should be used not as a final statement of government policy but as an open-ended iterative process that is aimed at encouraging discussion and debate by the players in the GIE and by relatively independent analysts such as academics and journalists. (In making this suggestion it is also necessary to acknowledge and accept that *all* GIEs also contain *vested interests* and *conflicts* between players that should be expected and should be viewed as part of the political economy of the modus operandi of GIEs. As far as possible these vested interests and conflicts should be made explicit rather than hidden and therefore subject possibly to sensible policies. Since these issues are often very sensitive and difficult for government politicians and bureaucrats to handle, it may be that relatively independent analysts such as academics and journalists could play this role.)

Based on the representations and comments received, the report should regularly be updated. This process will allow the *evolution of the GIE* to be encouraged and policy adapted to changing circumstances.

It is worth noting here another key market failure that justifies an important role for the state. The point simply is that the players in any GIE are not able to analyse objectively and critically the innovation ecosystem as a whole, and its performance, of which they are a part. To begin with, individual players lack the necessary information. But, more importantly, they are and must inevitably be self-interested players with vested interests who accordingly cannot be expected to articulate and evaluate the ecosystem as a whole.

This leads me to the next suggestion. This is that whichever agency of the Chinese state is given responsibility for the analysis and policy of the selected sector GIEs, it is necessary for *Sector GIE Teams* to be set up. The role of these teams is to develop an in-depth understanding of the sector, how it works, and its strengths and weaknesses and to take overall responsibility for doing so. The members of these teams will be able over time to develop expert understanding of 'their' sectors and will also be able to develop *networks*, both within China and globally, to include people and organisations with an *analytical* interest in the sector as a whole or some of its key parts.

But there is a further complication that affects all countries. This is that the organs of government are themselves fragmented so that it is difficult for any one organ to analyse a sector GIE as a whole. Typically, for example, the areas of enterprise, science and technology, finance, education and universities, and international trade are the responsibility of different ministries and bodies. This raises an important question: Who should be responsible in government for the *governance* (including analysis and policy) of sector GIEs; i.e. where in government should this function be located? (In the Chinese case it may be that the Development Research Center of the State Council is well placed to play this role because of its supra-positioning vis-à-vis ministries and other government bodies. Another candidate would be the National Development and Reform Commission.)

Example of a Sector GIE

[The original report to the Chinese government included my study of the ICT ecosystem as an example of a sector GIE. Since this topic is the theme of Chapter 4 of the present book it has been omitted here.]

The Bio-Medical Global Innovation Ecosystem

An example of a sector innovation ecosystem is the Bio-Medical Global Innovation Ecosystem, a simplified diagram of which is shown in Exhibit 9.2. This diagram shows the Bio-Medical Innovation Ecosystem and comes from research I am currently doing on connecting the British and Chinese Bio-Medical Innovation Ecosystems. It shows

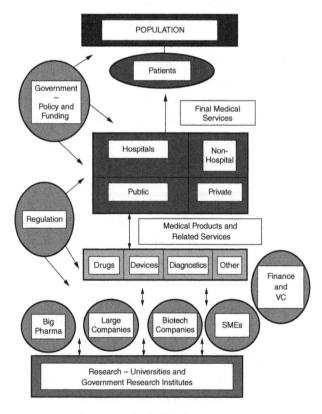

EXHIBIT 9.2 The Bio-Medical Global Innovation Ecosystem

the main players in the ecosystem who jointly create value for the customer-users of the ecosystem.

The first group of players are the companies, divided here into big pharmaceutical companies, other large companies, specialist biotechnology companies, and small- and medium-sized companies (e.g. contract research organisations). It is these companies that produce the main medical products and related services that are used by the health system. These medical products and services may be divided into drugs, medical devices, diagnostics, and other products and services. The health system and its various players (doctors, nurses, medical technicians, support staff, etc.) use these products and services in order to provide health services. Supporting these players are researchers in universities, government research institutes (such as the National Institutes of Health in the United States and the Chinese Academy of Sciences in China) and the R&D laboratories of companies. But this research needs to be funded. The players who provide some of this funding are shown in the grey circle on the right.

Specialised institutions (that define both formal and informal rules of the game) play a key role in this innovation ecosystem. Examples are the regulations that govern clinical trials necessary for the introduction of new drugs and devices, practices that deal for instance with the rules that will be used in deciding who should get particularly expensive drugs, and ethical considerations that determine what medical staff should and should not do.

Government policymakers also play a key role, for example, deciding what share of national resource should be allocated to health and what kinds of organisations and practices are needed for the delivery of health services.

A particularly important, but extremely complicated, question is how well the health system is performing, both absolutely and relative to other systems both nationally and globally. As we know, a great deal of sensitivity attaches to different performance measures, which affect different agents in different ways and which therefore have significant political consequences. A detailed discussion is essential in order to decide what performance measures should be adopted to judge the performance of any particular Bio-Medical Innovation Ecosystem.

But is any value provided by analysing the bio-medical sector in this way? My answer is that value is added as a result of the use of the system concept, which identifies the key players and highlights interdependencies, bottlenecks, and opportunities for improving the performance of the ecosystem. A good example is the detailed strategic analysis of the Life Sciences Ecosystem produced by the British Department of Business, Innovation and Skills pointed to earlier.[16] Interested readers are invited to read this document in order to form their own opinions on this question.

Regional-Level Global Innovation Ecosystems

As we know very well, economic activity is not spread evenly in geographical terms but tends to cluster in specific locations. The iconic example is Silicon Valley in California. These 'industrial districts' where complementary companies cluster, and where innovation is, in the words of nineteenth-century Cambridge economist Alfred Marshall, 'in the atmosphere', have long been a focus of attention for economists. There is a huge and growing literature on the analysis and policy of so-called clusters and much is to be learned from the experiences documented. It remains the case, however, that contrary to the hopes and aspirations of regional policymakers in virtually all countries of the world, there are no 'Silicon Valleys' outside the real Silicon Valley, including in the United States. Having said this, a good deal of progress can be made through a combination of the right kind of companies collocated in an appropriate area, the right kind of facilitators, and the right kind of policies.

China may not be able to grow its own Silicon Valley, but if any country is to have a good shot at trying to do so, it is China. The

---

[16] See http://bis.gov.uk/assets/biscore/economics-and-statistics/docs/i/12-1140-industrial-strategy-uk-sector-analysis.

reason, simply, is China's absolute size; its absolute and relative GDP growth rate; its rapidly increasing supply of skilled person-power; its fast-growing science, technology, and innovation capabilities and related institutions; the physical presence in China of some of the world's most talented players; and the gradual emergence in China of globally competitive Chinese companies, whether SOEs, POEs, SMEs, or Chinese MNCs.

China's three main Regional Global Innovation Ecosystems are in the greater areas of Beijing, Guangdong (including Shenzhen and Hong Kong), and Shanghai, although other regions are also trying to compete. As with any GIE if the most is to be made of the systemic interdependencies that exist among the components of the innovation ecosystem, it will be necessary for a single agency to have responsibility for its analysis and policy. This suggests that, as in the case of sector GIEs, it is necessary to establish (if they do not already exist) region-specific *Regional GIE Teams*. Presumably, these should be based in the regions concerned to facilitate their communication with the players in the regional GIE, rather than being centralised in Beijing.

However, it is important that there is a degree of coordination and information-sharing between those with overall responsibility for the development of national, sector, and regional GIEs because of the interactions and interdependencies that exist between them. For example, any regional GIE is bound to have representation from more than one sector, suggesting that there will be issues at the sector level that will also have implications at the regional level. Similarly, sector and regional GIEs will be heavily influenced by national institutions and policies. I see this coordination and information-sharing being realised through cooperation between the GIE teams that have responsibility for analysis and policy formulation at the national, sector, regional, and societal challenge levels.

Company-Level Global Innovation Ecosystems

Not to be neglected are company-level GIEs, although the overall design, organisation, and management of these should be left to the focal companies themselves to undertake even though government may be able to provide support in various ways. A greater interest in company-level GIEs is a result of the increasing division of labour, both within companies and between them. This was foreseen long ago by Alfred Marshall, who stressed that 'organisation aids knowledge [creation]; it has many forms, e.g. that of a single business, that of various businesses in the same trade, that of various trades relatively to one another, and that of the State providing security for all and help for many'.[17]

Indeed, from an innovation perspective it does not make sense to see a single firm as the appropriate unit of analysis. Firms are *always* embedded in a dense web of other firms and organisations. The knowledge that they acquire over time is *always* a function not only of their own internal knowledge-creating activities but also of knowledge acquired from their interactions with other firms and organisations. This is shown in Exhibit 9.3.

Exhibit 9.3 comes from my own research on the evolution and design of company-level GIEs. It shows a number of symbiotic innovation relationships between the focal firm (shown in the centre) and the other players in its web beginning with four prime co-innovating groups of players, namely customers, suppliers, partners, and competitors. The diagram goes on to show a wider circle of other players with whom focal firms often also establish symbiotic innovation relationships. The focal firm itself is not homogeneous. Intrafirm players, involved closely in the firm's innovation processes, include players in the areas of corporate strategy, researchers in research laboratories, developers in business units, and people in marketing and sales (the latter are not shown in the diagram).

In the diagram the focal firm is involved in external symbiotic innovation relationships with a total of eight groups of external players. In constructing, organising, and managing a global innovation ecosystem, the challenge that the firm faces lies in *designing* these

---

[17] Marshall, A., 1969. *Principles of Economics*. London: Macmillan.

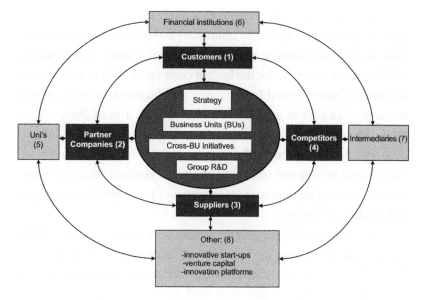

EXHIBIT 9.3 A Generic Company-Level Global Innovation Ecosystem (GIE)
(Copyright: M. Fransman)

symbiotic relationships so that all the players in the innovation eco-system are *incentivised* and therefore *motivated* to *jointly* create value through innovation, value that will significantly benefit the focal firm and its customer-users.

In some cases, the focal firm's symbiotic relationships with other players are structured by its *innovation platforms* around which the firm constructs its global innovation ecosystem. An innovation platform is something – e.g. a product, technology, or software – that serves as a foundation for complementary value-adding activities by other players. Good examples are the innovation platforms of Apple, Android/Google, and Samsung in the area of smartphones. There is a large literature on innovation platforms but unfortunately there is not enough space here to discuss it.

Research on company innovation ecosystems is revealing that the traditional model of company R&D is becoming obsolete, and, as a result, companies are experimenting with new innovative forms of organisation as they seek to more effectively acquire and use external knowledge. According to the traditional model, there is a relatively clear distinction between research and development. Development, which usually accounts for the bulk of companies' R&D expenditures, is almost always located in the company's business units. However, research is located in separate laboratories. The aim of these laboratories is twofold: first, to do exploratory research aimed at developing new and improved products/services and technologies for 'tomorrow' and, second, to respond to requests from the business units for assistance in making incremental improvements to 'today's' technologies and products/services.

However, under the influence both of 'open innovation' thinking and the incentives provided by the greater creation of relevant knowledge externally, companies are increasingly realising that the research and knowledge that they need do not necessarily have to be produced by themselves. It can be done by outside players.

This much is obvious and well known. Less well known and well tested, however, are answers to questions such as: Who in the company should play the External Knowledge Search role? Where in the company's internal division of labour should these External Knowledge Seekers be located and where globally? How should they be doing their jobs? How should they *design* the new external-knowledge-acquiring symbiotic relationships that they are forging with different kinds of external players in different parts of the world? And, finally, how should they be organising and managing their increasingly complex Global Innovation Ecosystem as a whole?[18]

Clear answers have not yet emerged to these kinds of complex questions. As a result, companies are still searching and experimenting with possible answers. There is much learning still to take place, both within and between companies. The implications are enormous

---

[18] Note: Answers to these and other key questions about designing and implementing competitiveness-increasing company innovation ecosystems are provided in the author's Fransman Innovation Programme (FIP).

for the attempt to grow increasingly globally competitive Chinese companies, whether SOEs, POEs, SMEs, or Chinese MNCs.

Societal-Challenge Global Innovation Ecosystems

The idea of Global Innovation Ecosystems is also useful in the area of societal challenges in fields such as health and the environment.[19] It can provide a governance and organisational framework for activities intended to meet the challenges. Several steps are needed in order to establish such GIEs (although the ordering of these steps can be altered).

To begin with and having selected a societal challenge, it is necessary to establish a Societal-Challenge GIE Team that will be given responsibility for establishing, coordinating, and monitoring the GIE that will generate the innovations needed to meet the challenge. As discussed earlier, the decision will also have to be made regarding where in the government structure the team should be located.

The next step is for the team to specify in detail two issues. The first is the nature of the societal challenge and the detailed objectives that are to be achieved. The second related issue is the specification of the performance criteria that are to be used in evaluating the success of the GIE. The clarification of these two issues will allow the players in the GIE to be clear about what they are trying to achieve and how their performance will be evaluated.

The third step is to decide who should be invited to become major players in the GIE. Since companies will be the engine of the GIE, they will have to be immediately identified. In some societal challenge areas, foreign MNCs will be potentially important players. However, as discussed earlier, careful thought will also have to be given to the question of which Chinese companies (SOEs, POEs,

---

[19] For an example using the idea of a societal challenge innovation ecosystem in dealing in China with problems such as pollution, congestion, and global warming, see Fransman (2018).

SMEs, and emerging Chinese MNCs) should also be included in order to facilitate their development and growth. In selecting companies, an important question, obviously, relates to the innovations that will be required to meet the challenge and, correspondingly, the innovation capabilities possessed by potential corporate players.

An important consideration that must constantly be kept in mind – one that is stressed in the designation of this organisation as a *global* innovation ecosystem – is that it is necessary to have an understanding of good activities and practices in this area in other parts of the world so as to learn from them and perhaps emulate some of their methods and activities. The monitoring of relevant activities and practices elsewhere is a key task that will have to be performed by the GIE team.

Fourth, it will be necessary to decide which other players, apart from the companies, should be included in the GIE. Examples are universities; other research institutions; financers; intermediaries such as lawyers, accountants, and consultants; and regulators. It will be necessary to give careful thought to the role that these players are expected to play and how they may be incentivised to play this role. This is a difficult issue since effective cooperation between the players in the GIE cannot be taken for granted.

Fifth, an analysis will have to be undertaken by the team of the facilitators that will be required and the frustrators that may inhibit the achievement of the GIE's goals. A key question here is whether steps can be taken to strengthen the facilitating factors and to weaken the frustrating factors. Government policymakers and regulators may have to be included in order to do so.

Once all this has been done and the GIE has been successfully established, it will be necessary for the team to 'embed' itself amongst the players by establishing organic connections with them (e.g. formal and informal methods of listening to and working with players and sharing information and concerns with them regarding how the goals may be achieved and effectiveness increased). In addition, the team will also have to measure and monitor performance and provide the results to all the players. It is also desirable that the team network with best-practice similar projects in other parts of the world so that mutual learning can take place. This is an area where innovative solutions can play an important role (e.g. the creation of information-sharing and interactive websites). Independent players should also be involved in these activities such as academics and high-level analysts and journalists who could make an important contribution.

Inevitably, there will be many problems and pitfalls that will arise in taking these steps. Coordinating and motivating independent players and creating the right set of facilitating (rather than frustrating) conditions is no easy task. But this is not to say that important progress cannot be made, particularly when careful attention is paid to the *design* of the GIE and the *incentives* and *motivation* engendered by this design. Openness, transparency, and honesty regarding what is being achieved and, even more importantly, what is failing to be achieved will also be a crucial ingredient of the design.

An Important Requirement for All Kinds of GIEs: Embeddedness and Coordination Rather than Command and Control
In view of the complexity of GIEs and the inherent uncertainty surrounding the evolution of their products and services, their technologies, and their markets, it is important to understand that it is simply impossible for an omnipotent visible hand to control the players and their innovation ecosystem in such a way as to achieve the chosen goals. This has important implications for the role of the GIE teams envisaged in this chapter.

Most significantly it means that the role of the GIE team is not to command and control but rather to analyse and propose sensible evolving policies. In order to do this effectively, GIE teams need to be 'embedded' in their GIE through a multitude of organic links with the main players in the ecosystem. Creating and developing these organic links is itself a form of organisational innovation that will have to be undertaken in the GIE. The purpose of the links is to generate the information that will provide both the GIE team members and all the players in the ecosystem with an understanding of how the GIE is working and of its strengths and weaknesses. The *GIE Evidence Database* referred to earlier plays an important role here by making it possible to understand strengths and weaknesses in a more rigorous way.

We need to be aware, however, that it is all too easy for a GIE team, and for policy-making more generally, to degenerate into a top-heavy, bureaucratic, and insensitive kind of organisation that loses touch with the dynamics and potential of the innovation ecosystem and its players. It is this kind of organisation that leads to 'government failure', which in some circumstances may become worse than market failure. A key challenge for Chinese policymakers will be to ensure that this does not happen. To actually do so is an essential ingredient in the design of successful innovation ecosystems; indeed, it is a necessary condition.

CONCLUSION

The aim of this chapter has been to illustrate the potential role of innovation ecosystems thinking in the area of government innovation policy. The chapter focuses on the case of China and on five kinds of innovation ecosystem: national, sectoral, regional, company, and societal challenge.

What value is added by thinking in terms of innovation ecosystems? It is important to ask this question since the inherent complexity of these systems implies that there can be considerable cost in rigorously analysing and using them.

The most important contribution made by innovation ecosystems thinking comes from seeing innovation as a *systemic* phenomenon. From this perspective the many determinants of innovation, including both players and processes, are seen as part of a single system. The components of the system interact and they are therefore interdependent. The innovation that we are seeking – which, in turn, drives other desirable effects such as increases in productivity, output, and employment at country level, and competitiveness, profitability, and growth at company level – is the output of this innovation ecosystem.

All the components of the ecosystem play an important role in generating innovation. Ecosystems thinking requires (1) that we identify these components, (2) understand their interactions and interdependencies, and (3) identify where the system is not working as well as it might. One of the strongest arguments in favour of such ecosystems thinking is that it is so much better than the alternative, which is not to think in terms of systems. The danger in not thinking in systems terms is that important determinants are left out of the picture and therefore not taken into account in the attempt to produce results.

Having said this, it is also important to recognise the significant challenges that confront attempts to think in terms of innovation ecosystems. As pointed out at many points in the present book, an ecosystem is not a real, observable entity. Rather, it is a conceptual construct created by an analyst in order to achieve particular chosen purposes. The construct that results, accordingly, is contingent on the analyst and the purposes. But different analysts with the same purposes may well come up with different conceptualisations of the makeup of the ecosystem and how it works. This can lead to misunderstanding.

Is this an insurmountable problem that is so great that it undermines the rationale for thinking in terms of ecosystems? I think not, for two reasons. The first has already been mentioned, namely the consequences of abandoning ecosystems thinking and the absence of any viable alternative when it comes to innovation, which has many interacting causes. The second is that it is far better to have even a rough understanding of why innovation outcomes are what they are, but to be in touch with the causal forces that are at work, than it is to base the attempt at understanding on oversimplified models that leave out many of the crucial determinants.

Will this conclusion satisfy all analysts interested in innovation? Surely not. There will always be those who are willing to trade off the complexities of the real world for the comfort, however illusory, of a simplification that provides straightforward conclusions even if, going beyond the simplification, there is little evidence that a robust explanation of the real-world phenomenon has been provided. But this should not be sufficient to discourage those analysts and policymakers who, in search of a deeper understanding, are willing to grapple with the complexities of real-world innovation. For them the concept of innovation ecosystems should be rewarding.

10 Keynes's General Theory of Employment, Interest, Money, and Innovation*

As pointed out in Chapter 1 of the present book, over time innovation is the main driver of socioeconomic change. In the case of the economy it is innovation that determines productivity, competitiveness, and economic growth and employment. And as the present book shows, innovation happens through the systemic activities of players and processes. But this raises an interesting puzzle. Why is it that arguably the most important book ever written about the economy and its functioning, *The General Theory*, by John Maynard Keynes, says virtually nothing about innovation?

In this chapter we examine some aspects of the famous book written by Keynes, the most important economist of the twentieth century. The point of departure in the present discussion is the absence of innovation and technical change in this book.

Why did Keynes not include innovation and technical change in the *General Theory*? If he had decided to include them, where might he have 'fitted' them into the book that he did write? What might some of the consequences have been if he had included innovation?

To examine these questions, we compare two different investment decisions: investing in a new, existing machine, on the one hand, and investing in innovating a completely new machine on the other. The examination of these two decisions leads to the conclusion that there is significantly more uncertainty involved in

---

* This chapter can be profitably read in conjunction with the following article that came to the author's attention after the present book had gone into production: Faulkner, P., Feduzi, A., and Runde, J., 2017. 'Unknowns, black swans and the risk/uncertainty distinction'. *Cambridge Journal of Economics*, 41: 1279–302.

the latter, innovation investment, decision. The case of the Concorde supersonic 'flying machine' is taken as an example.

The discussion then moves on to show that this example, together with the analysis that Keynes provides in chapter 12 of his book, has extremely important implications for the way in which economists should do their economics. This is shown through a book review written by Nobel Laureate Paul Krugman of a book by Mervyn King, former governor of the Bank of England.

The conclusion of the chapter is that Keynes would have considerably strengthened his argument in chapter 12 had he added a discussion of innovation. But why didn't he? Several possible answers to this question are considered. The final conclusion is that Keynes might well have found the problem of innovation too slippery to handle in his book.

INTRODUCTION: *THE GENERAL THEORY OF EMPLOYMENT, INTEREST, MONEY, AND INNOVATION*

This is the title of a book that Keynes did *not* write. Why did he not write such a book? If he had decided to write it, where would he have 'fitted' innovation into the *General Theory*[1] that he did write? What might some of the consequences have been if he had included innovation in the *General Theory*? These are the three questions that this chapter will tackle.

KEYNES'S OMISSION OF INNOVATION

At first sight it is indeed surprising that Keynes did not include innovation in his 'general' theory. A perusal of the index to his book shows no reference to the terms 'innovation' or 'technical change'. The reason this is so surprising is that innovation and technical change have an obvious and significant impact on variables such as

---

[1] Keynes, J. M., 1961 (originally published 1936). *The General Theory of Employment, Interest and Money*. London: Macmillan.

investment, consumption, output, and employment, which are central concerns in the *General Theory*. Furthermore, they are important determinants of growth over time (although Keynes was less concerned with growth in the *General Theory*).

So why did Keynes omit innovation? There was a good reason that might explain Keynes's omission.

Writing in the aftermath of the Great Depression, Keynes's concern was very much with how to restore output and employment when the economy failed to achieve a full-employment equilibrium. The problem of insufficient output and employment at the time, however, had little to do with innovation and technical change. Perfectly good machines, technically speaking, were sitting idle whilst the people who knew how to operate them to produce output (and at the same time further jobs) were standing idle in the dole queues. It is not surprising, therefore, that for Keynes the problem, rather than insufficient innovation and technical change, was insufficient aggregate demand. It was on this that he therefore concentrated.

But this reason is based on Keynes's main preoccupations at the time. What about his desire to understand the functioning of the capitalist economy more generally, in good times as well as bad, as well as his use of the term 'general theory' and his frequent references to optimism as well as pessimism? Surely, a 'general theory' and the implications of both optimism and pessimism warranted, indeed necessitated, a consideration of innovation and technical change? We shall return later to this issue.

WHERE COULD KEYNES HAVE 'FITTED' INNOVATION INTO THE GENERAL THEORY?

Had Keynes wanted to include innovation, his chapter 12 in the *General Theory* would have provided an ideal home for the discussion.

Chapter 12 deals essentially with the demand for investment. Such investment includes investment in physical assets like machinery as well as financial assets. In deciding whether or not to invest,

Keynes notes, potential investors try to assess what he called the 'prospective yield' that can be expected on the asset.

But this simple proposition opens up a can of difficult worms. The investment decision is made at a point in time, t0, which we may call the present. The investment, however, will be held over time, and in the case of durable assets such as machinery this period of time may be considerable. The problem is that over time, as the potential investor knows, things change and this may well include the investor's knowledge. The result may well be that at a later point time, t1, some of the knowledge, beliefs, and assumptions made by the investor at t0 may turn out to have been incorrect, negatively affecting the originally expected prospective yield on the basis of which the investment was made.

Keynes's statement that 'in the long run we are dead' is famous. This statement related to the mainly short-run concerns of the *General Theory*. But in order to delve into the determinants of the demand for investment Keynes was forced to consider the longer term. It is not surprising, therefore, that the title of chapter 12 is: 'The State of Long-Term Expectation'. Neither is Keynes's comment on chapter 12 surprising: 'Our conclusions [regarding these questions] must mainly depend upon the actual observation of markets and business psychology. This is the reason why the ensuing digression is on a different level of abstraction from most of this book.'[2]

The problem of uncertainty and uncertain expectations can be held at arm's-length, Keynes notes, if the assumption is valid that knowledge and information held at time t0 remains correct in the future: 'How then are these ... investments carried out in practice? In practice we have tacitly agreed as a rule, to fall back on what is, in truth a *convention*. The essence of this convention ... lies in assuming that the existing state of affairs will continue indefinitely, except in so far as we have specific reasons to expect a change.'[3]

However, whilst this may in some cases be correct, there is no guarantee that it will be correct in all cases. It is not possible, by

---

[2] Keynes (1961), p. 149.   [3] Ibid., pp. 151–2.

definition, to have valid knowledge and information about the future. Data on the future are not possible. Probabilities regarding the future cannot, therefore, be calculated. Accordingly, Keynes concludes, 'our existing knowledge does not provide a sufficient basis for a calculated mathematical expectation'.[4] In short, in the words of Frank Knight,[5] investors face 'uncertainty' as opposed to risk where probabilities can be calculated.

Referring to his now-famous idea of 'animal spirits' Keynes concludes:

> Most ... of our decisions to do something positive, the full consequences of which will be drawn out over many days to come, can only be taken as a result of animal spirits – of a spontaneous urge to action rather than inaction, and not as the outcome of a weighted average of quantitative benefits multiplied by quantitative probabilities.

What will happen if animal spirits turn negative?

> if the animal spirits are dimmed and the spontaneous optimism falters, leaving us to depend on nothing but a mathematical expectation, enterprise will fade and die ... individual initiative will only be adequate when reasonable calculation is supplemented and supported by animal spirits, so that the thought of ultimate loss ... is put aside as a healthy man puts aside the expectation of death.[6]

INVESTING IN A NEW, EXISTING MACHINE VERSUS
INNOVATING A COMPLETELY NEW MACHINE

Keynes's discussion in chapter 12 is tacitly based on investment in assets that embody *current* technology, which is assumed to remain constant over time. We have already noted that Keynes omitted

---

[4] Ibid., p. 152.
[5] Knight, F. H., 1921. *Risk, Uncertainty, and Profit*. Boston, MA: Houghton Mifflin.
[6] Keynes (1961), p. 162.

Exhibit 10.1 *Investing in a New, Existing Machine versus Innovating a Completely New Machine*

	A	B
Influencing variables	Investing in a new, existing machine	Innovating a completely new machine
Current cost	Knowable	Uncertain
Output	Relatively knowable	Uncertain
Unit price	Knowable in the short run	Uncertain

innovation. But is there a substantive difference between, say, investing in a new, existing machine versus investing in the innovation of a completely new machine? And, if there is, what are the implications for Keynes's arguments in chapter 12?

To answer these questions, let us identify some of the key variables that must be taken into account in deciding whether to make two kinds of investment: (1) investing in a new existing machine and (2) innovating a completely new machine. This comparison is shown in Exhibit 10.1.

Three key variables that will influence the investment decision are common to both cases, A and B. The first is current cost: in the case of A, the cost of the machine; in the case of B, the cost involved in trying to make the innovation happen.

The second variable is output. In both cases, A and B, the potential investor would need to know the output that the machine will produce over its life. Third, the investor needs to know the unit price of the output over time. This will enable a calculation of revenue generated (output multiplied by unit price).

How knowable are these three variables? The *current cost* in the case of A can reasonably be assumed to be knowable. The manufacturer and sellers of the machine are likely to possess this information as a result of tests done with the machine. Other users of the machine are also likely to have this information. In the case of B, however, current cost will be uncertain for the simple reason that the machine has not yet been created.

For similar reasons, *output* is likely to be relatively knowable for A. Only relatively because it may be that the machine in question is still relatively recent in design and long-term data have not yet been accumulated. Output in the case of B, however, will be uncertain since the machine has not yet been created and therefore no data can be available regarding output of the machine.

For A, current *unit price* is likely to be knowable since, if the machine is already in existence, it is likely that there have been cases where the output has been sold at a price that is in principle determinable. Over time, however, the unit price will be subject to the vagaries of the market and therefore will be less knowable. In the case of B, however, unit price will be uncertain. The reason is that this type of machine has not been created, the nature of the output is not known, and no opportunity has arisen to test customer demand.

Therefore, it seems reasonable to conclude that the decision to invest in innovation, case B, will confront significantly more uncertainty than the decision to invest in a new, existing machine.

Furthermore, and this is crucial for Keynes's argument in chapter 12, it is also fair to conclude that for case B it is not possible to decide ex ante what constitutes a 'reasonable' expectation. Since the machine does not yet exist, it has not yet been tested. Without the feedback yielded by testing, it will not be possible to decide what is a reasonable estimate. Of course, this does not stop a guess being made. But one guess will be as good as another. And different people, even in the same situation, may come up with different guesses. But there is no basis for deciding which of the guesses is most reasonable.

As is clear from the last quotation presented above, in chapter 12 Keynes was explicit that he thought that 'reasonable calculation' is possible under the conditions he postulated (explicitly and implicitly, including the absence of innovation and technical change). Even then, he felt that this was not sufficient to permit a definitive decision on whether the investment was justifiable. As he shows in chapter 12, he felt that despite this reasonable calculation there were many other factors influencing the outcome of the investment – including the psychology and actions of others – such that positive 'animal spirits' are also necessary to persuade a potential investor to invest.

Keynes's argument, therefore, would have been considerably strengthened had he included innovation. The reason is that in the case of innovation, as we have just demonstrated, it is not possible to determine a 'reasonable' calculation and distinguish it from one that is 'unreasonable'. Under conditions of innovation, accordingly, there are only 'hunches' and 'positive feelings' (Keynes's positive animal spirits) to go by. But as considerable empirical evidence reveals, entrepreneurs and other investors are often willing to make their investment decisions solely the basis of these kinds of animal spirit–influenced determinants without the help of reasonable calculations.

INVESTING IN INNOVATING A COMPLETELY NEW MACHINE: THE CASE OF CONCORDE

The innovation of Concorde, the world's first commercial supersonic 'flying machine', provides an illustration. Whilst Concorde is certainly atypical in terms of its high profile, the amount that its innovation and commercialisation cost, and the range of players involved in its innovation ecosystem, it is by no means atypical in terms of the errors made that over time and with hindsight became evident. Concorde therefore serves as an appropriate illustration.

The first supersonic flight was made in 1947. In 1956 Britain established a Supersonic Transport Aircraft Committee to consider options for supersonic commercial flights. The committee's recommendations resulted in the establishment of the British Aircraft Corporation. In 1962 France joined the project. The first commercial flight took place in 1976. In 2003 the Concorde project was terminated, deemed to be a commercial failure.

Five players were involved in the Concorde innovation ecosystem intended to make this innovation happen: (1) the British and

French governments, (2) the organisation created that was intended to develop the necessary innovations, (3) airlines potentially buying Concorde, (4) final customer-users of Concorde services, and (5) a Russian would-be competitor that eventually dropped out.[7]

Cost: The technological challenges facing the project were considerable. This contributed to the serious cost-overrun that occurred. In 1962, Concorde was projected to cost £160m (about £2bn in 2003 prices). By 1975, the year before commercial launch, more than £1.2bn (about £11bn in 2003 prices) had been spent.[8]

Output: 'By the time the first prototype took flight, sixteen airlines had signed contract options to purchase seventy-four airplanes. It appeared as though the Concorde would be welcomed into service by airlines from around the world. However, the Concorde never achieved such commercial success as only fourteen planes were ever put into commercial operation, and by only two airlines: British Airways and Air France.'[9]

Price: 'In 2003, at the retirement of the Concorde, a typical round-trip ticket on the Concorde cost $8,000–$12,000, where a typical transatlantic flight cost approximately $4,000 for business class and less than $1,000 for [economy].'[10]

An ex post study has concluded that one of the primary reasons for the failure of Concorde was 'the failure to realize that the personal travel market had matured to the point where value and price, not performance [i.e. the significantly shorter flight times of Concorde], were the dominant factors influencing consumer choice'.[11]

Accordingly, whilst the ex ante expectations of the players that decided to become involved in the Concorde project seemed to be reasonable at the time, ex post they proved to be in error. It is

---

[7] This discussion of Concorde is not intended to be detailed. Attention is restricted to several points of relevance to the three variables considered in Exhibit 10.1, namely, cost, output, and price. See Hooks, M., Isaacs, P., Miles, E., and Moreau, M., 2009. 'The Concorde: failure to create a breakthrough innovation in the aircraft industry'. The Tuck School at Dartmouth (mimeo).

[8] BBC, 10 October 2003. http://news.bbc.co.uk/1/hi/business/2935337.stm.

[9] Hooks (2009), p. 14. [10] Ibid., p. 16. [11] Ibid., p. 1.

abundantly evident that a similar fate regularly befalls many investments in innovation, of which entrepreneurial ventures are a prime example.

IMPLICATIONS FOR THE WAY IN WHICH ECONOMICS SHOULD BE DONE

The present discussion has extremely important implications for the way in which economics should be done. This may be illustrated by a recent book review by economics Nobel Laureate Paul Krugman.

The review by Krugman[12] is of a book by Mervyn King, former governor of the Bank of England.[13] In this book King offers his thoughts about the global financial crisis from 2007.

The details of the financial crisis and the implications, however, need not detain us here. Of interest, rather, is the chapter of King's book devoted to the implications for economics methodology and Krugman's comments on this chapter.

According to Krugman, in this chapter 'King sees the need for a complete rethinking of how we do economics.'[14] Related to this, 'King calls for what he says is a fundamental rethinking of bank regulation.'[15]

How does King come to this drastic conclusion (with which Krugman takes issue)? As Krugman points out, King's argument depends essentially on his approach to two key concepts central to the methodology adopted by most economists: 'equilibrium' and the 'rational economic man of the [economics] textbooks'.[16]

Krugman defines equilibrium 'roughly' as 'a situation in which the economy's participants are each doing what they imagine is in their self-interest, given what everyone else is doing'.[17] Equilibrium implies that all participants in the economic system are satisfied with

---

[12] Krugman, P., 2016. 'Money: the brave new uncertainty of Mervyn King'. *New York Review of Books*, 14 July, 21–3.

[13] King, M., 2016. *The End of Alchemy: Money, Banking, and the Future of the Global Economy*. New York, NY: W. W. Norton.

[14] Krugman (2016), p. 22.   [15] Ibid., p. 23.   [16] Ibid., p. 22.   [17] Ibid.

their current position and therefore do not feel the need to make changes. The economic system as a whole, therefore, will be in a state of rest, which is implied in the notion of equilibrium.

Krugman observes that King's views reflect a wider debate amongst economists. These economists are divided into two approaches. The first is what Krugman calls 'mainstream economic analysis'. The second he refers to as 'a more or less radical fringe that rejects the mainstream's methods', a 'relatively small but vociferous group of economists'.[18]

What does all this have to do with the present discussion about innovation and Keynes's chapter 12 in the *General Theory*? The answer is Krugman's suggestion that 'Both positions can find support in Keynes's own writings, indeed within ... *The General Theory*.' He goes on the describe 'these two factions' as 'Part-one-ers' [i.e. mainstream economists] and 'Chapter 12ers' [i.e. their critics]. The latter draw their inspiration from chapter 12.

Krugman provides his own summary of chapter 12:

> Chapter 12 of *The General Theory* is ... a discussion of the
> problems people have making decisions involving the future. In
> that chapter Keynes argues that the future is inherently
> unknowable, and that we deal with that uncertainty essentially by
> kidding ourselves, telling and acting on stories about the future that
> are grounded in little more than convention. And these stories,
> Keynes asserts, are subject to occasional drastic revisions, with
> huge economic implications. No equilibrium there![19]

In King's view, 'the story' changed fundamentally after the 2007 global financial crisis leading to the serious knock-on effects that followed.

For the economics mainstream, however, 'irrationality and volatility are at the fringes of their worldview'. In contrast, they concentrate on the first three chapters of the *General Theory* from 'that very same book ... that are described [by the mainstreamers] as

---

[18] Ibid., pp. 21–2.   [19] Ibid., p. 22.

presenting his essential argument – and the argument very much involves equilibrium reasoning, with the assumption that spending has a stable relationship with income, and that the economy settles at the level of employment at which desired spending equals income'.[20]

But as a self-styled Keynesian, how does Krugman (as well as those he calls mainstreamers) come to terms with chapter 12, which is, after all, also included by Keynes in the *General Theory*? Krugman's answer is central in understanding this debate:

> [King's argument is] not entirely clear, even though King spends a whole chapter explaining why radical uncertainty, not quantifiable risk, is the essence of economic life. Yes, economic forecasts are often grossly wrong; yes, even smart people often have far too much confidence in their ability to assess risks. Every serious economist knows this, yet most don't consider it sufficient reason to abandon conventional tools of analysis [including equilibrium]. At most, it's a reason to use them in the subjunctive – *to analyse economic issues as if people were making reasonable choices, while being aware that they might not.*[21]

THE RELEVANCE OF INNOVATION

Krugman suggests that serious economists 'analyse economic issues as if people were making reasonable choices'. Going back to the innovation example that we analysed in Exhibit 10.1, namely innovating a completely new machine and the example of Concorde and similar innovation decisions, how can we define an ex ante reasonable choice in these cases? In view of the uncertainty that exists as summarised in Exhibit 10.1, and the necessary absence of probability distributions under the circumstances of innovation, it obviously is impossible to define a 'reasonable' choice.

---

[20] Ibid., p. 22.   [21] Ibid., emphasis added.

In short, innovation is precisely an example of the situation that Keynes had in mind when in chapter 12 he analysed the 'state of long term expectation'. In case A, also included in Exhibit 10.1 – namely investing in a new, existing machine – it might be possible to 'push it' and suggest, on the basis of the information that is available at time t0, that a 'reasonable choice' can be made. But even here there is the problem that Keynes anticipates, which he discusses in detail in chapter 12, namely that given the remaining relevant unknowns an estimate of the 'prospective yield' (necessary to make the decision) remains 'extremely precarious'. In the innovation case B, however, defining a 'reasonable' decision is simply impossible.

For these reasons we may justifiably conclude that Keynes would have considerably strengthened his argument in chapter 12 had he included a discussion on innovation. Furthermore, this would have been a 'natural' thing to do since his concern in this chapter with issues such as uncertainty, expectations, and emotions are central to the way in which innovation happens. This is shown in Chapter 6 of the present book, which contains a detailed examination of how innovation happened in the case of the innovation of the transistor, microprocessor, optical fibre, and laser – innovations that literally changed the world as well as the economy that generates the output and employment that were Keynes's main concerns.

SO WHY DID KEYNES IGNORE INNOVATION?

If innovation would have considerably strengthened his argument in chapter 12 why did Keynes ignore it? I think there were two reasons.

The first appears in a statement made by the Cambridge economist Edith Penrose in her book *The Theory of the Growth of the Firm*:[22] 'Economists have, of course, always recognized the dominant role that increasing knowledge plays in economic processes but have,

---

[22] Penrose, E. T., 1959. *The Theory of the Growth of the Firm*. Oxford: Basil Blackwell, p. 77.

for the most part, found the whole subject of knowledge too slippery to handle.'

To his considerable credit, Keynes did not ignore the problem of knowledge and its change over time. Chapter 12 is a testimony to the insightful ways in which he handled the issue. However, he did not take the crucial further step to go on and examine the case of innovation, which, as we pointed out at the beginning of this chapter, is a crucial part of economic change. In this chapter we suggest that this was a missed opportunity.

But I think there was also a second, related reason why Keynes ignored innovation. In the first three chapters of the *General Theory*, the part of the book that Krugman notes inspires the economics mainstream, Keynes employs a formal analysis that includes, centrally, equilibrium. This both aids his exposition whilst giving him determinate outcomes for the variables on which his system depended, variables such as the rate of interest, investment, consumption, savings, output, and employment. Without this formality and the use of equilibrium, his exposition would have lacked the clarity and credibility that in the event it enjoyed.

But this does not mean that he believed that the assumptions that he incorporated into his formal analysis, both explicit and implicit, such as the absence of uncertainty, were features of the real world and of decision-making in this world. This explains why in chapter 12 Keynes said: 'Our conclusions [regarding the state of long-term expectation] must mainly depend upon the actual observation of markets and business psychology. This is the reason why the ensuing digression is on a different level of abstraction from most of this book.'[23]

In other words, his method in the first three chapters required a more abstract form of reasoning, including the use of equilibrium. However, in his discussion in chapter 12 of the demand for investment, a central concern for his general theory, he was no longer able

---

[23] Keynes (1961), p. 149.

to keep at arm's-length the issues that arise from the 'actual observation of markets' and the long-term expectations that play such a crucial role in the functioning of these markets as he had hitherto done in the earlier chapters. The meaning of Keynes, as evident in chapter 12, accordingly, differed from his method in the first part of the book.

CONCLUSION

As it is, the disjuncture between the first part of the *General Theory* and its chapter 12 is considerable, leaving his followers in some disarray, as Krugman's discussion of the debate between the 'mainstream' Keynesians and the 'radical' Keynesians suggests. Adding innovation, Keynes might have concluded, would only add to the complexity of the book and muddy its waters. It is therefore not inconceivable that Keynes did consider adding innovation to chapter 12 but found the prospect too slippery to handle.[24]

---

[24] Keynes was not the first, of course, to find a conflict between his meaning and his method. The same happened to his predecessor at Cambridge University, Alfred Marshall. In the introduction to his book *Principles of Economics*, Marshall noted that the 'Mecca of the economist lies in economic biology'. However, he also observed that 'biological conceptions are more complex than those of mechanics'. Accordingly, he chose to use the formal method of 'mechanical analogies' which included the use of equilibrium even whilst he insisted that the 'central idea of economics ... must be that of living force and movement'. This has important connections with the concept of 'innovation ecosystems', the central concern of the present book. Marshall, A., 1969. *Principles of Economics*. London: Macmillan.

11 Conclusions

This book is about innovation, how it happens, who makes it happen, and how it should be conceptualised to understand and explain it.

Those in search of the comforts of a predictable, controllable world that can be manipulated at will to satisfy our demands will likely find this book disappointing. Understandable though these desires may be, this book shows in detail why these desires cannot be fulfilled in a real world with innovation.

The reason is that the real innovating world is inevitably and irreducibly a world that includes

- uncertainty (where probabilities cannot be derived to assist decision-making)
- ignorance
- error and mistakes
- surprises
- frustrated expectations.

In such an innovating world theoretical postulates such as equilibrium, maximisation, and optimisation simply do not make sense. Indeed, they are misleading.

The unease of theorists confronted by such a world is well captured by Edith Penrose: 'Economists', she notes, 'have, of course, always recognized the dominant role that increasing knowledge plays in economic processes but have, for the most part, found the whole subject of knowledge too slippery to handle.'[1]

But surely we cannot leave it at that, turning our backs on the dilemma and avoiding it? Surely innovation is too fundamentally an

---

[1] Penrose, E., 1959. *The Theory of the Growth of the Firm*, p. 77.

essential, indeed necessary in the strict meaning of the word, component of the world we inhabit? Surely it cannot be ignored? For innovation, as we know and accept, is a key determinant of important things such as productivity, growth, and improvement without which all our lives would be significantly worse. In short, it seems we have no option but to embrace the innovating world, conceptually and practically, no matter how uncomfortable this embrace may at times be.

So how may be go about doing this? The general conclusion of this book is that there is no choice. We have to create conceptualisations that allow us to come effectively to grips with the complexities that are innovation. Many of these conceptualisations are discussed in this book.

Doubtless, however, there will be a price to pay. The price includes the difficulties and discomforts just referred to. But it is important and encouraging to realise that there is also a gain: the benefits that flow from a deeper, more rigorous understanding of this essential element of the world that is ours, a world of innovation.

Bibliography

Adner, R. and Kapoor, R. (2010). Value creation in innovation ecosystems: how the structure of technological interdependence affects firm performance in new technology generations. *Strategic Management Journal* 31: 306–33. Available at: http:// faculty.tuck.dartmouth.edu/images/uploads/faculty/ron-adner/Adner_Kapoor_ SMJ_-_Value_creation_in_innovation_ecosystems.pdf (accessed 28 November 2017).

American Physical Society (2017). *Laser History: Early History.* Available at: http:// laserfest.org/lasers/history/early.cfm (accessed 28 November 2017).

Antonelli, C. (2002). *The Economics of Innovation, New Technologies and Structural Change.* London: Routledge.

Antonelli, C. (ed.) (2006). *New Frontiers in the Economics of Innovation and New Technology: Essays in Honour of Paul A. David.* Cheltenham: Edward Elgar.

Baldwin, C. Y. and Clark, K. B. (2000). *Design Rules: The Power of Modularity.* Boston, MA: MIT Press.

Banerjee, A. V. (1992). A simple model of herd behavior. *The Quarterly Journal of Economics* 107(3): 797–817.

BBC (2003). Why economists don't fly Concorde. 10 October. Available at: http:// news.bbc.co.uk/1/hi/business/2935337.stm (accessed 28 November 2017).

Berlin, L. (2006). *The Man behind the Microchip.* Oxford: Oxford University Press.

BT (2015). Huawei–BT collaboration case study. Available at: www.globalservices .bt.com/static/assets/pdf/case_studies/EN_NEW/huawei-bt-collaboration-case-study.pdf (accessed 28 November 2017).

Business Week (2002). Special report – how corrupt is Wall Street? 13 May.

Cassidy, J. (2002). *Dot.com.* London: Allen Lane.

Cerf, V. (1996). Is there a future for the net? David Pitchford finds out from the man who invented it, Vinton Cerf. *Internet 75.*

Chapuis, R. J. and Joel, A. E. (1990). *100 Years of Telephone Switching, volume II: Electronics, Computers and Telephone Switching: A Book of Technological History, 1960–1985.* Amsterdam: North Holland.

China Government (2009). Opinions on deepening the reform of the scientific and technological system and speeding up the building of a national innovation system. Available at: www.most.gov.cn/eng/pressroom/201211/t20121119_ 98014.htm (accessed 28 November 2017).

Christensen, C. M. (1997). *The Innovator's Dilemma: When New Technologies Cause Great Firms to Fail*. Boston, MA: Harvard Business School Press.

CNN (2013). Viagra: the little blue pill that could. Available at: http://edition.cnn.com/2013/03/27/health/viagra-anniversary-timeline/ (accessed 28 November 2017).

Day, G. S. and Fein, A. (2003). Shakeouts in digital markets. *California Management Review* 45(2): 131–50.

Department for Business, Innovation and Skills (2011). Innovation and research strategy for growth. BIS Economics Paper No. 15. UK Government Department for Business, Innovation and Skills, London.

Department for Business, Innovation and Skills (2012). Industrial strategy: UK sector analysis. BIS Economics Paper No. 18. UK Government Department for Business, Innovation and Skills, London. Available at: http://bis.gov.uk/assets/biscore/economics-and-statistics/docs/i/12-1140-industrial-strategy-uk-sector-analysis (accessed 29 November 2017).

Dertouzos, M. L., Lester, R. K., and Solow, R. M. (1989). *Made in America: Regaining the Productive Edge*. Boston, MA: MIT Press.

District Court, S.D. (1987). *Corning v. Sumitomo Electric USA Inc.*, 21 December, 1545–71. New York.

Dretske, F. I. (1982). *Knowledge and the Flow of Information*. Cambridge, MA: MIT Press.

Duke, D. A. (1983). *A History of Optical Communications, Special Report, Telecommunication Products Department*. New York, NY: Corning Glass Works.

Economist (2002). The unfinished recession: a survey of the world economy. 28 September.

Edquist, C. (1997). *Systems of Innovation: Technologies, Institutions and Organizations*. London: Pinter.

Faulkner, P., Feduzi, A., and Runde, J. (2017). Unknowns, black swans and the risk/uncertainty distinction. *Cambridge Journal of Economics* 41: 1279–302.

Fein, A. J. (1998). Understanding evolutionary processes in non-manufacturing industries: empirical insights from the shakeout in pharmaceutical wholesaling. *Journal of Evolutionary Economics* 8: 231–70.

Financial Times (2012). Japanese manufacturing in search of salvation. January.

Fransman, M. (1988). The Japanese system and the acquisition, assimilation and further development of technological knowledge: organizational form, markets and government. In: B. Elliott (ed.), *Technology and Social Process*. Edinburgh: Edinburgh University Press.

Fransman, M. (1990). *The Market and Beyond: Information Technology in Japan*. Cambridge: Cambridge University Press.

Fransman, M. (1994a). AT&T, BT and NTT: a comparison of vision, strategy and competence. *Telecommunications Policy* 18(2): 137–53.

Fransman, M. (1994b). AT&T, BT and NTT: the role of R&D. *Telecommunications Policy* 18(4): 295–305.

Fransman, M. (1994c). Information, knowledge, vision and theories of the firm. *Industrial and Corporate Change* 3(3): 713–58.

Fransman, M. (1994d). Information, knowledge, vision and theories of the firm. *Industrial and Corporate Change* 3(2): 1–45. Reprinted in G. Dosi, D. J. Teece and J. Chytry (eds.) (1998). *Technology, Organisation, and Competitiveness: Perspectives on Industrial and Corporate Change.* New York, NY: Oxford University Press.

Fransman, M. (1994e). Knowledge segmentation–integration in theory and in Japanese companies. In: O. Granstrand (ed.), *Economics of Technology.* Amsterdam: North-Holland, pp. 172–5.

Fransman, M. (1994f). The Japanese innovation system: how it works. In: M. Dodgson and R. Rothwell (eds.), *The Handbook of Industrial Innovation.* Aldershot: Edward Elgar.

Fransman, M. (1995a). Is national technology policy obsolete in a globalised world? The Japanese response. *Cambridge Journal of Economics* 19: 95–119.

Fransman, M. (1995b). *Japan's Computer and Communications Industry: The Evolution of Industrial Giants and Global Competitiveness.* Oxford: Oxford University Press.

Fransman, M. (1997). Towards a new agenda for Japanese telecommunications. *Telecommunications Policy* 21(2): 185–94.

Fransman, M. (1999). *Visions of Innovation.* Oxford: Oxford University Press.

Fransman, M. (2002a). *Telecoms in the Internet Age: From Boom to Bust to … ?* Oxford: Oxford University Press.

Fransman, M. (2002b). Mapping the evolving telecoms industry: the uses and shortcomings of the layer model. *Telecommunications Policy.* Special Issue on Mapping the Evolving Telecommunications Value Chain and Market Structure 26 (9–10): 473–84.

Fransman, M. (2003). Evolution of the telecommunications industry. In: G. Madden (ed.), *The International Handbook of Telecommunications Economics,* vol. III. Aldershot: Edward Elgar, pp. 15–38.

Fransman, M. (2007). *Edinburgh, City of Funds.* Edinburgh: Kokoro.

Fransman, M. (2010). *The New ICT Ecosystem: Implications for Policy and Regulation.* Cambridge: Cambridge University Press.

Fransman, M. (2014). Models of innovation in global ICT firms: the emerging global innovation ecosystems. JRC Scientific and Policy Reports, EUR 26774 EN,

European Commission. Seville: JRC-IPTS. Available at: https://ec.europa.eu/ jrc/sites/default/files/jrc90726.pdf (accessed 28 November 2017).

Fransman, M. (2017). Lachmann and Schumpeter: some reflections and reminiscences. Presented at The Legacy of Ludwig Lachmann: Interdisciplinary Perspectives on Institutions, Agency, and Uncertainty. University of the Witwatersrand, Johannesburg, 11–13 April.

Fransman, M. (2018). Inventing and designing a Mobility Innovation Ecosystem for Chinese cities to combat congestion, pollution and global warming: putting it all together and making it happen. In: Jin Zhang and Zhang Laiming (eds.), *China and the World Economy: Transition and Challenges*. London: Routledge.

Freeman, C. (1987). *Technology Policy and Economic Performance: Lessons from Japan*. London: Pinter.

Freeman, C. (1988). Japan: a new national innovation system? In: G. Dosi, C. Freeman, R. R. Nelson, G. Silverberg, and L. Soete (eds.), *Technology and Economy Theory*. London: Pinter.

Freeman, C. (1995). The 'national system of innovation' in historical perspective. *Cambridge Journal of Economics* 19(1): 5–24.

Gawer, A. and Cusumano, M. A. (2002). *Platform Leadership: How Intel, Microsoft, and Cisco Drive Industry Innovation*. Boston, MA: Harvard Business School Press.

Gordon, R. (2012). Is US economic growth over? Faltering innovation confronts the six headwinds. National Bureau of Economic Research Working Paper 18315. Available at www.nber.org/papers/w18315.pdf (accessed 28 November 2017).

Gordon, R. (2016). *The Rise and Fall of American Growth: The U.S. Standard of Living since the Civil War*. Princeton, NJ: Princeton University Press.

Grove, A. S. (1996). *Only the Paranoid Survive*. London: Profile Books.

Harari, Y. N. (2011). *Sapiens: A Brief History of Humankind*. London: Harvill Secker.

Hayek, F. A. (1945). The use of knowledge in society. *American Economic Review* 35(4): 519–30.

Henderson, R. M. and Clark, K. B. (1990). Architectural innovation: the reconfiguration of existing product technologies and the failure of established firms. *Administrative Sciences Quarterly* 35(1): 9–30.

Henten, A. (2016). Interview with Martin Fransman. *Digiworld Economic Journal* 102(Q2): 95–100. Note: Some slight changes have been made to the originally published interview.

Hicks, J. R. (1972). Nobel Prize address. Available at: www.nobelprize.org/nobel_prizes/ economic-sciences/laureates/1972/hicks-lecture.html (accessed 28 November 2017).

Hooks, M., Isaacs, P., Miles, E., and Moreau, M. (2009). The Concorde: failure to create a breakthrough innovation in the aircraft industry. The Tuck School at Dartmouth (mimeo).

Hughes, T. P. (1993). *Networks of Power: Electrification in Western Society, 1880–1930*. Baltimore, MD: Johns Hopkins University Press.

Hume, R. (2015). From Velcro to Viagra: 10 products that were invented by accident. *HistoryExtra.com*, 15 October. Available at: www.historyextra.com/article/feature/velcro-viagra-10-products-were-invented-accident (accessed 28 November 2017).

Iansiti, M. and Levien, R. (2004a). *The Keystone Advantage: What the New Dynamics of Business Ecosystems Mean for Strategy, Innovation, and Sustainability*. Boston, MA: Harvard Business School Press.

Iansiti, M. and Levien, R. (2004b). Strategy as ecology. *Harvard Business Review* 82 (3): 68–78.

Kao, C. and Hockham, G. A. (1966). Dielectric-fibre surface waveguides for optical frequencies. *Proceedings of the IEEE* 113: 1151–8.

Keynes, J. M. (1921). *A Treatise on Probability*. London: Macmillan.

Keynes, J. M. (1961, originally published 1936). *The General Theory of Employment, Interest and Money*. London: Macmillan.

Kindleberger, C. P. (2000). *Manias, Panics and Crashes: A History of Financial Crises*. Basingstoke, Hampshire, UK: Palgrave.

Kindleberger, C. P. and Aliber, R. Z. (2005). *Manias, Panics and Crashes: A History of Financial Crises*. Hampshire, UK: Palgrave Macmillan.

King, M. (2016). *The End of Alchemy: Money, Banking, and the Future of the Global Economy*. New York, NY: W. W. Norton.

Klepper, S. (1997). Industry life cycles. *Industrial and Corporate Change* 6(1): 145–82.

Klepper, S. and Miller, J. (1995). Entry, exit, and shakeouts in the United States in new manufactured products. *International Journal of Industrial Organization* 13: 567–91.

Klepper, S. and Simons, K. (1996). Technological extinctions of industrial firms: an inquiry into their nature and causes. *Industrial and Corporate Change* 6: 379–460.

Knight, F. H. (1921). *Risk, Uncertainty and Profit*. Boston, MA: Houghton Mifflin.

Krugman, P. (2016). Money: the brave new uncertainty of Mervyn King. *New York Review of Books*, 14 July.

Kuhn, T. S. (1996). *The Structure of Scientific Revolutions*, 3rd edition. Chicago, IL: University of Chicago Press.

Lackie, J. M. (2007). *Chambers Science and Technology Dictionary*. Edinburgh: Chambers.

Laserlab Europe (2015). When lasers first saw the light of day. Available at: www.laserlab-europe.net/events-1/light2015/light-links/when-lasers-first-saw-the-light-of-day (accessed 28 November 2017).

The Lean Startup (2017). Available at: www.theleanstartup.com (accessed 28 November 2017). See also Ries (2011).

Loasby, B. (1996). The imagined deemed possible. In: E. Helmstadter and M. Perlman (eds.), *Behavioral Norms, Technological Progress and Economic Dynamics*. Ann Arbor, MI: University of Michigan Press, pp. 17–31.

Loasby, B. (2001). Cognition, imagination and institutions in demand creation. *Journal of Evolutionary Economics* 11(1): 7–22.

Loasby, B. (2003). The innovative mind. Paper presented at the DRUID Conference on Creating, Sharing and Transferring Knowledge, Copenhagen.

Lundvall, B.-Å. (1985). *Product Innovation and User-Producer Interaction, Industrial Development*. Industrial Development Research Series, No. 31. Aalborg: Aalborg University Press.

Lundvall, B.-Å. (ed.) (1992). *National Innovation Systems: Towards a Theory of Innovation and Interactive Learning*. London: Pinter.

Maiman, T. (1987). The laser – its origins, applications and future. Japan Prize 1987 Official Brochure, pp. 15–16. See also www.japanprize.jp/en/prize_past_1987_prize02.html (accessed 29 November 2017).

Malerba, F. (ed.) (2004). *Sectoral Systems of Innovation: Concepts, Issues and Analyses of Six Major Sectors in Europe*. Cambridge: Cambridge University Press.

Malerba, F. (2005). Sectoral systems: how and why innovation differs across sectors. In: J. Fagerberg, D. C. Mowery, and R. R. Nelson (eds.), *The Oxford Handbook of Innovation*. Oxford: Oxford University Press.

Malone, M. S. (2014). *The Intel Trinity*. New York, NY: Harper Collins.

Marshall, A. (1969). *Principles of Economics*. London: Macmillan

Mehrling, P. (1999). The vision of Hyman P. Minsky. *Journal of Economic Behavior & Organization* 39: 125–58.

Metcalfe, S. (1995). The economic foundations of technology policy: equilibrium and evolutionary perspectives. In: P. Stoneman (ed.), *Handbook of the Economics of Innovation and Technological Change*. Oxford: Blackwell Publishers.

Metcalfe, S. (1998). *Evolutionary Economics and Creative Destruction: The Graz Schumpeter Lectures*. London: Routledge.

Metcalfe, S. (2002). Knowledge of growth and the growth of knowledge. *Journal of Evolutionary Economics* 12 (1–2): 3–16.

Metcalfe, S. (2004). The entrepreneur and the style of modern economics. *Journal of Evolutionary Economics* 14 (2): 157–76.

Miller, M. (2014). The birth of the microprocessor. Available at: http://uk.pcmag.com/opinion/38270/opinion/the-birth-of-the-microprocessor (accessed 28 November 2017).

Minsky, H. P. (1975). *John Maynard Keynes*. New York, NY: Columbia University Press.

Minsky, H. P. (1982). The financial instability hypothesis: capitalistic processes and the behavior of the economy. In: C. P. Kindleberger and J.-P. Laffargue (eds.), *Financial Crises: Theory, History and Policy*. Cambridge: Cambridge University Press.

Moore, J. F. (1993). Predators and prey: a new ecology of competition. *Harvard Business Review*, May–June, pp. 75–86.

Moore, J. F. (1996). *The Death of Competition: Leadership and Strategy in the Age of Business Ecosystems*. New York, NY: Harper Business.

Mowery, D. C. and Nelson, R. R. (eds.) (1999). *Sources of Industrial Leadership: Studies of Seven Industries*. Cambridge: Cambridge University Press.

Nairn, A. (2002). *Engines That Move Markets: Technology Investing from Railroads to the Internet and Beyond*. New York, NY: Wiley.

NASA (2017). What is a laser? Available at: http://spaceplace.nasa.gov/laser/en/ (accessed 28 November 2017).

Nelson, R. R. (ed.) (1993). *National Innovation Systems: A Comparative Analysis*. New York, NY: Oxford University Press.

Nelson, R. R. (2012). Why Schumpeter has had so little influence on today's main line economics, and why this may be changing. *Journal of Evolutionary Economics* 22(5): 901–16.

Nelson, R. R. and Winter, S. G. (1982). *An Evolutionary Theory of Economic Change*. Cambridge, MA: Harvard University Press.

Nobel Foundation (2009). The Masters of Light. The Nobel Prize in Physics 2009. 6 October. See also www.nobelprize.org/nobel_prizes/physics/laureates/2009/ (accessed 29 November 2017).

OECD (1997). National innovation systems. Organisation for Economic Cooperation and Development (OECD), Paris. Available at: www.oecd.org/science/inno/2101733.pdf (accessed 28 November 2017).

Owen, G. (2010). Industrial policy in Europe since the Second World War: what has been learnt. ECIPE Occasional Paper No. 1/2012, Department of Management, London School of Economics.

Patel, P. and Pavitt, K. (1994). The nature and economic importance of national innovation systems. *STI Review*, No. 14, Organisation for Economic Cooperation and Development (OECD), Paris.

PBS (1999). Transistorized! Available at: www.pbs.org/transistor/album1/ (accessed 28 November 2017).

Penrose, E. T. (1959). *The Theory of the Growth of the Firm.* Oxford: Basil Blackwell.

Perez, C. (2002). *Technological Revolutions and Financial Capital: The Dynamics of Bubbles and Golden Ages.* Cheltenham: Edward Elgar.

Planet Science (2017). What is a laser? Available at: www.planet-science.com/cat egories/over-11s/technology/2012/01/what-is-a-laser.aspx (accessed 28 November 2017).

Rabin, M. and Schrag, J. L. (1999). First impressions matter: a model of confirmatory bias. *The Quarterly Journal of Economics* 114(1): 37–82.

Ries, E. (2011). *The Lean Startup: How Constant Innovation Creates Radically Successful Businesses.* Portfolio Penguin. See also: www.theleanstartup.com (accessed 28 November 2017).

Riordon, M. and Hoddeson, L. (1998). *Crystal Fire: The Invention of the Transistor and Birth of the Information Age.* New York, NY: W. W. Norton.

Rodrik, D. (2008). Normalising industrial policy. Working Paper No. 3, Commission on Growth and Development, Washington, DC. Available at: https://drodrik .scholar.harvard.edu/files/dani-rodrik/files/normalizing-industrial-policy.pdf (accessed 28 November 2017).

Rosenberg, N. (1994). *Exploring the Black Box: Technology, Economics and History.* Cambridge: Cambridge University Press.

Scharfstein, D. S. and Stein, J. C. (1990). Herd behavior and investment. *The American Economic Review* 80(3): 465–79.

Schumpeter, J. A. (1939). *Business Cycles.* New York, NY: McGraw Hill.

Schumpeter, J. A. (1943). *Capitalism, Socialism, and Democracy.* London: Unwin.

Schumpeter, J. A. (1947a). The creative response in economic history. *The Journal of Economic History* 7(2): 149–59.

Schumpeter, J. A. (1947b). Theoretical problems: theoretical problems of economic growth. *The Journal of Economic History* 7: 1–9.

Schumpeter, J. A. (1961). *The Theory of Economic Development.* New York, NY: Oxford University Press.

Shackle, G. L. S. (1972). *Epistemics and Economics: A Critique of Economic Doctrines.* Cambridge: Cambridge University Press.

Shapira, P., Smits, R., and Kuhlmann, S., (eds.) (2010). *The Theory and Practice of Innovation Policy: An International Research Handbook.* Cheltenham: Edward Elgar.

Shiller, R. J. (2000). *Irrational Exuberance.* Princeton, NJ: Princeton University Press.

Shockley, W. (1950). *Electronics and Holes in Semiconductors, with Applications to Transistor Electronics.* New York, NY: Van Nostrand.

Sildenafilakaviagra.com (2017). History of Viagra. Available at: www
.sildenafilakaviagra.com/history-of-viagra (accessed 28 November 2017).

Simon, H. A. (1959). Theories of decision making in economics and behavioral
science. *American Economic Review* 49: 253–83.

Simon, H. A. (2002). Organizing and coordinating talk and silence in organizations.
Industrial and Corporate Change 11(3): 616–17.

Smith, A. (2010). *An Inquiry into the Nature and Causes of the Wealth of Nations.*
London: J. M. Dent & Sons.

Stiglitz, J. E. (2003). *The Roaring Nineties: Seeds of Destruction.* London: Allen
Lane.

Stiglitz, J. E., Sen, A., and Fitoussi, J.-P. (2009). Report by the Commission in the
Measurement of Economic Performance and Social Progress. Available at:
http://ec.europa.eu/eurostat/documents/118025/118123/Fitoussi+Commission
+report (accessed 4 December 2017).

Townes, C. H. (1965). 1964 Nobel lecture: production of coherent radiation by
atoms and molecules. *IEEE Spectrum* 2(8): 31.

Townes, C. H. (1984). Ideas and stumbling blocks in quantum electronics. *IEEE
Journal of Quantum Electronics* 20(6): 547–50.

Townes, C. H. (1999). *How the Laser Happened: Adventures of a Scientist.* New York,
NY: Oxford University Press. Excerpt available at: www.acamedia.info/sciences/
J_G/references/Townes_How_the_Laser_Happened.pdf (accessed 28 November
2017).

Wikipedia (2017a). History of the transistor. Available at: https://en.wikipedia.org/
wiki/History_of_the_transistor (accessed 28 November 2017).

Wikipedia (2017b). Laser. Available at: https://en.wikipedia.org/wiki/Laser
(accessed 28 November 2017).

Zwiebel, J. (1995). Corporate conservatism and relative compensation. *The Journal
of Political Economy* 103(1): 1–25.

Index